NEW ACCENTS

General Editor: TERENCE HAWKES

Making a Difference:
Feminist Literary Criticism

IN THE SAME SERIES

Making a Difference:

Feminist Literary Criticism

Edited by GAYLE GREENE
and COPPÉLIA KAHN

METHUEN

London and New York

First published in 1985 by
Methuen & Co. Ltd
11 New Fetter Lane, London EC4P 4EE
Published in the USA by
Methuen & Co.
in association with Methuen, Inc.
29 West 35th Street, New York, NY 10001

© *1985 Gayle Greene and Coppélia Kahn*

Photoset by Rowland Phototypesetting Ltd
Bury St Edmunds, Suffolk
Printed in the United States of America

British Library Cataloguing in Publication Data
Making a difference: feminist literary criticism.
– (New accents)
1. English literature – History and criticism
2. Feminism and literature
3. Women critics
I. Greene, Gayle   II. Kahn, Coppélia   III. Series
820.9'9287   PR65.w6

ISBN 0-416-37470-0
ISBN 0-416-37480-8 Pbk

Library of Congress Cataloging in Publication Data
Making a difference.
(New accents)
Includes index.
1. Feminist literary criticism – Addresses,
essays, lectures.
I. Greene, Gayle, 1943–   II. Kahn, Coppélia.
III. Series: New accents (Methuen & Co.)
PN98.w64M35   1985   801'.95'088042   85-11427

ISBN 0-416-37470-0
ISBN 0-416-37480-8 (pbk.)

Contents

General editor's preface

It is easy to see that we are living in a time of rapid and radical social change. It is much less easy to grasp the fact that such change will inevitably affect the nature of those disciplines that both reflect our society and help to shape it.

Yet this is nowhere more apparent than in the central field of what may, in general terms, be called literary studies. Here, among large numbers of students at all levels of education, the erosion of the assumptions and presuppositions that support the literary disciplines in their conventional form has proved fundamental. Modes and categories inherited from the past no longer seem to fit the reality experienced by a new generation.

New Accents is intended as a positive response to the initiative offered by such a situation. Each volume in the series will seek to encourage rather than resist the process of change; to stretch rather than reinforce the boundaries that currently define literature and its academic study.

Some important areas of interest immediately present themselves. In various parts of the world, new methods of analysis have been developed whose conclusions reveal the limitations of the Anglo-American outlook we inherit. New concepts of literary forms and modes have been proposed; new notions of the nature of literature itself and of how it communicates are current; new views of literature's role in relation to society flourish. *New Accents* will aim to expound and comment upon the most notable of these.

In the broad field of the study of human communication, more and more emphasis has been placed upon the nature and function of the new electronic media. *New Accents* will try to identify and discuss the challenge these offer to our traditional modes of critical response.

The same interest in communication suggests that the series should also concern itself with those wider anthropological and sociological areas of investigation which have begun to involve scrutiny of the nature of art itself and of its relation to our whole way of life. And this will ultimately require attention to be focused on some of those activities which in our society have hitherto been excluded from the prestigious realms of Culture. The disturbing realignment of values involved and the disconcerting nature of the pressures that work to bring it about both constitute areas that *New Accents* will seek to explore.

Finally, as its title suggests, one aspect of *New Accents* will be firmly located in contemporary approaches to language, and a continuing concern of the series will be to examine the extent to which relevant branches of linguistic studies can illuminate specific literary areas. The volumes with this particular interest will nevertheless presume no prior technical knowledge on the part of their readers, and will aim to rehearse the linguistics appropriate to the matter in hand, rather than to embark on general theoretical matters.

Each volume in the series will attempt an objective exposition of significant developments in its field up to the present as well as an account of its author's own views of the matter. Each will culminate in an informative bibliography as a guide to further study. And, while each will be primarily concerned with matters relevant to its own specific interests, we can hope that a kind of conversation will be heard to develop between them; one whose accents may perhaps suggest the distinctive discourse of the future.

TERENCE HAWKES

Acknowledgements

We are grateful to the extended community of feminist critics and scholars whose work has enabled our own, and to our contributors. We wish especially to thank Agnes Greene, Jack Greenberg, Michael F. Harper, Gabriel Kahn, and Avi Wortis and to acknowledge the support of Scripps College and Wesleyan University.

The publisher and editors wish to thank *Feminist Studies*, Inc., (c/- Women's Studies Programme, University of Maryland, College Mark, MD 20742) for permission to reprint the article by Bonnie Zimmerman which appears on p. 177. This article is reprinted from *Feminist Studies*, 7, 3 (1981), pp. 451–75.

Notes on contributors

Nelly Furman is an Associate Professor in the Department of Romance Studies at Cornell University where she teaches nineteenth-century French literature and French feminist theories. She organized the literary section of the book *Women and Language in Literature and Society*, edited by Sally McConnell-Ginet, Ruth Borker and Nelly Furman (Praeger 1980).

Judith Kegan Gardiner teaches English literature and Women's Studies at the University of Illinois at Chicago. Her publications centre on Renaissance English literature, modern women writers, and feminist theory. Her book, *The Hero as her Author's Daughter: Jean Rhys, Christina Stead, Doris Lessing*, is forthcoming from Indiana University Press.

Gayle Greene is an Associate Professor of English at Scripps College, Claremont, California. She has published numerous articles on Shakespeare, feminist criticism, and contemporary women writers. She co-edited *The Women's Part: Feminist Criticism of Shakespeare* (University of Illinois 1980), and is currently working on a book, *Re-Visions: Contemporary Women Writers and the Tradition*.

Ann Rosalind Jones is an Associate Professor of Comparative Literature at Smith College, Northampton, Massachusetts, where she teaches literary theory and women-authored fiction. Her research interests include Marxist and feminist criticism, narrative theory, and political dimensions of the culture of the European Renaissance. She has published on Renaissance poetry and fiction, on the French feminists, and on contemporary novel theory, and she is working on a book about women love poets of the sixteenth century.

Coppélia Kahn is Professor of English at Wesleyan University, Middletown, Connecticut, and the author of *Man's Estate: Masculine Identity in Shakespeare* (University of California Press 1981). She also co-edited *Representing Shakespeare: New Psychoanalytic Essays* with Murray Schwartz (The Johns Hopkins University Press 1980), and is working on a semiotic study of sexuality and gender in Jacobean drama.

Cora Kaplan teaches at the University of Sussex, Brighton, England, and is a member of the Feminist Review Collective. Her writing on feminism and culture includes the critical anthology *Salt and Bitter and Good: Three Centuries of English and American Women Poets* (Paddington 1975), and an edition, with introduction, of *Aurora Leigh and Other Poems* (The Women's Press 1978) by Elizabeth Barret Browning. She is now writing a book on class, gender, sexuality and literature to be called *A Romantic Twist of the Mind*, for Virago Press.

Sydney Janet Kaplan is Director of the Women Studies Programme and Associate Professor of English at the University of Washington. She has published *Feminine Consciousness in the Modern British Novel* (University of Illinois Press 1975) and numerous articles on feminist criticism and on Doris Lessing, Rosamond Lehmann, Katherine Mansfield and other women writers. She is currently working on a critical re-evaluation of Katherine Mansfield.

Adrienne Auslander Munich, who teaches at the State University of New York at Stonybrook, has published feminist criticism on James Joyce, Gilbert and Sullivan, and the movie *Tootsie*. She is editor of *Browning Institute Studies: An Annual of Literary and Cultural History*. Her recent work includes studies of the engendering of war in Virgil and Tennyson and of the Andromeda myth in Victorian England.

As an academic, Susan Willis is something of an anomaly. In the great tradition of José Marti, she defines herself as an Americanist on a hemispheric plane. Her teaching and writing bring together North American, Latin American and Caribbean writers upon the basis of shared culture and history.

Bonnie Zimmerman is a professor in the Department of Women's Studies at San Diego State University. She has published articles on George Eliot and on lesbian literature and critical theory in a number of journals and anthologies. She is currently working on a study of the contemporary lesbian-feminist novel.

Feminist scholarship and the social construction of woman

GAYLE GREENE
and COPPÉLIA KAHN

Literary criticism, like history and the social sciences, has traditionally asked questions that exclude women's accomplishments. Feminist scholarship undertakes the dual task of deconstructing predominantly male cultural paradigms and reconstructing a female perspective and experience in an effort to change the tradition that has silenced and marginalized us. This chapter describes these efforts in anthropology (Part II), history (III) and literature (IV). In investigating the purposes cultural paradigms serve, feminist scholars expose the collusion between ideology and cultural practices; but we need to be aware of the ideological implications of our own assumptions and make sure that we are not recuperating the ideology of the systems we repudiate. In literary criticism, as in the social sciences, the inclusion of women raises questions that reshape it – challenging traditional notions of what constitutes evidence and excellence, redefining both the subjects and the methods of study, we enrich and enlarge the discipline.

Feminist literary criticism is one branch of interdisciplinary enquiry which takes gender as a fundamental organizing cat-egory of experience. This enquiry holds two related premises about gender. One is that the inequality of the sexes is neither a biological given nor a divine mandate, but a cultural construct, and therefore a proper subject of study for any humanistic discipline. The second is that a male perspective, assumed to be 'universal', has dominated fields of knowledge, shaping their paradigms and methods. Feminist scholarship, then, has two concerns: it revises concepts previously thought universal but now seen as originating in particular cultures and serving particular purposes; and it restores a female perspective by extending knowledge about women's experience and contributions to culture. Feminist scholarship received impetus from the women's movement of the late 1960s and 1970s, but it participates in the more general dethroning of authority begun by Freud, Marx and Saussure – a redefinition of ideas of human nature and reality which has called into question traditional concerns of literary criticism, including established canons and ways of reading.

A feminist perspective leads to a critique of our sex–gender system – 'that set of arrangements by which the biological raw material of human sex and procreation is shaped by human social intervention' (Rubin 1975, p. 165; Fox-Genovese 1982, pp. 14–15). That men have penises and women do not, that women bear children and men do not, are biological facts which have no determinate meaning in themselves but are invested with various symbolic meanings by different cultures. Feminists do, however, find themselves confronting one universal – that, whatever power or status may be accorded to women in a given culture, they are still, in comparison to men, devalued as 'the second sex'. Feminist scholars study *diverse* social constructions of femaleness and maleness in order to understand the *universal* phenomenon of male dominance. That 'one is not born, but rather becomes a woman . . . it is civilization as a whole that produces this creature' is the thesis of Simone Beauvoir's *The Second Sex* (1952, p. 301), the pioneering and most comprehensive study of the ideology of woman; and it is a central assumption of feminist scholarship, which undertakes to 'deconstruct' the social construction of gender and the cultural paradigms that support it. Feminist scholarship both originates and participates in the larger efforts of feminism to liberate women from the structures that have marginalized them; and as such it seeks not only to reinterpret, but to change the world.

The social construction of gender takes place through the workings of ideology. Ideology is that system of beliefs and assumptions – unconscious, unexamined, invisible – which represents 'the imaginary relationships of individuals to their real conditions of existence' (Althusser 1971, p. 162); but it is also a system of practices that informs every aspect of daily life – the clothes we wear, the machines we invent, the pictures we paint, the words we use. Though it originates in particular cultural conditions, it authorizes its beliefs and practices as 'universal' and 'natural', presenting 'woman' not as a cultural construct but as eternally and everywhere the same. Thus that women, who happen to bear children, should be more responsible for rearing them than the men who father those children is presented as 'the way things naturally are', though this social arrangement has been challenged by feminist scholars from several standpoints (Dinnerstein 1976; Chodorow 1978; Rich 1977). Ideology masks contradictions, offers partial truths in the interests of a false coherence, thereby obscuring the actual conditions of our existence and making people act in ways that may actually contradict their material interests – as, for example, when wives refuse to strike for equal pay in the belief that their wages only provide extra income for the family while their husbands are the true breadwinners.

The oppression of woman is both a material reality, originating in material conditions, and a psychological phenomenon, a function of the way women and men perceive one another and themselves. But it is generally true that gender is constructed in patriarchy to serve the interests of male supremacy. Radical feminists argue that the construction of gender is grounded in male attempts to control female sexuality (Barrett 1980, p. 45; Firestone 1970, p. 11), an objective that accounts for the 'madonna/whore dichotomy': the

> twin images of woman as, on the one hand, the sexual property of men and, on the other, the chaste mothers of their children . . . [are] the means whereby men . . . ensure both the sanctity and inheritance of their families and their extra-familial sexual pleasure.
>
> (Barrett 1980, p. 45)

This objective also helps explain the dichotomization of masculine and feminine in terms of such polarities as 'culture and nature', 'truth and duplicity', 'reason and passion', 'day and night' – the term associated with the female always requiring control by the superior male. Thus the meaning of gender in patriarchal ideology is '*not* simply "difference", but . . . division, oppression, inequality, interiorized inferiority for women' (Barrett 1980, pp. 112–13).

The ideology of gender is inscribed in discourse – in our ways of talking and writing – and it is 'produced and reproduced in cultural practice' (Barrett 1980, p. 99). An example from Roland Barthes's *Mythologies* (1972) shows how such production occurs in a process that invisibly cements the imaginary to the actual. Barthes examines a group photograph from the French women's magazine *Elle* which depicts seventy women novelists, captioned thus: 'Jacqueline Lenoir (two daughters, one novel); Marina Grey, one son, one novel; Nicole Dutreil, two sons, four novels', etc. He remarks that, while *Elle* singled these women out because they actually do 'have access, like men, to the superior status of creation', the effect of the caption is to reinforce the ideology in which women are inscribed – to remind us all that 'Women are on the earth to give children to men; let them write as much as they like, let them decorate their condition, but above all, let them not depart from it' (Barthes 1981, p. 50). Further noting the total absence of men from the picture, the caption and the magazine as a whole, Barthes writes:

> where then is man in this family picture? Nowhere and everywhere, like the sky, the horizon, an authority which at once determines and limits a condition. . . . Man is never inside, femininity is pure, free, powerful; but man is everywhere around, he presses on all sides, he makes everything exist . . . the feminine world of *Elle*, a world without men, but entirely constituted by the gaze of man, is very exactly that of the gynaeceum.
>
> (Barthes 1981, p. 51)

In their creation of fictions, writers call upon the same signifying codes that pervade social interactions, re-presenting in fiction the rituals and symbols that make up social practice. Literature itself is a 'discursive practice' (Michele Foucault's term; Eagleton 1983, p. 205) whose conventions encode social conventions and are ideologically complicit.[1] Moreover, since each invocation of a code is also its reinforcement or reinscription, literature does more than transmit ideology: it actually creates it – it is 'a mediating, moulding force in society' (Hawkes 1977, p. 56) that structures our sense of the world. To invoke the conventional narrative resolutions of marriage or death, for example, as most nineteenth-century novelists did, was to sanction them, make them prescriptive as well as descriptive, to perpetuate them as the working myths of the culture.

Feminist literary critics attend to the collusion between literature and ideology, focusing on the ways ideology is inscribed within literary forms, styles, conventions, genres and the institutions of literary production. Like feminist scholars in other areas, they are – in Barthes's term – myth decipherers.

I

We turn to a short story by Isak Dinesen to show how a feminist mode of reading is at the same time, and inevitably, a reading of culture. 'The Blank Page' is told by an old woman who learned the art of storytelling from her grandmother, who learned it, in turn, from her grandmother. This art has been passed down with the admonition 'Where the storyteller is loyal, eternally and unswervingly loyal to the story, there, in the end, silence will speak' (Dinesen 1975, p. 100). The story concerns a convent whose nuns are renowned for growing, spinning and weaving the finest flax in Portugal. For centuries, they have enjoyed the privilege of supplying linen bridal sheets for the princesses of the royal house – sheets which, blood-spotted, are hung on the balcony of the palace the morning after the wedding as the Chamberlain or High Steward proclaims, '*Virginem eam tenemus*' ('We declare her to have been a virgin') (pp. 102–3). The sisters' privilege extends even further, for they also maintain a gallery lined with gilt frames, 'each of them adorned with a coroneted plate of pure gold, on which is engraved the name of a princess', each frame displaying a square cut from a royal wedding sheet which bears the 'faded markings' of the wedding night (p. 103). In their later years, the princesses make 'sacred and secretly gay' pilgrimages to the convent to ponder the stories told by the sheets (p. 103); and the old woman recounts:

in the midst of the long row there hangs a canvas which differs from the others. The frame of it is as fine and as heavy as any, and as proudly as any carries the golden plate with the royal crown. But on this one plate no name is inscribed, and the linen within the frame is snow-white from corner to corner, a blank page.   (p. 104)

This tale, like the linen of Convento Velho, is woven from the social fabric of western European patriarchy. It can be unravelled only by a reader who understands that patriarchy, its social practices, psychological dynamics and symbol-making, and its power to mould women and men as social beings. With the image of the sheets, Dinesen evokes an ideology built on male control, through the institution of marriage, of female sexuality and reproductive power. The nuns preserve their virginity and the princesses surrender theirs, but the ideology informing both practices holds female sexuality to be dangerous and powerful, requiring men to exercise strict control over it. In a custom observed widely throughout Europe well into the nineteenth century, the sheets are meant to validate the virginity of daughters who are passed on by fathers to husbands, to ensure the legitimacy of the heirs they will bear and to attest to the honour of both fathers and husbands. It is this honour that the various structures of male dominance – property, the law, social status, political authority – exist to protect.

The arresting analogies Dinesen draws between bloodstained sheet and printed page, between female body and male authority, make the story a critique of culture. And the contrast between the story told by the spotted bridal sheets and that which speaks in the silence of 'the blank page' may be seen as a metaphor for the two major foci of feminist scholarship: deconstructing dominant male patterns of thought and social practice; and reconstructing female experience previously hidden or overlooked. Thus a feminist interpretation of literature involves decoding many of the same systems of signification with which social scientists are concerned.

II

Though anthropology gathers much of its data from so-called 'primitive cultures' rather than from Europe in the periods during which literature flourished, it addresses some of the same questions that concern feminist scholars in all areas – how patriarchal power arose and what makes it persist – and its debates focus ideas about gender in a way that is helpful to feminist literary critics.

Two anthropological theories of the origin and dynamics of gender have attracted attention from feminists. The first is put forth by Claude Lévi-Strauss in his monumental *Elementary Structures of Kinship* (1969). Though the book is conceived as a theory of the basis of human society and not as a radical critique of its sex–gender systems, feminists have discerned such a critique within it (as they also have in Freud's theories). A dichotomy between nature and culture is basic to Lévi-Strauss's structuralist approach. It can readily be seen in his analysis of kinship, in which sexuality is seen as an element of nature which, by means of the imposition of the incest taboo and exogamy, is transformed into culture. For Lévi-Strauss, such binary structures are rooted in the unconscious but exfoliate endlessly in the ways people cook, worship, build houses or make up stories.

Briefly, he proposes that any social order is based on its kinship system. The incest taboo, a prohibition against marriage with certain kin, creates two opposing groups of permitted and prohibited marriage partners. Since each group is thus enjoined to marry with the other, a social link is created between them which, in its various aspects – kinship, commerce, rivalry and reciprocity – also gives rise to forms of social organization. Women are the gifts which men exchange between each other. Like the princesses in Dinesen's story, they are gifts, not givers. They have no significant power or influence within a system which is controlled by men and works to their benefit. Men, not women, have the power to determine the value of women in the exchange and the meanings associated with them.

This paradigm of male dominance has been criticized from several angles. First, it identifies male control over the exchange of women with culture *per se* and makes culture itself dependent on the subjugation of women by men. Actually, however, it may be possible to see the subordination of women 'as a product of the relationships by which sex and gender are organized and produced' in kinship rather than as the origin of those relationships. Kinship systems produce many kinds of exchanges – of statuses, rights, property, people. The 'traffic in women' is but one of these (Rubin 1975).

Another challenge to Lévi-Strauss's paradigm of gender construction, closely related to the first, holds that 'prestige structures' are prior to sex–gender systems, which are themselves codes articulating prestige in which men always, finally, rank higher than women. The sources of prestige are multiple: they include political power, personal skill or presence, kinship, property and reputation, among others. Any conception of prestige is constituted by the network of beliefs, categories, assumptions and symbols which make up a culture. While kinship and marriage are important parts of this network, they 'are filtered through the perspective of the male ego situated within the prestige structure (or structures) of the society in question' (Ortner and Whitehead 1982, p. 20). In this view, cultures may define woman's nature and status variously, but always from a male standpoint.

A third critique of Lévi-Strauss holds that the exchange of women by men in marriage operates at a psychological even more than a social level to create the structures of gender differentiation within individuals. Joining psychoanalytic theory to Lévi-Strauss's anthropological approach, Gayle Rubin (1975) argues that the exchange of women works to create the genders by enforcing heterosexuality and constraining female sexuality. To begin with heterosexuality: it is not only one group which must marry the other, but men who must marry women. Each sex is ideologically constructed as people identify with the same gender and direct their sexual desire solely towards the other. Exogamy thus enforces a pervasive, absolute symbolic opposition of men to women, suppressing their similarities and oppressing them both by preventing either from enjoying the traits associated with the other. This opposition, moreover, is hierarchical, in that maleness is valued over femaleness as well as simply being opposed to it – as male control over the exchange of women testifies. To employ the terms proposed by Lacan, the penis thus becomes the phallus – symbol of the male power which determines all order and meaning (Lacan 1977). And marriage becomes 'an expression of the transmission of male dominance ... [which] passes through women and settles upon men' (Rubin 1975, p. 192). What is really being exchanged is not the women themselves but the phallus, the symbol of male power. Through the use made of her reproductive power in marriage, woman's sexuality is in effect co-opted; she is the vehicle, not the object, of the real exchange. Only by accepting a definition of herself as the one who lacks a penis, and consenting to her role as childbearer (that is, reproducer of the phallus) in the marital exchange, does she take her place in the symbolic and social order.

The second influential theory of sex–gender systems builds on an opposition between nature and culture. Sherry B. Ortner begins with the assumption that 'The secondary status of woman in society is one of the true universals, a pan-cultural fact' (1974, p. 67). Culture, she holds, is 'equated relatively unambiguously with men', while women are seen as being '*closer* to nature than men' for three reasons. First, woman's body space and life cycle are more taken up with the natural processes of reproduction than is man's body, which leaves him freer to use tools and symbols, to hunt and make war. Second, her social role as the bearer but especially the nurturer of infants who are 'barely human and utterly unsocialized', and her close association with the domestic unit as opposed to the public domain, place her closer to nature. (None the less, Ortner stresses, woman in her mothering, homemaking role might also be associated with culture for the same reason – as the one who performs the basic, quintessential tasks of culture: changing babies into socially acceptable people and turning the raw into the cooked.) Finally, drawing on Chodorow's theory that a distinctly female personality is created by the structure of the family, Ortner holds that women tend to experience things, feelings and people as concrete rather than abstract, subjectively and interpersonally rather than objectively:

> women tend to enter into relations with the world that culture might see as being more 'like nature' – immanent and embedded in things as given – than 'like culture' – transcending and transforming things through the superimposition of abstract categories and transpersonal values.

(p. 82)

Ortner concludes that, although woman's body and mothering role align her closely with nature, her obvious participation in culture places her in an intermediate position, 'performing some sort of synthesizing or converting function between nature and culture' (p. 84). Because she mediates between the two realms somewhat ambiguously, she is liable to more stringent restrictions and circumscriptions than men are.

Ortner's paradigm attracted much comment because of its boldness, simplicity and apparent applicability to the humanities. But it has since been widely challenged, and as a result anthropologists have moved even further from universalizing propositions and towards greater awareness of the ethnocentrism likely to underlie them. They point out that, although organizing dichotomies such as nature and culture, female and male, may be vital in certain cultural contexts, their meaning is not universal and certainly not value-free:

> the 'myth' of nature is a system of arbitrary signs which relies on a social consensus for meaning. Neither the concept of nature nor that of culture is 'given', and they cannot be free from the biases of the culture in which the concepts were constructed.
>
> (MacCormack 1980, p. 6; see also Davis 1976, p. 92)

Specifically, Lévi-Strauss, and Ortner as well, can be seen as the intellectual descendants of Rousseau, who himself entered into an ideological discourse already established in the Enlightenment – a discourse which polarized nature and culture and which endowed woman in particular with contradictory meanings. When nature was taken to be 'that part of the world which human beings have understood, mastered, and made their own', woman was seen as the repository of the natural law which made nature intelligible; when it was taken as 'that which has not yet been penetrated (either literally or metaphorically), the wilderness and deserts', she was conceived as a creature of uncontrolled passion which made her a dangerous source of disorder (Jordanova 1980, p. 66).

It is evident that the nature–culture opposition exists in a matrix common to other value-laden oppositions (including those of gender ideology) by which western culture organizes itself, and that it must be understood in relation to them. With regard to the social sciences, the opposition derives from 'that distinctive tradition in European thought long concerned with the opposition between things as they are and things as they might be; separation of subject from object and . . . a dialectic between participation and objectivity' (Strathern 1980, p. 177). Such patterns of thought, however significant or useful they may be, can be seen as part of the intellectual framework of male dominance. If feminist scholars are concerned with challenging and changing the ideology which has subjugated women, then they must beware of borrowing analytical categories from it. If it seems 'natural' for us to align female and male with nature and culture, perhaps that is because we still participate unconsciously in that very ideology. We must seek to avoid making oppositions out of what might be, more elusively, differences.

Finally, we may direct the same criticism at both these paradigms of the sex–gender systems – the exchange of women, as well as the association of woman with nature and man with culture. Neither paradigm recognizes the possibility or presence of a female point of view. Lévi-Strauss, for example, considers women to be the passive objects of male activity in the marital exchange, and disregards their frequent involvement as matchmakers and sharers in wealth or higher status. Ortner assumes that, if women are kept from the public realm in which men prevail, they are therefore necessarily inferior to men, and fails to question the priority assigned to public life or women's importance in less formal private roles (Rogers 1978). One anthropologist suggests that women and men may, in some cultures at least, hold two distinct models of the universe. Men, he claims, articulate the dominant structure in terms of their position in the world, while women, rendered inarticulate within this structure, form a 'muted group' whose model of the universe exists at 'deeper levels'. It is this which accounts for men's association of women with the non-social realm, the wilderness (Ardener 1975). Furthermore, he argues, anthropology trains its practitioners to think in male-oriented categories and models, so that they tend to accept male versions of the world and overlook women's less accessible, contrasting views. We must beware of adopting assumptions and terms from the very ideology we are trying to challenge.

Dinesen's tale evokes the association of female with nature and male with culture in order to subvert it. The 'natural' blood of defloration (which suggests the blood of menstruation and childbirth as well) makes the framed sheets function as testaments of the patriarchal order and, in effect, as contracts between fathers and sons-in-law. But the empty frame, the blank page, mutely speaks of a female experience outside that order, and by its very presence calls attention to the order as a cultural construct.

III

The nunnery which is the setting of Dinesen's tale is a female community engaged in traditional 'women's work', yet in that its purpose is to validate the honour of the brides of the royal family – to provide testimony to women's value as defined by patriarchal ideology – it serves the dominant culture. The nuns are entrusted with keeping the records, with preserving the histories of the royal women as recorded on their marriage sheets and then framed and displayed for the edification of future generations. In this respect they function like traditional historians whose focus has been the history of dynasties and who, if they have attended to women at all, considered them within a domestic sphere and in relation to the ruling families. Yet the nuns' records also tell a different story; for, whereas the frames they display 'suggest the traditional framework which has contained women in history, the blank page which is emphasized by Dinesen's larger narrative frame implies other possibilities, suggesting the existence of a subtext which is subversive of the main text. These two taken together represent the traditional paradigm and alternatives to it which are the dual concerns of feminist historians and literary critics.

History has been a record of male experience, written by men, from a male perspective. What has been designated historically significant has been deemed so according to a valuation of power and activity in the public world. History has 'been written primarily from the perspective of the authoritative male subject – the single triumphant consciousness', with a view to justifying the values of the politically dominant west – individualism, progress, conquest – i.e. to providing 'worthy pedigrees for individuals, rising classes, nations, cultures, and ideologies' (Fox-Genovese 1982, p. 29). As long as 'the transmission and experience of power' are its primary focus, as long as 'war and politics are seen as more significant to the history of humankind than child-rearing', women remain marginalized or invisible (Lerner 1979e, p. 166). Its androcentric framework – the criteria of significance and selection which have determined the questions it asks as well as its methodology and notion of evidence – has excluded from its consideration not only women but the poor, the anonymous and the illiterate.

It is the task of historians of women to reconstruct the female experience, 'the buried and neglected female past' (Lerner 1979e, p. 166), to fill in the blank pages and make the silences speak. Historians of women, like feminist scholars in other disciplines, reject universalizing assumptions, exposing the 'universality imperative' as 'a strategy of male hegemony' (MacKinnon 1983, p. 537). Indeed, they reveal that sexist history, by virtue of its assumption of 'immutable and inherent ... character attributes', is bad history, since it cannot 'deal with change over time' (Gordon *et al.* 1976, p. 55).

In their first efforts to incorporate women into history, historians concerned themselves with exceptional women. Gerda Lerner describes these initial stages as 'compensatory' and 'contributory' history – attempts to compensate for what has been missing and to note women's contributions. But both these stages defined achievement according to the standards of the male, public world, and, appending women to history as it has been defined, left unchallenged the existing paradigm (Lerner 1979d, pp. 145–59). Historians of women soon extended their enquiries to the majority of women unaccounted for by traditional historiography, in search of 'the actual *experiences* of women in the past' (Lerner 1979d, p. 153). They asked questions about the quality of their daily lives, the conditions in which they lived and worked, the ages at which they married and bore children; about their work, their role in the family, their class and relations to other women; their perception of their place in the world; their relation to wars and revolutions.

Women present a special case to the historian: neither class nor caste nor minority, they are more closely allied to the men in their lives than they are to women of other classes and races, and so are more closely integrated with the dominant culture than is any other subordinate group. They have in some sense consented to their subordination, internalizing the ideology of the oppressor, indoctrinating 'their children of both sexes in the very values by which they themselves have been indoctrinated to subordination' (Lerner 1979f, p. 170). Such considerations require that historians add new categories and conceptual frameworks to those by which they traditionally organize their material: female sexuality and its regulation, birth control, birth rates, childbearing and childrearing, marriage behaviour patterns, female bonding, female role indoctrination and consciousness.

Historians of women assert the need for a 'woman-centred analysis' of the past, suggesting that women's social reality and experience of history are different from men's. They draw attention to

the female life cycle – especially to recurrent and risky childbirth, but also to the particular experiences of youth and age, to the paucity of rites of passage, to women's special experience of medical practice. They have stressed the gap that separates most female lives from public events and have reminded us that the invention of reliable contraception has more decisively affected the lives of women than the majority of political revolutions.   (Fox-Genovese 1982, p. 12)

Some historians of women posit the existence of a separate woman's culture, even going so far as to suggest that women and men within the same society may have different experiences of the universe – implying a model like that of Ardener in anthropology, of 'muted' and 'dominant' groups.

These sorts of enquiries imply criteria of historical significance and evidence different from those of traditional history. Since women rarely leave the usual kinds of evidence that historians rely on, historians of women turn to sources used by anthropologists – artefacts, folklore – and to those used by demographers and social historians ('census figures, parish birth records, property and tax records, wills . . . the records of churches and educational institutions, minutes of organizations, police and criminal records, hospital and medical records'; Lerner 1979f, p. 172). They ask questions similar to those asked by family historians concerning 'the functions and use of dowry, patterns of inheritance, the relations of families to their kin, the strength of family sentiment, and the varied relations between the generations' (Davis 1976, p. 87; Smith-Rosenberg 1983, p. 32).

In investigating the material conditions of women's lives, women's history goes hand in hand with the revisionist efforts of social historians, family historians and Marxist historians, who similarly try to reconstruct the experience of anonymous men and women and view history from the bottom up rather than the top down. But neither social nor family nor Marxist history can substitute for women's history. An emphasis on the material conditions of life does not necessarily yield insights into the experience of women, as the work of the Annales historians – Lucien Febvre, Fernand Braudel, Marc Bloch, Georges Duby, Le Roy Ladurie – indicates (Stuard 1981; Faure 1981). Marxist feminists such as Margaret Benston and Sheila Rowbotham, who extend the tools of class analysis to women's history, reveal the difference between Marxist and women's history, since, although women exist within social classes, they do not themselves constitute a class (Kelly 1976, p. 813; see also Eisenstein 1979; Zaretsky 1973). Yet many feminists are coming to understand the interdependence of patriarchal ideology and capitalism, a system that reduces both sexes, but particularly women, to objects for exploitation. And Marxist analyses and methods may be essential for the radical deconstruction of gender necessary to change woman's position, for, if woman is defined as a sexual being that exists for another, then she can be liberated only by redefinition of the very norms of gender identity – a process which requires a radical change in the society that produced such norms (MacKinnon 1982, pp. 533–4).[2]

In challenging the traditional categories of history, women's history asks questions that result in a redefinition of the discipline itself. One of the categories it questions is the traditional separation of society into the 'private' and 'public' spheres, with its relegation of woman to the family, to a domestic realm which is conceived of as a refuge from the world of work and the competition of men in market-place and empire. This division – as feminist anthropologists have also noted – perpetuates the belief that woman's childbearing 'naturally' placed her in the home and leads to an understanding of women 'not in terms of relationship – with other women and with men – but of difference and apartness . . . as beings who presently *are* and have at all times, been . . . not actors but mere subjects of male action and female biology' (Rosaldo 1980, p. 409). Feminist historians and anthropologists draw attention to the ideological function of the 'separation of the spheres' in mystifying woman's position and work, legitimizing her economic dependence, and curbing her activities in the public realm (Fox-Genovese 1982, pp. 23–4; see also Welter 1966).

The division of public from private has obscured an understanding of the family, in terms both of women's position in the family and of the family's position within society. Women's history considers 'how we are all, women and men, initially humanized, turned into social creatures by the work of that domestic order to which women have been primarily attached', and views 'women as agents and the family as a productive and social force' (Kelly 1976, pp. 822–3). Feminist analyses demonstrate that the 'private' and 'public' are interdependent – that 'the personal is political' – with experience in each realm affecting that in the other. In investigating this relation, historians of women turn to other disciplines – to studies of the institutionalization of motherhood by Nancy Chodorow, Adrienne Rich, Dorothy Dinnerstein – which demonstrate how seemingly private arrangements shape men and women and so affect life in the public realm.

The separation of spheres has also distorted our understanding of women's work, rendering much of it invisible by relegating it to the personal. The definition of work as something performed for wages discounts some traditional aspects of women's work – housekeeping, childrearing – as a part of production, whereas actually it has been women's unpaid labour in the home that has enabled men to work outside it. Feminist analyses of women's work in England and France from 1500 to 1700 (Tilly and Scott 1978) challenge the traditional view that industrialization separated the family from work, isolating one sphere from the other, and demonstrate the family's continued role in production. A fuller understanding of women's work – which, like the family, must be viewed in relation to social, economic and political factors – will provide crucial insights into women's experience:

> Since all women have always worked . . . the study of how working patterns, experiences, and perceptions have differed according to class, race, ethnic background, and place of residence can provide scholars with a broader basis for comparing women's lives than almost any other field of inquiry except perhaps childbearing.
>
> (Norton 1979, p. 332)

An understanding of the interdependence of the spheres reveals that women have wielded more power than has been apparent, and that aspects of women's lives which appear to be restrictive may actually be enabling. Women's history is concerned to see women, not as victims of oppression, as passive spectators of the drama of history, but as having an influence and a history of their own: 'While men conquered territory and built institutions which managed and distributed power, women transmitted culture to the young and built the social network and infra-structures that provide continuity in the community' (Lerner 1979f, p. 179). Historians of women broaden their conception of power to include subtler forms – informal, invisible, collective – recognizing that 'the location of power' is 'a tricky business' (Davis 1975, p. 90). The sexual repression of Victorian women, for example, has been reinterpreted in terms of its usefulness to women, as providing them with a means of control over reproduction and a source of 'power and self-respect'. It was their supposed 'passionlessness' that gave them a claim to moral superiority, and this claim allowed them some participation in the public sphere (Cott 1977).

As these questions suggest, ascertaining the criteria for measuring women's status is itself a central problem for historians of women. No single criterion can be singled out: 'Woman's role in . . . economics, or religion, or education, or the family, or reproduction, or sexual life, or her image in philosophy and literature, or her legal rights, or her physical weakness or her temperament' – none can be used as the sole measure of her position (Lerner 1979c, p. 81). Woman may have high status in the family, for example, and low status economically. Losses in one area may entail gains in another; or what appears to be a disadvantage may entail hidden advantages, as is suggested by the reassessment of Victorian sexuality. Conversely, apparent advantages may conceal disadvantages, as in the case of Renaissance English wives, who impressed sixteenth-century travellers as having 'the most spirited and independent temperaments and the most freedom from their husbands' supervision', while they actually had 'less protection from economic exploitation or general mistreatment by husbands than any women in Western Europe' (Johannson 1976, p. 408).

In considering such issues, historians question the correlation between ideology and social reality, revealing some startling relationships. The contrast between the image of woman in Greek tragedy, for example, which invests woman with terrifying emotional power, and her complete exclusion from Athenian public life, has been accounted for by a hypothesis similar to that of Chodorow and Dinnerstein concerning the effects of female-dominated childrearing (Slater 1968). Some historians of women go so far as to posit an inverse relation between ideology and social reality, suggesting that prescriptive literature implies 'the reality of prohibited behavior which alone made the prescriptions necessary' (Lougee 1977, p. 635). Still others see prescriptive literature as a form of coercion, a kind of 'sexual propaganda': since

> it has never been possible to exclude women in the same ways as it has been to exclude other out-groups ... it has been necessary to bombard them with a massive literature of religious, social, and biological content explaining why they should remain in a role secondary to men.
>
> (Hilda Smith 1976, p. 374)

Actual behaviour is likely to be more varied than is suggested by social myths or stereotypes, and the relation of the ideology of woman to social reality remains difficult to measure.

One of the most important contributions of women's history

is its reshaping of traditional periodization. History has customarily been periodized 'according to wars, conquests, revolution and/or vast cultural and religious shifts' – categories which are – 'appropriate to the major activities of men' (Lerner 1979f, p. 175) but which render invisible the experience of women. Women's history reveals that periods of progress for men often involved losses for women. If we assume 'that the emancipation of women is an index of the general emancipation of an age – our notions of so-called progressive developments, such as classical Athenian civilization, the Renaissance, and the French Revolution, undergo a startling re-evaluation' (Kelly 1976, p. 811). Kelly contrasts women's position in pre-industrial society, where her labours were essential, to her economic and sexual dependence in post-industrial society, arguing that the same factors that liberated men from the social and ideological constraints of the past – the new capitalist economy and humanist learning – impinged on the lives of women, moulding the noblewoman especially into 'an aesthetic object, decorous, chaste, dependent'. Kelly concludes that 'there was no Renaissance for women, at least not in the Renaissance' (1977, pp. 161, 154; see also Casey 1976).

Kelly's generalizations may be challenged on the grounds that the backbreaking work required of both men and women in a pre-industrial society liberated neither sex (Sicherman 1975, p. 464). Yet it is also true that, although early capitalism in Europe in the fifteenth and sixteenth centuries and industrialization in Europe and America in the nineteenth century improved the material quality of many people's lives, these very improvements depended on the introduction of a money standard which devalued women. In this century, technology, medical advances and urbanization offer women unparalleled opportunities, but these advances are mitigated by 'new denigrations of female nature . . . new celebrations of female needs for protection . . . [which] exclude women from full social and political participation' (Fox-Genovese 1982, pp. 21–2).

It may be that 'women's ability to control their own fertility [is] the single most important determinant of their status' (Sicherman 1975, p. 464; de Beauvoir 1952, p. 136), and that the periods when women acquire such control constitute their

'Renaissance' – though this control is dependent on ideology as well as on technology. Some historians even suggest that, because of woman's connection with reproduction, women's history should be rewritten from the point of view of major events in her reproductive cycle (Vann 1974). But a new periodization based solely on such criteria threatens to detach women's history from other types of history. It is clear that the history of women differs from the history of men, but a new periodization should relate the history of women to that of men and consider social change from the perspective of both sexes. Only by considering each in relation to the other can we begin to understand such complex questions as the effects of industrialization on women's lives; for

> the important point about preindustrial work may not be that for women . . . it was arduous, precarious, and unrewarding but that it was the same for men. Thus the relevant comparison would not juxtapose the work experiences of seventeenth and nineteenth-century women but would measure the extent to which the work of women and men differed in the seventeenth and then in the nineteenth century.
>
> (Lougee 1977, p. 633)[3]

Similarly, in their analyses of female subcultures, feminist scholars, including anthropologists, historians and literary critics, must consider 'the dialectic, the tension between the two cultures' (Lerner 1979d, p. 159; see Sklar (1973), Smith (1976), Cott (1977), Auerbach (1978), Smith-Rosenberg (1983). As Dinesen's story suggests, such subcultures exist in complex relation to the dominant ideology, and are as likely to exist in collusion with it as to challenge it. Merely to substitute women's history for 'mainstream history' is to perpetuate the terms and categories which have kept women subordinate. What is needed is a more inclusive notion of history which is 'based on the recognition that women have always been essential to the making of history and that *men and women* are the measure of significance' (Lerner 1979f, p. 180).

An understanding of the interdependence of the private and public, family and society, work and home, has created a more comprehensive view of historical and social processes than that which characterized traditional history. Traditional historians 'looking only at male experience . . . frequently saw homogeneity where, in fact, complexity and conflict predominated' (Smith-Rosenberg 1983, p. 32). The new history, avoiding both heroic models and models of oppression, encompasses the complexity of women's past. Women have collaborated with the oppressor but they have also identified with other women and created counter-cultures; they have contributed to 'the building of slave societies, the suppression of *jacqueries*, the consolidation of big business and the efforts at counter-revolution', but they have also 'participated in slave revolts, *jacqueries*, strikes and revolutions':

> The history we know has been written primarily from the perspective of the authoritative male subject. . . . [But] women share the experience of having been denied access to an authoritative self. . . . In this sense, women's history challenges mainstream history not to substitute the chronicle of the female subject for that of the male, but rather to restore conflict, ambiguity and tragedy to the centre of historical process.
>
> (Fox-Genovese 1982, p. 28)

IV

The complex, ambivalent relation of women to the patriarchy is suggested by Dinesen's tale, which concerns two types of 'communities of women' – both those that serve the dominant culture and those that subvert it. Each of these communities is the custodian of a tradition: the nuns, of the ancient craft of weaving; the storytellers, of the equally ancient art of narrative which has been handed down from one generation of women to the next. But though the nuns with their traditional 'frames', like the royal brides whose stories they keep, serve the interests of patriarchy, the storytellers, keepers of another kind of record, comprise a counter-culture existing outside and as a challenge to it.

'Storytellers' in western culture, however, as often legitimize the dominant culture as challenge it; even when literature is potentially subversive, it has been made to function as part of a literary tradition that inscribes the dominant ideology and marginalizes women. Feminist critics find that the critical tradition reinforces – even when literature does not – images of character and behaviour that encourage women to accept their subordination, either ignoring or degrading women, or praising them for such virtues as obedience, meekness and humility. Moreover, literary history has canonized, designated as 'great', certain texts which are claimed to embody 'universal human truths'; but such truths only appear so because of their congruence with the dominant ideology. The criteria that have created the literary canon have, like the traditional conception of history, excluded the accomplishments not only of women but of people of races, ethnic backgrounds and classes different from the politically dominant one, which is western and white.

Feminist criticism questions the values implicit in the Great Works, investigating the tradition that canonized them and the interests it serves. It exposes the collusion between literature and ideology, 'demanding that we understand the ways in which [structures of primarily male power] have been – and continue to be – reified in our literature and by our literary criticism' (Kolodny 1980a, p. 20). It is alert to the omissions, gaps, partial truths and contradictions which ideology masks – it attends to the silences. In this, feminist criticism is allied with the deconstructive criticism advocated by Barthes and Macherey, which 'seeks out the process of production of the text; the organization of the discourses which constitute it and the strategies by which it smoothes over the incoherences and contradictions of the ideology inscribed in it' (Belsey 1980, p. 129). It attends to 'the processes by which the work of gender ideology is done' – processes that include 'stereotyping, compensation, collusion and recuperation' (Barrett 1980, p. 108).[4]

In refusing the received ideas of greatness and investigating the political interests they serve, feminist critics embark upon 'a revisionist rereading of our entire literary inheritance', a *revisionary rereading*' (Kolodny 1980b, pp. 464–5). As in the social sciences, so in literary criticism, feminist scholarship does more than merely append women to the discipline as it exists, for the inclusion of women raises questions that reshape the discipline.[5] In the same way that women's history has modified notions of historical evidence and periodization, the reading of women writers alters standards of literary excellence, redefines literary periods and reshapes the canon. To view a literary movement such as modernism from the perspective of women writers alters our conception of it (see Chapter 2). Moreover, the existence of a black women's tradition and a lesbian tradition raises questions analogous to those that women's literature raises in relation to the male-dominated tradition: how will women's literature be altered when the work of lesbian and black women writers is not merely added to but really incorporated into it? (Robinson 1983, pp. 92–3; see also Barbara Smith 1982; and Chapter 7.)

Such changes will create a new literary history, though the nature of this history remains disputed. Some feminist critics are concerned with revisionary readings of the literary canon (Millett, Figes, Janeway, Greer, Heilbrun, Kolodny, Fetterley; see Robinson 1983, p. 85); others direct their attention to the recovery of neglected women writers and the establishment of an alternative canon (Spacks, Moers, Pratt, Bayme, Gilbert and Gubar, Walker; see Chapter 2). These concerns correspond to the dual focus of feminist efforts in other areas – revising the traditional paradigm and restoring the female perspective.[6] Showalter refers to rereadings of the canon as the 'feminist critique', 'a historically grounded inquiry which probes the ideological assumptions of literary phenomena . . . [including] the images and stereotypes of women in literature, the omissions and misconceptions about women in criticism, and the fissures in male-constructed literary history' (Showalter 1979, p. 25). She terms the focus on women writers 'gynocriticism', which she describes as 'the history of styles, themes, genres, and structures of writing by women; the psychodynamics of female creativity; the trajectory of the individual or collective female career; and the evolution and laws of a female literary tradition' (Showalter 1981, pp. 181–5). Basing her ideal of gynocriticism on a model of women's culture like the woman-centred history advocated by Lerner and the 'muted' female half of society described by the Ardeners, Showalter argues for a 'programme of gynocritics [which] constructs a female framework for the analysis of women's literature [and] develops new models based on the study of female experience . . . on the newly visible world of female culture' (Showalter 1979, p. 28):

> Before we can even begin to ask how the literature of women would be different and special, we need to reconstruct its past, to rediscover the scores of women novelists, poets and dramatists whose work has been obscured by time, and to establish the continuity of the female tradition from decade to decade, rather than from Great Woman to Great Woman.
>
> (Showalter 1979, pp. 34–5)

Showalter's argument is compelling, and gynocriticism may be a necessary stage in redressing the imbalances of a male-dominated tradition. But in referring to the 'feminist critique' as 'ideological', 'essentially political and polemical' for its 'affiliations to Marxist sociology and aesthetics', Showalter implies that gynocriticism is somehow less ideological, more value-free. Feminist criticism should avoid representing its own ideals as politically neutral, for, if a feminist approach has taught anything, it is that all critical stances are ideological. And we must recall – as Dinesen's tale cautions – that 'female subcultures' exist in complicated relation to the dominant culture, in collusion with as well as 'counter' to it.

In the same way that substituting women's history for 'mainstream history' reduplicates the central assumption – of woman as 'other', separate and apart – that we are trying to change, merely to substitute one canon for another is to perpetuate the terms which feminist literary criticism should challenge. This question reflects a general tension in feminist scholarship today between the celebration of the 'female' and the advocation of 'androgyny' – a tension that may be productive:

> Instead of celebrating the feminine, we need to retain a vital tension between androgynous and female-centered visions. We need to recognize contradiction and to apply a critical perspective that distinguishes between giving value to traditionally female qualities and celebrating the female in a universalistic and essentialist manner.
>
> (Stacey 1983, p. 575)[7]

Feminist criticism should avoid 'the women's literature ghetto – separate, apparently autonomous, and far from equal'; and 'while not abandoning our new-found female tradition ... return to confrontation with "the" canon, examining it as a source of ideas, themes, motifs, and myths about the two sexes' (Robinson 1983, pp. 95–6; see Chapter 9). The value of gyno-criticism may be, like that of the study of female subcultures in history and anthropology – as an intermediary stage on the way towards a more comprehensive literary criticism which considers both male and female traditions in their interactions, avoiding the 'model of oppression' that presents women's literature as merely subordinate, and illuminating works by women in relation to a mainstream which it will redirect.

Moreover, the assumption that women's experience is 'directly available in the texts written by women' and that 'the more "authentic" the experience is felt to be by the critic, the better and more valuable the text will be', leaves unquestioned the view of 'the text as the transmitter of authentic "human" experience' (Moi 1985). Implicit in Showalter's argument – as in much Anglo-American feminist criticism – is the assumption that the text, and language itself, are transparent media which reflect a pre-existent objective reality, rather than signifying systems which inscribe ideology and are actually constitutive of reality. But this is precisely the view of literature on which the canon has been predicated; and it is a view that conceals assumptions – concerning epistemology, language, 'objectivity' and subjectivity – which feminists would do well to question. If we hope to challenge the ideology which has so long passed for 'truth', we must be careful not to recuperate its terms and assumptions in our own positions. Feminist criticism should heed the radical implications of post-Saussurean linguistics which, in revealing language as a signifying system, 'implicitly put in question the "metaphysics of presence" which had dominated western philosophy', and, in liberating the text 'from the authority of a presence behind it', released it 'from the constraints of a single and univocal reading', making it 'available for production, plural, contradictory, capable of change . . . unfixed, a process' (Belsey 1980, pp. 136, 134).

Such a criticism would question 'not whether a literary work has been written by a woman and reflects her experience of life, or how it compares to other works by women', but the way the text works as a signifying process which inscribes ideology (see Chapter 3). If Anglo-American feminist criticism has drawn back from the more far-reaching implications of its positions,

French feminist criticism, which participates in Derridian deconstruction and Lacanian psychoanalysis, has presented a radical challenge to humanist-empiricist assumptions. The most radical feminist literary criticism has been informed by structuralist and post-structuralist French thought (see Chapter 4).[8] Since, as Derrida has demonstrated, thinking in terms of binary opposition always implies the subordination of the second element to the first, to reverse the order of the pairing – which an alternative literary canon based on redefined values does – can only reduplicate the initial system (Chapter 3). Deconstruction aims to expose and dismantle an epistemology based on the construction of a sovereign subject – man as 'the central reference point of an epistemology built on a set of hierarchical oppositions in which "man" . . . always occupies the privileged position' (Chapter 4). Only the undermining of such oppositions, the dismantling of the system that sanctions them, can undo the hierarchical opposition between men and women. In this way an epistemologically radical feminist criticism may be allied with deconstruction in seeking a 'leverage for displacing or undoing the system of concepts or procedures of male criticism' (Culler 1982, p. 63). Though deconstruction may lead to a scepticism which is used to justify the evasion of political positions, this need not be its implication; a deconstructive feminist criticism is potentially revolutionary. In order to understand the collusion between literature and ideology – to become 'myth decipherers' – we need to evolve a theory and practice true to the most radical implications of our positions. Only in this way can feminist scholars hope to change the tradition that has silenced and marginalized us.

Such criticism seeks out 'the lack in the work, what it is unable to say' – what is 'unspoken' (Belsey 1980 on Macherey, pp. 135–6). Like the blank page in Dinesen's tale, it enables the 'silence to speak'. And 'listening for the silences' is, as Adrienne Rich suggests, difficult and essential in understanding women's experience:

> listening and watching in art and literature, in the social sciences, in all the descriptions we are given of the world, for the silences, the absences, the unspoken, the encoded – for there we will find the true knowledge of women. And in breaking those silences, naming our selves, uncovering the

hidden, making ourselves present, we begin to define a reality which resonates to *us*, which affirms *our* being.

(Rich 1979, p. 245)

If the nuns in Dinesen's tale are traditional historians or literary critics in their relegation of women to a patriarchal 'frame', the storytellers with their tale of the blank page allow for more revolutionary – and more open-ended – possibilities. The blank page 'tells . . . a finer tale than any of us' (Dinesen 1975, p. 104), and, in the end, commands the attention of women of all classes, ages and 'occupations':

> It is in front of this piece of pure white linen that the old princesses of Portugal – worldly wise, dutiful, long-suffering queens, wives and mothers . . . have most often stood still. It is in front of the blank page that the old and young nuns, with the Mother Abbess herself, sink into deepest thought.
>
> (p. 105)

And it is the blank page that arrests the attention of the reader of the tale. Though contained in a conventional 'frame' like the others, it is, as Susan Gubar suggests, 'radically subversive, the result of one woman's defiance which must have cost either her life or her honour . . . a mysterious but potent act of resistance' (1981, p. 259). It is subversive in that it may imply any one of a number of alternative scripts for women. Was this woman not a virgin, or was she consecrated to chastity? Did she run away, or spend her wedding night telling stories like Scheherazade to escape the fate of her predecessors (Gubar 1981, p. 259)?

It is also subversive in that it is unnamed, without an author, for, as Barthes suggests, 'To give the text an Author is to impose a limit on that text, to furnish it with a final signified, to close the writing', whereas to refuse 'to assign . . . an ultimate meaning to the text (and to the world as text), liberates what may be called an anti-theological activity, an activity that is truly revolutionary, since to refuse to fix meaning is, in the end, to refuse God and his hypostases – reason, science, law' (Barthes 1977, p. 147). Feminist criticism can gain from a practice that does not privilege the author's intentions, for such a practice is 'a serious act of insubordination [which] puts into question the authority of authors, that is to say the propriety of paternity . . . [and] implies denial of patriarchal rule' (Chapter 3).

Dinesen's tale implies a connection between patriarchal authority and authorship, suggesting that a challenge to one is a challenge to both. Though her female subculture of nuns and princesses is circumscribed and inscribed by the patriarchal system which it serves, that system is itself circumscribed – and subverted – by the storytellers and by the wider narrative framework of the tale itself, which resonates with radically new possibilities. Providing a framework which exists in complex, subversive relation to the social system that it addresses, Dinesen reminds us that history itself is narrative and suggests that a feminist perspective enables us to read both in a way that allows the silences to speak.

Notes

1 Roland Barthes (1974) argues this in relation to realism, and Fredric Jameson discusses the 'strategies of containment' of narrative (Jameson 1981, p. 53).

2 See Catherine A. MacKinnon's persuasive analysis of 'gender socialization' as 'the process through which women come to identify themselves as sexual beings, as beings that exist for men. It is that process through which women internalize . . . a male image of their sexuality *as* their identity as women' (1982, p. 531). She suggests that 'If being *for* another is the whole of women's sexual construction, it can be no more escaped by separatism, men's temporary concrete absence, than eliminated or qualified by permissiveness . . . [by] women emulating male roles' (pp. 533–4).

3 Studies of the effects of industrialization suggest that 'women's roles changed radically between the seventeenth and nineteenth centuries' in response to 'technological and economic forces', yet 'women's status and power relative to men's changed little'. This 'unique pattern of constancy in a world in which all else was in flux' is somewhat inexplicable, suggesting perhaps, a 'male social cohesion' that 'cuts across class lines' 'in the face of violent economic change' (Smith-Rosenberg 1983, pp. 30, 28).

4 Barrett defines 'compensation' as 'the presentation of imagery and ideas that tend to elevate the "moral value" of femininity', citing Mariolatry, Romanticism and the 'ideology of domesticity' as examples. By 'collusion' she means 'attempts made to manipulate and parade women's "consent" to their subordination and objectification'; and 'recuperation' is 'the ideological effort that goes into negating and defusing challenges to the historically dominant mean-

ing of gender', as in the co-opting of women's liberation by the media (Barrett 1980, pp. 109–11).

5 A similar modification of traditional paradigms is occurring in psychology. As Carol Gilligan demonstrates, studies of sex-role stereotypes suggest

> that the qualities deemed necessary for adulthood – the capacity for autonomous thinking, clear decision-making, and responsible action – are those associated with masculinity. . . . Yet looked at from a different perspective, these stereotypes reflect a conception of adulthood that is itself out of balance, favoring the separateness of the individual self over connection to others, and leaning more toward an autonomous life of work than toward the interdependence of love and care.
>
> (Gilligan 1982, p. 17)

Gilligan concludes that 'The disparity between women's experience and the representation of human development . . . [which is] generally . . . seen to signify a problem in women's development' may rather point to a problem in the models themselves (Gilligan 1982, pp. 1–2).

6 But see Judith Kegan Gardiner's slightly different categorization of feminist ideologies as 'liberal, radical, and social feminisms' (Gardiner 1982, p. 629).

7 Stacey's 'The New Conservative Feminism' (1983) discusses the danger of recuperating traditional and even reactionary ideas under feminist guises.

8 See Margaret Homans's distinction between American and French criticism: 'The French writers . . . accept the premise that language and experience are coextensive . . . [whereas American] feminist criticism . . . has pragmatically assumed that experience is separable from language' (1983, p. 186).

References

Abel, Elizabeth (ed.) (1981) 'Writing and Sexual Difference', *Critical Inquiry* (special issue), 8, 2 (Winter).

Althusser, Louis (1971) 'Ideology and State Apparatuses'. In *Lenin and Philosophy and Other Essays*, trans. Ben Brewster. New York: Monthly Review Press.

Ardener, Edward (1975) 'Belief and the Problem of Women'. In Shirley Ardener (ed.), *Perceiving Women*. New York: John Wiley.

Auerbach, Nina (1978) *Communities of Women: An Idea in Fiction*. Cambridge, Mass.: Harvard University Press.

Barrett, Michele (1980) *Women's Oppression Today: Problems in Marxist Feminist Analysis*. London: Villiers Publications.

Barthes, Roland (1974) *S/Z*. New York: Hill & Wang.

Barthes, Roland (1977) *Image–Music–Text*, trans. Stephen Heath. London: Fontana.

Barthes, Roland (1981) *Mythologies*, trans. Annette Lavers. New York: Hill & Wang.

Baym, Nina (1978) *Woman's Fiction: A Guide to Novels by and about Women in America 1820–1870*. Ithaca, NY: Cornell University Press.

Beauvoir, Simone de (1952) *The Second Sex*, trans. H. M. Parshley. New York: Vintage.

Belsey, Catherine (1980) *Critical Practice*. New Accents. London and New York: Methuen.

Benston, Margaret (1970) *The Political Economy of Women's Liberation*. New York: Monthly Review Press.

Braudel, Fernand (1974) *Capitalism and Material Life: 1400–1800*. New York: Harper & Row.

Bridenthal, Renate, and Koonz, Claudia (eds) (1977) *Becoming Visible: Women in European History*. Boston, Mass.: Houghton Mifflin.

Brown, Cheryl L., and Olson, Karen (1978) *Feminist Criticism: Essays on Theory, Poetry and Prose*. Metuchen, NJ, and London: Scarecrow Press.

Carroll, Berenice A. (1972) 'Peace Research: The Cult of Power', *Journal of Conflict Resolution* (December), pp. 585–616.

Carroll, Berenice A. (ed.) (1976) *Liberating Women's History: Theoretical and Critical Essays*. Urbana, Ill.: University of Illinois Press.

Casey, Kathleen (1976) 'The Cheshire Cat: Reconstructing the Experience of Medieval Woman'. In Carroll (1976), pp. 224–49.

Chodorow, Nancy (1978) *The Reproduction of Mothering: Psychoanalysis and the Sociology of Gender*. Berkeley, Cal.: University of California Press.

Cott, Nancy F. (1977) *The Bonds of Womanhood: 'Women's Sphere' in New England 1780–1835*. New Haven, Conn.: Yale University Press.

Cott, Nancy F. (1978) 'Passionlessness: An Interpretation of Victorian Sexual Ideology 1790–1850', *Signs*, 4, 2 (Winter), pp. 219–33.

Culler, Jonathan (1982) *On Deconstruction: Theory and Criticism after Structuralism* Ithaca, NY: Cornell University Press.

Davis, Natalie Zemon (1975) *Society and Culture in Early Modern France*. Stanford, Cal.: Stanford University Press.

Davis, Natalie Zemon (1976) ' "Women's History" in Transition: The European Case', *Feminist Studies*, 3, pp. 83–103.

Diamond, Arlyn, and Edwards, Lee R. (eds) (1977) *The Authority of Experience: Essays in Feminist Criticism*. Amherst, Mass.: University of Massachusetts Press.

Dinesen, Isak, (1975) *Last Tales*. New York: Vintage.

Dinnerstein, Dorothy (1976) *The Mermaid and the Minotaur: Sexual Arrangements and Human Malaise*. New York: Harper & Row.

Donovan, Josephine (ed.) (1975) *Feminist Literary Criticism: Explorations in Theory*. Lexington, Ky: University of Kentucky Press.

Eagleton, Terry (1983) *Literary Theory: An Introduction*. Minneapolis, Minn.: University of Minnesota Press.

Edwards, Lee R. (1979) Review of Nina Auerbach, *Communities of Women*, and Judith Fetterley, *The Resisting Reader*, *Signs*, 5, 5 (Winter), pp. 351–4.

Eisenstein, Zillah R. (1979) 'Developing a Theory of Capitalist Patriarchy and Socialist Feminism' and 'Some Notes on the Relations of Capitalist Patriarchy'. In Zillah R. Eisenstein (ed.) *Capitalist Patriarchy and the Case for Socialist Feminism*. New York: Monthly Review Press.

Ellmann, Mary (1968) *Thinking about Women*. New York: Harcourt Brace and World.

Faure, Christine (1981) 'Absent from History', *Signs*, 7, 1 (Autumn), pp. 71–80.

Fetterley, Judith (1978) *The Resisting Reader: A Feminist Approach to American Fiction*. Bloomington, Ind.: Indiana University Press.

Firestone, Shulamith (1970) *The Dialectic of Sex: The Case for Feminist Revolution*. New York: Bantam.

Fox-Genovese, Elizabeth (1982) 'Placing Women's History in History', *New Left Review* (May–June), pp. 5–29.

Gardiner, Judith Kegan (1982) 'An Interchange on Feminist Criticism: On "Dancing through the Minefield"'; with Elly Bulkin, Rena Grasso Patterson and Annette Kolodny, *Feminist Studies*, 8 (Fall), pp. 629–75.

Gilbert, Sandra M., and Gubar, Susan (1979) *The Madwoman in the Attic: The Woman Writer and the Nineteenth-Century Literary Imagination*. New Haven, Conn.: Yale University Press.

Gilligan, Carol (1982) *In a Different Voice: Psychological Theory and Woman's Development*. Cambridge, Mass.: Harvard University Press.

Gordon, Ann D., Buhle, Mari Jo, and Dye, Nancy Schrom (1976) 'The Problem of Women's History', (revision of 'Women in American Society', *Radical America*, 5, 4 (July–August 1971)). In Carroll (1976).

Gordon, Linda, Hunt, Persis, Pleck, Elizabeth, Rutchild, Rochelle Goldberg, and Scott, Marcia (1976) 'Historical Phallacies: Sexism in American Historical Writing'. In Carroll (1976), pp. 55–75.

Gornick, Vivian, and Moran, Barbara K. (1971) *Woman in Sexist Society: Studies in Power and Powerlessness*. New York: New American Library.

Greene, Gayle (1981) 'Feminist and Marxist Criticism: An Argument for Alliances', *Women's Studies: An Interdisciplinary Journal*, 9, pp. 29–45.

Greer, Germaine (1971) *The Female Eunuch*. New York: McGraw-Hill.

Gubar, Susan (1981) '"The Blank Page" and the Issues of Female Creativity', *Critical Inquiry* (Winter), pp. 243–63.

Hawkes, Terence (1977) *Structuralism and Semiotics*. Berkeley, Cal.: University of California Press.

Heilbrun, Carolyn G. (1974) *Toward a Recognition of Androgyny*. New York: Harper & Row.

Homans, Margaret (1980) *Women Writers and Poetic Identity*. Princeton, NJ: Princeton University Press.

Homans, Margaret (1983) '"Her Very Own Howl": The Ambiguities of Representation in Recent Women's Fiction', *Signs*, 9, 2 (Winter), pp. 186–205.

Hull, Gloria T., Scott, Patricia Bell, and Smith, Barbara (eds) (1982) *All the Women are White, All the Blacks are Men, But Some of us are Brave: Black Women's Studies*. Old Westbury, NY: Feminist Press.

Jacobus, Mary (ed.) (1979) *Women Writing and Writing about Women*. New York: Barnes & Noble.

Jameson, Fredric (1981) *The Political Unconscious: Narrative as a Socially Symbolic Act*. Ithaca, NY: Cornell University Press.

Janeway, Elizabeth (1971) *Man's World, Woman's Place: A Study in Social Mythology*. New York: William Morrow.

Jehlen, Myra (1981) 'Archimedes and the Paradox of Feminist Criticism', *Signs*, 6, 4 (Summer), pp. 575–601.

Johansson, Sheila Ryan (1976) '"Herstory" as History: A New Field or Another Fad?' In Carroll (1976), pp. 400–30.

Jordanova, L. J. (1980) 'Natural Facts: A Historical Perspective on Science and Sexuality'. In Carol P. MacCormack and Marilyn Strathern (eds) *Nature, Culture and Gender*. Cambridge: Cambridge University Press.

Kelly, Joan (1976) 'The Social Relation of the Sexes: Methodological Implications of Women's History', *Signs*, 1, 4 (Summer), pp. 809–23.

Kelly, Joan (1977) 'Did Women Have a Renaissance?' In Renate Bridenthal and Claudia Koonz (eds) (1977) *Becoming Visible: Women in European History*, pp. 139–64. Boston, Mass.: Houghton Mifflin.

Kelly, Joan (1979) 'The Doubled Vision of Feminist Theory: A Postscript to the "Women and Power" Conference', *Feminist Studies*, 5, 1 (Spring), pp. 216–27.

Kolodny, Annette (1975) *The Lay of the Land: Metaphor as Experience in American Life and Letters*. Chapel Hill, NC: University of North Carolina Press.

Kolodny, Annette (1980a) 'Dancing through the Minefield: Some Observations on the Theory, Practice and Politics of a Feminist Literary Criticism', *Feminist Studies*, 6, 1 (Spring), pp. 1–25.

Kolodny, Annette (1980b) 'A Map for Rereading; or, Gender and the Interpretation of Literary Texts', *New Literary History*, 11, 3 (Spring), pp. 451–67.

Lacan, Jacques (1977) 'The Signification of the Phallus'. In *Ecrits*, trans. Alan Sheridan. London: Tavistock.

Ladurie, Emmanuel Le Roy (1979) *Montaillou: The Promised Land of Error*. New York: Vintage.

Landy, Marcia (1977) 'The Silent Woman: Towards a Feminist Critique'. In Diamond and Edwards (1977), pp. 16–27.

Lenz, Carolyn Ruth Swift, Greene, Gayle, and Neely, Carol Thomas (eds) (1980) *The Woman's Part: Feminist Criticism of Shakespeare*. Urbana, Ill.: University of Illinois Press.

Lerner, Gerda (1979a) *The Majority Finds its Past: Placing Women in History*. London: Oxford University Press.

Lerner, Gerda (1979b) 'New Approaches to the Study of Women in American History', *The Journal for Social History*, 3, 1 (Fall 1969), pp. 53–62. In Lerner (1979a), pp. 3–14.

Lerner, Gerda (1979c) 'Black Women in the United States: A Problem in Historiography and Interpretation' (1973). In Lerner (1979a), pp. 63–82.

Lerner, Gerda (1979d) 'Placing Women in History: Definitions and Challenges', *Feminist Studies*, 3, 1–2 (Fall 1975), pp. 5–14. In Lerner (1979a), pp. 145–59.

Lerner, Gerda (1979e) 'The Majority Finds its Past', *Current History*, 70, 416 (May 1976), pp. 193–6. In Lerner (1979a), pp. 160–7.

Lerner, Gerda (1979f) 'The Challenge of Women's History' (1977). In Lerner (1979a), pp. 168–80.

Lerner, Gerda (1979g) 'Autobiographical Notes, by way of an Introduction'. In Lerner (1979a).

Lévi-Strauss, Claude (1969) *The Elementary Structures of Kinship*, trans. James Harle Bell, John Richard von Sturmer and Rodney Needham. Rev. edn. Boston, Mass.: Beacon Press.

Lougee, Carolyn C. (1977) 'Review Essay: Modern European History', *Signs*, 2, 3 (Spring), pp. 628–50.

Lougee, Carolyn C. (1981) 'Women, History, and the Humanities: An Argument in Favor of the General Studies Curriculum', *Women's Studies Quarterly*, 9, 1 (Spring), pp. 4–7.

MacCormack, Carol P. (1980) 'Nature, Culture and Gender: A Critique'. In Carol P. MacCormack and Marilyn Strathern (eds), *Nature, Culture and Gender*. Cambridge: Cambridge University Press.

Macherey, Pierre (1978) *A Theory of Literary Production*, trans. Geoffrey Wall. London: Routledge & Kegan Paul.

MacKinnon, Catharine A. (1982) 'Feminism, Marxism, Method, and the State: An Agenda for Theory', *Signs*, 7, 3, pp. 515–44.

Mitchell, Juliet (1973) *Woman's Estate*. New York: Vintage.

Mitchell, Juliet (1975) *Psychoanalysis and Feminism: Freud, Reich, Laing and Women*. New York: Vintage

Moers, Ellen (1977) *Literary Women: The Great Writers*. Garden City, NY: Anchor Press/Doubleday.

Moi, Toril (1985) *Sexual/Textual Politics: Feminist Literary Theory*. London: Methuen.

Norton, Mary Beth (1979) 'Review Essay: American History', *Signs*, 5, 2 (Winter), pp. 324–37.

Offen, Karen (1982) Review of Bonnie G. Smith, *Ladies of the Leisure Class: The Bourgeoises of Northern France*, *Signs*, 8, 2 (Winter), pp. 372–6.

Ortner, Sherry B. (1974) 'Is Female to Male as Nature is to Culture?' In Rosaldo and Lamphere (1974), pp. 67–87.

Ortner, Sherry B., and Whitehead, Harriet (eds) (1982) *Sexual Meanings*. Cambridge: Cambridge University Press.

Rich, Adrienne (1977) *Of Woman Born: Motherhood as Experience and Institution*. New York: Bantam.

Rich, Adrienne (1979) 'Taking Women Students Seriously'. In *On Lies, Secrets, and Silence: Selected Prose 1966–1978*. New York: Norton.

Robinson, Lillian S (1978) 'Dwelling in Decencies: Radical Criticism and the Feminist Perspective'. In *Sex, Class, and Culture*. Bloomington, Ind.: Indiana University Press.

Robinson, Lillian S. (1983) 'Treason Our Text: Feminist Challenges to the Literary Canon', *Tulsa Studies in Women's Literature*, 2, 1 (Spring), pp. 83–98.

Rogers, Susan Carol (1978) 'Woman's Place: A Critical Review of Anthropological Theory', *Comparative Studies in Society and History*, 20, pp. 123–62.

Rosaldo, Michelle Zimbalist (1980) 'The Use and Abuse of Anthropology: Reflections on Feminism and Cross-Cultural Understanding', *Signs*, 5, 3 (Spring), pp. 389–417.

Rosaldo, Michelle Zimbalist, and Lamphere, Louise (eds) (1974) *Woman, Culture and Society*. Stanford, Cal.: Stanford University Press.

Rowbotham, Sheila (1973) *Woman's Consciousness, Man's World*. Harmondsworth: Pelican.

Rowbotham, Sheila (1974) *Hidden from History: Rediscovering Women in History from the Seventeenth Century to the Present*. New York: Random House.

Rubin, Gayle (1975) 'The Traffic in Women: Notes on the "Political

Economy" of Sex'. In Rayna Rapp Reiter (ed.), *Toward an Anthropology of Women*, pp. 157–210. New York: Monthly Review Press.

Showalter, Elaine (1977) *A Literature of their Own: British Women Novelists from Brontë to Lessing*. Princeton, NJ: Princeton University Press.

Showalter, Elaine (1979) 'Towards a Feminist Poetics'. In Jacobus (1979), pp. 22–41.

Showalter, Elaine (1981) 'Feminist Criticism in the Wilderness', *Critical Inquiry*, 8, 2 (Winter), pp. 179–205.

Sicherman, Barbara (1975) 'Review Essay: American History', *Signs*, 1, 2 (Winter), pp. 461–85.

Sklar, Kathryn Kish (1973) *Catharine Beecher: A Study in American Domesticity*. New Haven, Conn.: Yale University Press.

Slater, Philip E. (1968) *The Glory of Hera: Greek Mythology and the Greek Family*. Boston, Mass.: Beacon Press.

Smith, Barbara (1982) 'Towards a Black Feminist Criticism'. In Hull, Scott and Smith (1982).

Smith, Bonnie G. (1981) *Ladies of the Leisure Class: The Bourgeoises of Northern France in the Nineteenth Century*. Princeton, NJ: Princeton University Press.

Smith, Hilda (1976) 'Feminism and the Methodology of Women's History'. In Carrol (1976), pp. 368–84.

Smith-Rosenberg, Carroll (1975) 'The Female World of Love and Ritual: Relations between Women in Nineteenth-Century America', *Signs*, 1, 1 (Autumn), pp. 1–29.

Smith-Rosenberg, Carroll (1983) 'The Feminist Reconstruction of History', *Academe* (September–October), pp. 26–37.

Spacks, Patricia Meyer (1975) *The Female Imagination*. New York: Knopf.

Stacey, Judith (1983) 'The New Conservative Feminism', *Feminist Studies*, 9, 3 (Fall), pp. 559–83.

Strathern, Marilyn (1980) 'No Nature, No Culture: The Hagen Case'. In Carol P. MacCormack and Marilyn Strathern (eds), *Nature, Culture and Gender*. Cambridge: Cambridge University Press.

Stuard, Susan Mosher (1981) 'The Annales School and Feminist History: Opening Dialogue with the American Stepchild', *Signs*, 7, 1 (Autumn), pp. 135–43.

Tilly, Louise A., and Scott, Joan W. (1978) *Women, Work, and Family*. New York: Holt, Rinehart & Winston.

Vann, Richard T. (1974) 'Towards a Periodization of Women's History'. Paper delivered at the second Berkshire Conference, Cambridge, Mass., October 1974. Cited in Sicherman (1975), p. 464.

Walker, Cheryl (1982) *The Nightingale's Burden: Women Poets and American Culture before 1900*. Bloomington, Ind.: Indiana University Press.

Welter, Barbara (1966) 'The Cult of True Womanhood 1820–1860', *American Quarterly*, 18 (Summer), pp. 151–74.

Zaretsky, Eli (1973) *Capitalism, the Family, and Personal Life*. San Francisco, Cal.: Agenda.

2

Varieties of
feminist criticism
SYDNEY JANET KAPLAN

Feminist criticism begins, according to Sydney Janet Kaplan, in the personal response of women readers to women writers, and in the implicit repudiation of any critical stance which claims to be objective. It then branches into several paths: revisionary criticism of the canon, the study of neglected or lost women writers, and the articulation of a distinctive female literary tradition. Surveying the attempts of Spacks, Pratt, Moers and Showalter to identify the patterns of influence and common concerns of such a tradition, Kaplan considers the extent to which they ground women's writing in the cultural moment of its time and place, and she assesses Showalter's use of the anthropological model of a woman-centred female subculture. Kaplan sees the diversity of feminist criticism, its eclecticism and ability to incorporate a variety of critical approaches, as its strength, but she points out the tension between this tendency – Kolodny's 'playful pluralism' – and the movement towards a monolithic theory advocated by Showalter.

*

For some of us, feminist criticism originated in a recognition of our love for women writers. In this we diverge from many of our sister critics whose awakening was hastened by their urge to reveal the diverse ways women have been oppressed, misinterpreted and trivialized by the dominant patriarchal tradition, and to show how these are reflected in the images of women in the works of male authors. The latter approach is important and necessary, but it should be apparent that it has its roots in suffering and anger, while the impetus for the first is passion and identification.

These two initiating impulses lead to a variety of critical methods and even converge in several places. For instance, studies of the images of women in the works of female authors might also concentrate on the ways in which such images reveal women's oppression, or on how an author's own absorption of patriarchal values might cause her to create female characters who fulfil society's stereotypes of women. By contrast, studies of women in the works of male authors might possibly reveal strong women characters and support of feminist values. The two impulses also converge when the interest in women writers leads to a questioning of the literary canon itself, not only for the stereotyping of women characters and the prevalent misogyny in so many of the famous works of literature, but also for the neglect of works by women writers.

How many of us had a favourite woman author whose works we read and reread, whose characters shared our lives and served as touchstones for our own achievements, models for our decisions, and listeners to our problems? But if we entered academia such ways of reading and such secret loves had to be abandoned. Perhaps this happens to some degree to everyone who takes up the academic study of literature. Left behind are the indiscriminate hours of reading whatever pleased us, abandoning whatever did not – or could not – because it was dull, boring or 'edifying'. We learned to accept boredom as part of the discipline of becoming educated. And, if we went even further and actually took up the task of studying literature as our life's vocation, then our connections with that child-self (who read with a flashlight to finish a book long after she was supposed to be asleep) were forgotten, if not broken entirely.

For graduate students during the early 1960s, the predominant approach to literary study was still the 'New Criticism'. Our experience and training in criticism was primarily devoted to a steady, detailed reading of the text in isolation from outside influences such as the author's life, historical and political events, and our own responses as readers. And when I refer to the 'text' I mean one of a carefully limited number of texts which had been designated to be among the best ever written. The distance between our methods of study and what we were experiencing in our own lives, as the social changes of that decade affected us, became increasingly apparent. I remember that during those years I found myself reading with a vague dissatisfaction, holding back an undercurrent of alienation, uneasiness, and a sense of living in the wrong time-frame – or mind-frame. Such near-melancholy was punctuated by moments of inexplicable fury, disgust, flashes of insight incompatible with the limitations my own methods had imposed upon me. I gradually began to question that assigned 'canon' of great literature that formed the basis of graduate education. I soon discovered that even the rigorous conditioning it had imposed had not destroyed my hidden preference for writers who were not included in that canon – or who barely held on to a place in the footnotes to it. These were all women writers. I also discovered that if I were to study them properly, and understand the consciousness of which the text was only a part, I would have to shake loose from the bias of my graduate training. My concern grew for the actual women who wrote these newly discovered or rediscovered texts. What were the experiences that affected their evolution as writers? To understand that evolution it would be necessary to seek information that the New Criticism had taught us to ignore: letters, diaries, fragments of autobiography; social and cultural analyses, biographies, histories; studies in anthropology, sociology, philosophy: in short, the knowledge, methodologies and theories that women's studies were quickly accumulating. Like those of many other feminist critics, my personal motivations and my own personal history were beginning to merge with those of a powerful women's movement.

I have emphasized the personal so far in this chapter out of a concern close to the heart of many feminist critics – a concern which expresses itself through the style and tone of much of our writing. Not only did many of us feel alienated by the content of the canon we were expected to 'master', but we also felt excluded by the assumed objectivity of the critical jargon we were expected to use, with its accompanying assumption of the generically masculine 'reader', its implied universality, as well as its estrangement from our lived experience. It is no wonder that one of the earlier collections of feminist criticism was entitled *The Authority of Experience* (Diamond and Edwards

1977). Frequently, feminist critics acknowledge their indebtedness to their students' challenges of accepted critical assumptions. Judith Fetterley has developed an entire theory of feminist reading on the basis of such correcting experiences (1978). Patricia Meyer Spacks used her class discussions at Wellesley College as the basis for her book on *The Female Imagination* (1975), incorporating many of her students' questions, revelations and critiques into the substance of her text.

The personal stance is even more assertive in an essay by Sandra Gilbert on Sylvia Plath, that begins:

> Though I never met Sylvia Plath, I can honestly say that I have known her most of my life. To begin with, when I was twelve or thirteen I read an extraordinary story of hers.
>
> (Gilbert 1979, p. 245)

Gilbert melds her own experience of being a guest editor of *Mademoiselle* with that of Plath. The exploration of the Plath myth, and the detailed analysis of Plath's poetry which follows, are thereby enriched by Gilbert's own personal associations and by her recognition that the life of the critic who is female has usually contained different experiences from those of her male colleagues.

This immediate connection between the critic's personal vision and the text characterizes much feminist criticism and is one of the main sources of its energy and creative power. Whether that personal response results from the first initiating impulse or the second, it is usually shared by other women who have made similar discoveries along parallel routes. From its beginning, feminist criticism's vital connection with the women's movement has encouraged joint efforts and collaborative research. As Judith Fetterley defines it, 'At its best, feminist criticism is a political act whose aim is not simply to interpret the world but to change it by changing the consciousness of those who read and their relation to what they read' (Fetterley 1978, p. viii). Arlyn Diamond and Lee Edwards recognize that all the writers of essays in their collection *The Authority of Experience*

> see art as the product of a particular cultural milieu, sometimes embodying a society's most deeply held convictions,

sometimes questioning these values, sometimes disguising an artist's own ambivalence with regard to these matters, but never disengaged from the claims of time or social order.

(Diamond and Edwards 1977, p. ix)

In fact, the power of the personal is intensified when the vision is shared. The integrity of that vision reveals its commonality, for, as Doris Lessing has remarked, 'nothing is personal, in the sense that it is uniquely one's own' (Lessing 1973, p. 21).

Once this is understood, it is possible to return to one's original love for women writers with a sense of assurance that one's interest and excitement are not merely idiosyncratic or narcissistic. A critic's return to the woman writer who first awakened her (whether it be Rosamond Lehmann, Kay Boyle, Kate Chopin, Jo Sinclair, Paule Marshall, Djuna Barnes, Marguerite Young, or any one of a large number of relatively neglected or underrated women authors) is an assertion of the validity of that author's interpretation of experience and her artistic power in conveying it. To make that assertion – in opposition to male critics' trivialization, contempt or neglect of the author – is one of the first steps in an emerging feminist critic's rebellion against the critical establishment.

Such a critic may ask why her favourite book is not included in literature classes or on lists of 'major' texts, while less serious or complex works written by men make their way easily into the same classes, the same lists. These questions lead to the issue of *who* establishes the literary canon and *whose* interests it serves. The feminist critic may choose to focus on the reasons behind that exclusion (and thus upon the ideology underlying the construction of the literary canon and the misogyny in so much of the literature that composes it), or she may choose to concentrate on understanding her own attraction to that particular author. This second choice takes her in the direction of the feminist criticism that is centred on the study of women writers. It opens up several exciting fields of enquiry: the rediscovery of other similarly neglected authors; the study of themes, images and ideas in the works of women writers; and the possibility of an alternative women's tradition or new literary history.

The rediscovery of lost women writers has been essential to

the development of feminist criticism. Annis Pratt refers to it as 'spadework criticism', and believes that 'many women authors were not haphazardly "forgotten" but deliberately buried', because their writing was 'far too critical of contemporary sexual norms for them to survive' the censorship of influential male critics (Pratt 1976, p. 176). Since a writer's critical reputation affects her ability to be republished, feminist critics recognize the crucial connection between the politics and economics of publishing and the course of women writers' careers – which of their books get printed, how long those books are allowed to remain in print, and why many of them disappear as if they had never been written.

It has been more than a decade since the Feminist Press brought out editions of two long-out-of-print, 'deliberately buried' works which have since become staples of reading lists for courses on women writers: Rebecca Harding Davis's *Life in the Iron Mills*, and Charlotte Perkins Gilman's *The Yellow Wallpaper*. The Feminist Press has continued with this recovery effort by publishing books by Agnes Smedley, Zora Neale Hurston, Paule Marshall, Meridel Le Sueur, and others. In Britain a similar effort to resurrect important 'lost' books by British women is carried out by Virago Books, which has published Dorothy Richardson's *Pilgrimage* (a central text for critics of women's fiction), as well as May Sinclair's *Mary Olivier* and Sarah Grand's *The Beth Book*.

The search for lost women writers continues to be necessary, since so many writers outside the mainstream remain unknown – especially those who were neither white, middle-class nor heterosexual. Such awareness informs Gloria T. Hull's '"Under the Days": The Buried Life and Poetry of Angelina Weld Grimké'. Hull asks in reference to Grimké: 'What did it mean to be a Black Lesbian/poet in America at the beginning of the Twentieth Century?' (Hull 1979, p. 17).

This process of rediscovery is intimately linked with an ongoing feminist transformation of the *teaching* of literature. These authors' works need to be available not only to scholars and critics but to students as well. Pedagogical discussions about the experiences of teaching women writers and courses in women and literature have been germane to feminist criticism from the beginning. An important example is Elaine

Showalter's early essay on 'Women and the Literary Curriculum', which appeared in 1970. The series of collections of essays on feminist pedagogy which were published by the Feminist Press under the title *Female Studies* (especially *Female Studies VI* (1972), edited by Nancy Hoffman, Cynthia Secor and Adrian Tinsley) influenced literature classes nation-wide. More recent collections, also published by the Feminist Press, include *All the Women are White, All the Blacks are Men, But Some of Us are Brave: Black Women's Studies* (1982, edited by Gloria T. Hull, Patricia Bell Scott and Barbara Smith) and *Lesbian Studies* (1982, edited by Margaret Cruikshank). These provide a much-needed revision of earlier work that tended to assume a homogeneity of race, class, ethnicity and sexual orientation in writing by women.

New anthologies which make the work of women poets, short-story writers and essayists available for classroom use introduce students to the richness and diversity of work by women. Poetry anthologies, such as those edited by Louise Bernikow (1974), Florence Howe and Ellen Bass (1973) and Cora Kaplan (1975), cover poetry written by women over several centuries. Of great value are Mary Helen Washington's *Midnight Birds: Stories by Contemporary Black Women Writers* (1980), Dexter Fisher's *The Third Woman: Minority Women Writers of the United States* (1980), and Cherríe Moraga and Gloria Anzaldúa's *This Bridge Called My Back: Writings by Radical Women of Color* (1981). Collections of earlier women writers such as *The Female Spectator: English Women Writers before 1800* (1977), edited by Mary R. Mahl and Helene Koon, and *First Feminists: British Women Writers from 1578–1799* (1984), edited by Moira Ferguson, make available important documents of women's experience.

While the process of rediscovery and dissemination of writing by women is essential, it alone cannot produce the radical transformation of literary study that is the final goal of feminist pedagogy. As Elaine Showalter cautions, 'The task of rediscovery, while altogether admirable, is self-limiting. The supply of Kate Chopins . . . cannot be infinite.' She continues:

> while the process of rediscovery is primary, minor women writers need to be treated historically as well as critically, to be placed in a theoretical framework which treats them as

more than the flotsam of popular culture, and to be connected to each other and to a female literary tradition. A
feminist literary history would describe the continuity and
coherence of women's writing and provide the hypotheses
against which individual writers could be assessed.

(Showalter 1975, p. 444)

Not only are the rediscovery and dissemination of writing by
women insufficient to bring about this radical transformation of
literary study; the limitation of feminist criticism to the close
reading of 'major' women writers (such as Austen, Eliot,
Dickinson and the Brontës) will not bring it about either. This is
especially true if these writers are studied in isolation, without
concern for their relationships with other writers. Moreover,
this sort of study of women's writing can result in a criticism
which actually reinforces cultural stereotypes. Feminist critics
have frequently attacked mainstream critics for their assumptions about women, for their imposition of culturally assumed
notions about women's nature on to a work by a woman author.
Mary Ellmann noted this tendency in one of the first critical
works to approach the question of bias in the treatment of
women in literature, *Thinking about Women* (1968). But we must
be careful to avoid this tendency in our own criticism.

Patricia Meyer Spacks was one of the first to group women
writers systematically in the 'female literary tradition' that
Showalter recommends. In *The Female Imagination* (1975) she
examined similarities of experience and response in writing by
women throughout the centuries. Spacks's book reflects the
pedagogical emphasis referred to earlier in this chapter. It is
based on her own teaching experience and, in particular, on
class discussions in which her students found connections between their own lives and those of characters in fiction written
by women – even in fiction written by women more than a
hundred years ago. Spacks considers aspects of women's experience such as power and passivity, adolescent development, the
female artist, independent women, and others. She begins by
questioning: 'What are the ways of female feeling, the modes of
responding, that persist despite social change? Do any characteristic patterns of self-perception shape the creative expres-
sions of women?' (Spacks 1975, p. 3). Obviously, this approach

is ahistorical and tends towards generalization. The use of the term 'female imagination' is in itself open to charges of stereo-typing, although Spacks uses the term loosely and allows it to encompass a multitude of subtle observations about the be-haviour and attitudes of women in literature. Yet, since it is not fully defined, the term is difficult to use without making certain assumptions about the inherent nature of 'woman'. Since Spacks concentrates her attention for the most part on 'major' writers, the implied 'universality' of her definitions is problem-atic and actually antithetical to the implications of feminist theory. In the context of recent efforts to enlarge the canon of women writers, it has become difficult to accept the notion of realities 'that persist despite social change'. Spacks has been criticized especially by those who insist that feminist criticism must be sensitive to differences in class, race, ethnicity, sexual orientation and historical contexts. Critics such as Barbara Smith (1977) and Elly Bulkin (1982) point out that Spacks concentrates on 'the lives of middle-class women' while pur-porting to include 'fundamental female experience'. Admit-tedly, she hesitates – borrowing Phyllis Chesler's words – 'to construct theories about experiences [she hasn't] had' (Spacks 1975, p. 3). Yet Spacks seems to feel comfortable interpreting texts by white, middle-class, nineteenth-century women whose experiences must surely be as distant from her own as those of black women. As Alice Walker suggests, 'Spacks never lived in 19th-century Yorkshire, so why theorize about the Brontës?' (Walker 1979, p. 50).

Although Annis Pratt's more recent *Archetypal Patterns in Women's Fiction* (1981) is also a synchronic study which de-emphasizes historical distinctions, it is more sensitive to issues of class and race. Pratt studied over 300 novels written by women in order to 'determine if these works constituted a field that could be investigated as a self-contained entity following its own organic principles'. Since Pratt needed 'the widest possible range of novels', she made sure not to limit herself to major writers or to assume middle-class experience as the norm. Pratt looks at working-class women in such novels as Edith Summers Kelley's *Weeds* (1923) and Marta Roberts's *Tumbleweeds* (1940). The observations of black novelists such as Margaret Walker, Paule Marshall, Ann Petry, Toni Morrison, and others, inform many of her conclusions. In addition, Pratt's discussions of love and sexuality in women's fiction do not assume that all women are heterosexual. She recognizes that women's love for each other is a major source of emotional sustenance and self-assertion. Pratt's chapter 'Love and Friendship between Women' (written in collaboration with Andrea Loewenstein) is not as extensive as the more precisely focused studies of lesbian novels by Catharine Stimpson (1982) or Bonnie Zimmerman (1983), but it attempts, at least, to incorporate lesbian experience into any definitions of 'women's' identity, values, sexuality and political ideologies.

As her title suggests, Pratt looks for similarities among women's experiences. She uses women's fiction to explore questions of women's identity and draws upon the theories of archetypal critics, while remaining cognizant of the male bias in their assumptions – especially in Jung's definitions of the feminine.

Pratt insists that her own method of archetypal analysis is different:

> Since I have been accused once or twice of 'believing in archetypes', as if this method derived from some freak of religious conversion, I want to reiterate the pragmatic basis of my approach. Archetypal patterns, as I understand them, represent categories of particulars, which can be described in their interrelationships within a given text or within a larger body of literature. A dogmatic insistence upon preordained, invariable sets of archetypal patterns would distort literary analysis: one must not deduce categories down *into* a body of material but induce them *from* images, symbols, and narrative patterns observed in a significantly various selection of literary works.

> (Pratt 1981, p. 5)

Pratt's explanation notwithstanding, I am not completely convinced that she has worked out these patterns through inductive reasoning alone. Underlying her examples are the traditional notions of the 'quest' described by Jung, Campbell and Frye, as well as those stages of Jungian individuation that are reflected in her book's organizational structure, which is based on the quest pattern: beginning with 'the novel of development', she moves on to 'novels of marriage' and 'social protest', then to chapters on love and friendship, and concludes with 'singleness and solitude' and 'rebirth and transformation'. Yet Pratt does transform traditional expectations of the quest pattern when she applies it to women, by giving it a different shape, since what distinguishes her archetypal criticism from that of her male predecessors is her understanding of the profound differences between what society allows women and what it makes possible for men. She brings the weight of evidence from hundreds of novels to conclude 'that even the most conservative women authors create narratives manifesting an acute tension between what any normal human being might desire and what a woman must become' (Pratt 1981, pp. 5–6).

But neither Pratt's 'archetypal patterns' nor Spacks's 'female imagination' completely satisfies Showalter's desire for a 'theoretical framework' adequate to illuminate 'a female literary tradition'. It is still necessary to go beyond similarities of image, theme and structure, and to consider issues that link women's writing to *specific* sociocultural realities. Such studies may concern the products of a particular age or school. For example, in *Woman's Fiction: A Guide to Novels by and about Women in America 1820–1870* (1978) Nina Baym treats – with a complex awareness of women's history – novels which have long been either ridiculed or forgotten by literary critics, but which served women readers of their time by making their own experiences seem worthy of attention. Baym does not pretend that these novels merit praise equal to fiction by Austen or Eliot, but she does note that

'purely' literary criteria, as they have been employed to identify the best American works, have inevitably had a bias in favor of things male – in favor, say, of whaling ships rather than the sewing circle as a symbol of the human community; in favor of satires on domineering mothers, shrewish wives, or betraying mistresses rather than tyrannical fathers, abusive husbands, or philandering suitors; displaying an exquisite compassion for the crises of the adolescent male, but altogether impatient with the parallel crises of the female.

(Baym 1978, p. 14)

My own *Feminine Consciousness in the Modern British Novel* (1975) is a study of the relationship between the rise of the feminist movement during the first decades of this century and the simultaneous development of the novel of consciousness by women writers. While it is not strictly a literary history, since its methodology is primarily textual, it links writers who were responding similarly to the same dramatic changes in women's expectations, and who were struggling with older definitions of femininity which ran counter to those expectations. I am concerned with the fictional devices created by innovative novelists such as Dorothy Richardson and Virginia Woolf to explore the internal reality of female characters as they struggled to deal with these conflicts in expectations. The term 'feminine consciousness' differs from 'female imagination', however, because it does not imply any *inherent* characteristics in women authors. Instead it refers to the methods created by women writers to depict the internal life of female characters in the process of self-discovery.

Studying groups of women writers within a particular time-frame and social class may actually lead to a redefinition of periods in literary history. The traditional parameters of a period may be shifted or its predominant preoccupations reassessed if it is studied through the perspective of women writers. The modernist period is a good case in point. The Standard literary histories tend to characterize modernism in terms of the reaction against Victorianism, the effects of the First World War and increasing alienation from a society overwhelmingly industrialized, along with a corresponding development of experimental modes in literature which were attempts to confront and counteract those dominant tendencies of the age. Yet, by shifting the focus to women, it is possible to link modernism to the rise of the suffrage movement (to note, for instance, that the major literary journal of the period, *The Egoist*, evolved out of the feminist publication *The New Freewoman*), and to recognize how experiments in style and structure correspond to significant changes in the relations between women and men, as well as to a growing uneasiness about sexuality (such as that expressed in *The Waste Land* or *The Sun Also Rises*).

So far I have been discussing books which concentrate largely on the *writing* of women. Ellen Moers's *Literary Women* (1977) concentrates on the women who did the writing. Highly idiosyncratic in its positions and preferences, limited in its choices of authors, and oddly unsystematic in its organization, it is none the less a brilliant, visionary study of the well-known women authors. Moers was one of the first critics to look at women authors in terms of a women's tradition. *Literary Women* is celebratory criticism. Moers does not ask why there were so few famous women writers; she does not ask why other talented women remained silent. Instead, she boldly asserts that 'the written word in its most memorable form, starting in the eighteenth century, became increasingly and steadily the work of women.' Moers looks at women like Jane Austen, Harriet Beecher Stowe, George Eliot, Charlotte Brontë, Willa Cather and Gertrude Stein, and reads them not as anomalous, eccentric or precious, but as vital, active precursors and innovators. She considers the bonds of friendship, shared interests, correspondence between writers – all the ways in which they gave support to each other in their struggles to create and publish.

Moers's explanation of her method illuminates both the startling intensity of her book and its highly original contributions to literary study:

> From the start my approach has been essentially a practical one. If there seemed something new worth saying about a major writer as a woman writer, that is what I say here: Jane Austen's precise concern with money, Mary Shelley's creation of a birth myth, Emily Dickinson's use of the metaphors of girlhood, George Sand's obsession with the illiterate, Harriet Beecher Stowe's access as a woman to the drama of landscape, Emily Brontë's access as a woman to the savagery of childhood, the ending of mothers in Virginia Woolf and modern fiction after her, George Eliot's place in a tradition of women's literature originated by Mme de Staël, which made a myth of glory, of the public appurtenances of fame, for the woman of genius.
>
> (Moers 1977, p. xiii)

The book that most lives up to Showalter's call for a 'feminist literary history' turns out to be, not surprisingly, her own *A Literature of their Own: British Women Novelists from Brontë to Lessing* (1977). (Of course we still need a comparably comprehensive history of American women writers as well.) Showalter begins by pointing out that 'each generation of women writers has found itself, in a sense, without a history, forced to rediscover the past anew, forging again and again the consciousness of their sex' (Showalter 1977, pp. 11–12). The task of rediscovery, discussed earlier in this chapter, has been aided immeasurably by Showalter, who has brought renewed attention to a surprising number of writers, such as Mary E. Braddon, Rhoda Broughton, Sarah Grand and George Egerton. Showalter's methodology proves to be especially productive. Rather than concentrating on a special vision inherently belonging to women, she studies their contributions to literature as part of 'the female subculture'. She emphasizes that 'it is important to see the female literary tradition in ... relation to the wider evolution of women's self-awareness and to the ways in which any minority group finds its direction of self-expression relative to a dominant society' (Showalter 1977, p. 11). Showalter's useful definition of women's literature as a subculture with its own patterns of relationship, themes, images and concerns provides a starting-place from which feminist criticism may counteract the ahistorical tendency of much work in the field. Showalter had been uncomfortable with Spacks's notion of a 'female imagination' which does not include an analysis of culture, history and tradition. She reminds her readers that 'the female literary tradition comes from the still-evolving relation between women writers and their society'. Showalter is firmly committed to a socially based theory that illuminates 'the ways in which the self-awareness of the woman writer has translated itself into a literary form in a specific place and time-span, how this self-awareness has changed and developed, and where it might lead' (p. 12).

Showalter replaces traditional literary periods with three stages in *women's* literary history, stages which mark their growth in consciousness as feminine, feminist and female. These correspond to phases of other literary subcultures:

First, there is a prolonged phase of *imitation* of the prevailing modes of the dominant tradition, and *internalization* of its standards of art and its views on social roles. Second, there is a phase of *protest* against these standards and values, and *advocacy* of minority rights and values, including a demand for autonomy. Finally, there is a phase of *self-discovery*, a turning

inward freed from some of the dependency of opposition, a
search for identity.

(p. 13)

Accordingly, Showalter discusses recent women novelists such
as Iris Murdoch, Doris Lessing and Margaret Drabble with
approval because they are 'able to incorporate many of the
strengths of the past with a new range of language and experience' (p. 35). Like the 'feminine' novelists, these contemporary
writers are concerned with conflicts between art and love,
self-fulfilment and duty; like the 'feminists', they are 'aware of
their place in a political system and their connectedness to other
women' (p. 35). Showalter praises them also for daring to use a
vocabulary previously reserved for men and for their boldness
in describing tabooed areas of sexuality. These new novelists,
then, provide us with a synthesis of the 'feminine' and the
'feminist'. Yet it seems to me that assuming such a dialectical
process forces too easy a synthesis.

Showalter's paradigm, while useful for organizational purposes, may actually distort the individual achievements of
particular authors. Since she tends to measure her authors
against an ideal of self-development and sexual awareness that
belongs to the late twentieth century, nearly all the women who
wrote earlier than the 1960s fail to achieve complete success in
her terms. She appears to assume that history moves towards
greater and greater improvements and more intense consciousness. But are the 'female' novelists of our time really more
successful in attaining their *own* goals as women than were the
less evolved 'feminine' and 'feminist' novelists? Should we
blame earlier authors for not achieving twentieth-century
modes of independence, for themselves or for their literary
creations? Showalter is especially hard on Olive Schreiner, for
example. Her analysis tends to undercut Schreiner's genuine
achievements. For a critic whose methodology is historical,
Showalter sometimes seems curiously ahistorical herself. Kathleen Blake notes Showalter's impatience and suggests that
'sympathy closely depends on historical perspective':

There is so much that is lamentable in women's heritage that
feminist critics may make a habit of lamenting, and too
often they lament that women writers did not give us more

successful heroines, more to celebrate. . . . I prefer to blame women's lot than the women artists who depicted it.

(Blake 1983, pp. x–xi)

Showalter's most recent critical essays show that she has become even more deeply immersed in the idea of women's culture as the basis for feminist criticism. She explains that 'a theory based on a model of women's culture . . . incorporates ideas about woman's body, language, and psyche but interprets them in relation to the social contexts in which they occur' (Showalter 1982, p. 27). Showalter is not alone in stressing the relationship between women's writing and women's culture. In 1975 Josephine Donovan had predicted that 'another series of concepts likely to be developed in the next several years revolves around the concept of a female culture' (Donovan 1975, pp. 76–7). And Cheri Register has observed:

If women's work is organized differently from men's, if the day is structured differently, if space is inhabited differently, if styles of verbal communication are different, then it follows that women will have a different sense of beauty and pleasure. Whether this shows up in literature depends on the extent to which women's literary forms are derived from a female culture, rather than determined by literary tradition and critical response.

(Register 1980, p. 272)

Currently, feminist critics are interested in studying relationships between women, including mothers and daughters, sisters, friends, lesbians and female communities (see, for example, Davidson and Broner 1980; Bernikow 1980; Todd 1979; Auerbach 1979; Faderman 1981). Such studies are extensions of Virginia Woolf's comment in *A Room of One's Own* that women are rarely portrayed in relation to each other in fiction written by men. Such a shift in focus allows feminist critics to explore a truly new area, one not addressed by male writers or critics. Moreover, this new focus also allows feminist critics to move away from what Carolyn Heilbrun fears are 'the effects of a feminist criticism or history that necessarily focuses on the constraints of female life, constraints that, however overcome or subverted or subtly recognized in novels and in life, remain nonetheless crippling' (Heilbrun 1982, p. 291).

This focus is consistent with Showalter's interest in women's culture as it has been described by the anthropologists Shirley and Edwin Ardener. Her insistence on 'a feminist criticism that is genuinely women centered, independent, and intellectually coherent' (Showalter 1982, p. 14) places her firmly on the side of criticism that is concerned with 'women as *writers*', for which she invents the term 'gynocritics' (pp. 14–15). Showalter sees more possibilities in 'gynocritics' than in what she calls 'the feminist critique', which considers 'the images and stereotypes of women in literature, the omissions and misconceptions about women in criticism, and woman-as-sign in semiotic systems', but is essentially 'redressing a grievance and is built upon existing models'.

Although Showalter maintains that this 'feminist obsession with correcting, modifying, supplementing, revising, humanizing, or even attacking male critical theory keeps us dependent upon it and retards our progress in solving our own theoretical problems' (Showalter 1982, p. 13), one cannot deny that some of the most challenging work in feminist criticism was produced through the very force of that obsession. Who can forget how powerfully Kate Millett's *Sexual Politics* (1970) acted as a catalyst for the subsequent explosion of reaction against misogyny in the works of male writers? Even now, after more than a decade, it still has the energy to unsettle and disturb a complacent reader. Annette Kolodny's *The Lay of the Land* (1975) and Judith Fetterley's *The Resisting Reader* (1978) are two other studies focused on the works of male writers that alter our ways of understanding the male literary tradition and how it has dealt with us. What I have called the second initiating impulse, anger, continues to generate important and increasingly sophisticated studies. I say this despite the fact that my own strongest preferences remain with the first initiating impulse – love, and women writers. Yet one must recognize the need for further explorations both of male authors and their stereotyping of women, and of masculinist critics and their mistrust of feminist criticism, for much work remains to be done in exposing the myriad ways patriarchal attitudes affect literary criticism.

It should be clear by now that my initial division of feminist criticism into two strands, the study of women writers and the analysis of women in literature, rapidly fractions itself into many sub-categories and complexities, depending upon a particular critic's theoretical framework. The issue of personal vision also becomes more complicated when the academic tendency towards theorization comes into conflict with individual experience. Annette Kolodny has admitted honestly that

> in our heart of hearts, of course, most critics are really structuralists (whether or not they accept the label) because what we are seeking are patterns (or structures) that can order and explain the otherwise inchoate; thus, we invent, or believe we discover, relational patternings in the texts we read which promise transcendence from difficulty and perplexity to clarity and coherence.
>
> (Kolodny 1980, p. 17)

Of course, the process of ordering and patterning changes the nature of the experience both of reading the text and of knowing its shape and content. Kolodny is one of the foremost feminist critics who continues to speak tentatively about this process of ordering, referring to it as something 'we invent', 'or believe we discover'.

She is not willing to discard the variety of approaches she discovers in feminist criticism in favour of a single theoretical model. She advocates, rather, 'a playful pluralism, responsive to the possibilities of multiple critical schools and methods, but captive of none', a recognition 'that the many tools needed for our analysis will necessarily be largely inherited and only partly of our own making' (Kolodny 1980, p. 19). Showalter, however, is uneasy about the notion of 'playful pluralism', and answers Kolodny with the following:

> If we see our critical job as interpretation and reinterpretation, we must be content with pluralism as our critical stance. But if we wish to ask questions about the process and the contexts of writing, if we genuinely wish to define ourselves to the uninitiated, we cannot rule out the prospect of theoretical consensus at this early stage.
>
> (Showalter 1982, p. 13)

Yet Showalter's call for a 'theoretical consensus', and her

dismissal of other types of feminist criticism in order to arrive at her own theory, have been challenged by Carolyn Allen, who asks

> why we need or would want a single model for all feminist criticism just now when we have finally begun to move away from close reading to investigate a range of theoretical directions. Non-feminist discourses are not monolithic, so it is difficult to see the value or purpose in limiting the theoretical basis of our work.
>
> (Allen 1982, p. 299)

Showalter's eagerness to formulate a theoretical model for feminist criticism is connected with her desire to distinguish feminist criticism from all other modes of literary criticism. Looking at the development of feminist criticism from a historical perspective, Showalter notes that 'an early obstacle to constructing a theoretical framework for feminist criticism was the unwillingness of many women to limit or bound an expressive and dynamic enterprise'. Showalter's tone here betrays her impatience with 'advocates of the anti-theoretical position'. The term 'unwillingness' seems to connote stubbornness, or short-sightedness, or lack of rigour. Showalter suggests genuine reasons behind the anti-theoretical position, however, and refers sympathetically to

> feminist visionaries, such as Mary Daly, Adrienne Rich, and Marguerite Duras, who had satirized the sterile narcissism of male scholarship and celebrated women's fortunate exclusion from its patriarchal methodolatry. Thus for some, feminist criticism was an act of resistance to theory, a confrontation with existing canons and judgements.
>
> (Showalter 1982, pp. 10–11)

Nevertheless, while Showalter expresses 'sympathy' for 'the suspicion of monolithic systems and the rejection of scientism in literary study that many feminist critics have voiced', her own impulse towards a theory of her own finally necessitates her rejection of the anti-theoretical position. It interests me to find that her method for doing so entails creating a pattern of historical *phases* similar to the one she had used earlier to describe women's literary history:

Yet it now appears that what looked like a theoretical impasse was actually an evolutionary phase. The ethics of awakening have been succeeded, at least in the universities, by a second stage characterized by anxiety about the isolation of feminist criticism from a critical community increasingly theoretical in its interests and indifferent to women's writing. The question of how feminist criticism should define itself with relation to the new critical theories and theorists has occasioned sharp debate in Europe and the United States.

(p. 11)

While I find this ongoing debate over theory to be provocative and invigorating, I am not yet convinced that resolving it will make feminist criticism less isolated from that 'critical community' which sets theory above experience in its claims to dominance. There may always be a split between the theoretical impulses of criticism practised 'in the universities' and those passions of love and anger that resist its categorization.

References

Allen, Carolyn (1982) 'Critical Response: Feminist(s) Reading: A Response to Elaine Showalter'. In Elizabeth Abel (ed.), *Writing and Sexual Difference*. Chicago, Ill.: University of Chicago Press.

Auerbach, Nina (1979) *Communities of Women: An Idea in Fiction*. Cambridge, Mass.: Harvard University Press.

Baym, Nina (1978) *Woman's Fiction: A Guide to Novels by and about Women in America 1820–1870*. Ithaca, NY: Cornell University Press.

Bernikow, Louise (ed.) (1974) *The World Split Open: Four Centuries of Women Poets in England and America 1552–1950*. New York: Random House.

Bernikow, Louise (1980) *Among Women*. New York: Harmony-Crown.

Blake, Kathleen (1983) *Love and the Woman Question in Victorian Literature: the Art of Self-Postponement*. New York: Barnes and Noble.

Bulkin, Elly (1982) 'An Interchange on Feminist Criticism: On "Dancing Through the Minefield"', with Judith Kegan Gardiner, Rena Grasso Patterson and Annette Kolodny, *Feminist Studies*, 8 (Fall), pp. 638–40.

Cruikshank, Margaret (ed.) (1982) *Lesbian Studies: Present and Future*. Old Westbury, NY: Feminist Press.

Davidson, Cathy N., and Broner, E. M. (eds) (1980) *The Lost Tradition: Mothers and Daughters in Literature*. New York: Frederick Ungar.

Diamond, Arlyn, and Edwards, Lee R. (eds) (1977) *The Authority of*

Experience. Amherst, Mass.: University of Massachusetts Press.

Donovan, Josephine (1975) *Feminist Literary Criticism: Explorations in Theory*. Lexington, Ky: University of Kentucky Press.

Ellmann, Mary (1968) *Thinking about Women*. New York: Harcourt Brace and World.

Faderman, Lilian (1981) *Surpassing the Love of Men: Romantic Friendship and Love between Women from the Renaissance to the Present*. New York: William Morrow.

Ferguson, Moira (ed.) (1984) *First Feminists: British Women Writers from 1578–1799*. Old Westbury, NY: Feminist Press.

Fetterley, Judith (1978) *The Resisting Reader: A Feminist Approach to American Fiction*. Bloomington, Ind.: Indiana University Press.

Fisher, Dexter (ed.) (1980) *The Third Woman: Minority Women Writers of the United States*. Boston, Mass.: Houghton Mifflin.

Gilbert, Sandra M. (1979) 'A Fine, White Flying Myth: The Life/Work of Sylvia Plath'. In Sandra M. Gilbert and Susan Gubar (eds), *Shakespeare's Sisters: Feminist Essays on Women Poets*. Bloomington, Ind.: Indiana University Press.

Heilbrun, Carolyn G. (1982) 'Critical Response: A Response to *Writing and Sexual Difference*'. In Elizabeth Abel (ed.), *Writing and Sexual Difference*. Chicago, Ill.: University of Chicago Press.

Hoffman, Nancy, Secor, Cynthia, and Tinsley, Adrian (eds) (1972) *Female Studies VI: Closer to the Ground*. Old Westbury, NY: Feminist Press.

Howe, Florence, and Bass, Ellen (eds) (1973) *No More Masks! An Anthology of Poems by Women*. Garden City, NY: Doubleday.

Hull, Gloria T. (1979) ' "Under the Days": The Buried Life and Poetry of Angelina Weld Grimké', *Conditions: Five: The Black Women's Issue*, pp. 17–25.

Hull, Gloria T., Scott, Patricia Bell, and Smith, Barbara (eds) (1982) *All the Women are White, All the Blacks are Men, But Some of us are Brave: Black Women's Studies*. Old Westbury, NY: Feminist Press.

Kaplan, Cora (ed.) (1975) *Salt and Bitter and Good: Three Centuries of English and American Women Poets*. New York: Paddington Press.

Kaplan, Sydney Janet (1975) *Feminine Consciousness in the Modern British Novel*. Urbana, Ill.: University of Illinois Press.

Kolodny, Annette (1975) *The Lay of the Land: Metaphor as Experience in American Life and Letters*. Chapel Hill, NC: University of North Carolina Press.

Kolodny, Annette (1980) 'Dancing through the Minefield: Some Observations on the Theory, Practice and Politics of a Feminist Literary Criticism', *Feminist Studies*, 6, 1 (Spring), pp. 1–25.

Lessing, Doris (1973) 'On the Golden Notebook', *Partisan Review*, 40, 1, pp. 14–30.

Mahl, Mary R., and Koon, Helene (eds) (1977) *The Female Spectator:*

English Women Writers before 1800. Bloomington, Ind.: Indiana University Press.

Millett, Kate (1970) *Sexual Politics.* Garden City, NY: Doubleday.

Moers, Ellen (1977) *Literary Women: The Great Writers.* Garden City, NY: Anchor Press/Doubleday.

Moraga, Cherríe, and Anzaldúa, Gloria (eds) (1981) *This Bridge Called My Back: Writings by Radical Women of Color.* Watertown, Mass.: Persephone Press.

Pratt, Annis (1976) 'The New Feminist Criticisms: Exploring the History of the New Space'. In Joan I. Roberts (ed.), *Beyond Intellectual Sexism; A New Woman, A New Reality.* New York: David McKay.

Pratt, Annis (1981) *Archetypal Patterns in Women's Fiction,* with Barbara White, Andrea Loewenstein and Mary Wyer. Bloomington, Ind.: Indiana University Press.

Register, Cheri (1980) 'Review Essay: Literary Criticism', *Signs: Journal of Women in Culture and Society,* 6, 2, pp. 268–82.

Showalter, Elaine (1970) 'Women and the Literary Curriculum', *College English,* 32, pp. 855–62.

Showalter, Elaine (1975) 'Review Essay: Literary Criticism', *Signs: Journal of Women in Culture and Society,* 1, pp. 435–60.

Showalter, Elaine (1977) *A Literature of their Own: British Women Novelists from Brontë to Lessing.* Princeton, NJ: Princeton University Press.

Showalter, Elaine (1982) 'Feminist Criticism in the Wilderness'. In Elizabeth Abel (ed.), *Writing and Sexual Difference.* Chicago, Ill.: University of Chicago Press.

Smith, Barbara (1977) 'Towards a Black Feminist Criticism', *Conditions: Two,* pp. 25–44.

Spacks, Patricia Meyer (1975) *The Female Imagination.* New York: Knopf.

Stimpson, Catharine R. (1982) 'Zero Degree Deviancy: The Lesbian Novel in English'. In Elizabeth Abel (ed.), *Writing and Sexual Difference.* Chicago, Ill.: University of Chicago Press.

Todd, Janet M. (1979) *Women's Friendship in Literature.* New York, Columbia University Press.

Walker, Alice (1979) '*One* Child of One's Own', *Ms,* 8, 2, pp. 47–50, 72–5.

Washington, Mary Helen (ed.) (1980) *Midnight Birds: Stories by Contemporary Black Women Writers.* New York: Doubleday.

Zimmerman, Bonnie (1983) 'Exiting from Patriarchy: The Lesbian Novel of Development'. In Elizabeth Abel, Marianne Hirsch and Elizabeth Langland (eds), *The Voyage In: Fictions of Female Development.* Hanover, NH: University Press of New England.

3
The politics of language:
beyond the gender principle?
NELLY FURMAN

In our culture, marriage is a privileged place for the interaction of the sexes. Marriage can be viewed as the blissful coming together of equal voices speaking in unison, or as an ongoing dialogue between individuals affirming in turn their differences. In the first instance, marriage is seen as a social structure where equality and unity can be achieved; in the second, it is the place which allows the play of difference. Lévi-Strauss suggests that linguists and sociologists are studying the same thing. Nelly Furman, following him, holds that understanding marriage as a human experience, a social structure or a verbal deed can help us perceive the ideological values at work in language as well as in society. Literary criticism is one of the places where feminism confronts patriarchal values. Feminist criticism unveils the prejudices at work in our appreciation of cultural artefacts, and shows us how the linguistic medium promotes and transmits the values woven through the fabric of our society. While the egalitarian argument in feminist criticism calls for equal representation in literature of women's and men's experience of life, post-structuralist feminism denounces representation itself as already a patriarchal paradigm. Marriage, like criticism, is a locus of interaction for the two sexes. Marriage thus can serve to illustrate how differing modes of feminist criticism relate to our patriarchal culture and its language.

*

If the function of the feminist endeavour is to unveil the workings of the patriarchal system of values and display the structures which control the social and cultural order, then we must begin, as Hélène Cixous points out, by confronting the politics of language:

> You'll understand why I think that no political reflection can dispense with reflection on language, with work on language. For as soon as we exist, we are born into language and language speaks (to) us, dictates its law, a law of death: it lays down its familial model, lays down its conjugal model, and even at the moment of uttering a sentence, admitting a notion of 'being', a question of being, an ontology, we are already seized by a certain kind of masculine desire, the desire that mobilizes philosophical discourse.
>
> (Cixous 1981, p. 45)

At the end of his study of *The Elementary Structures of Kinship*, Claude Lévi–Strauss suggests that 'linguists and sociologists do not merely apply the same methods but are studying the same thing' (Lévi-Strauss 1969, p. 493). For Lévi-Strauss, marriage is a form of human communication. In an exogamous matrimonial system, potential wives are assets in the service of society. Through the exchange of daughters and sisters, families are forced into a system of reciprocity whereby they establish enduring ties with other families which assure the formation of social communities. The prohibition of incest, which imposes the exchange of women, is not, according to Lévi-Strauss, a cultural option but a social necessity. Because it channels the biological family into the social organization, marriage is the agency that marshals the interaction of nature and culture. Since, in Lévi-Strauss's view, marriage operates like a communication device between groups, it functions fundamentally like a linguistic system; in marriage the exchange of women assures the continuity of the social structure, whereas the circulation of words performs a similar action for the linguistic system:

> The emergence of symbolic thought must have required that women, like words, should be things that were exchanged. In this new case, indeed, this was the only means of overcoming the contradiction by which the same woman was seen under two incompatible aspects: on the one hand, as the object of

personal desire, thus exciting sexual and proprietorial in-
stincts; and, on the other, as the subject of the desire of others,
and seen as such, i.e., as the means of binding others through
alliance with them. But woman could never become just a
sign and nothing more, since even in a man's world she is still
a person, and since in so far as she is defined as a sign she must
be recognized as a generator of signs. In the matrimonial
dialogue of men, woman is never purely what is spoken
about; for if women in general represent a certain category of
signs, destined to a certain kind of communication, each
woman preserves a particular value arising from her talent,
before and after marriage, for taking her part in a duet. In
contrast to words, which have wholly become signs, woman
has remained at once a sign and a value.

(Lévi-Strauss 1969, p. 496)

In a world defined by man, the trouble with woman is that she is
at once an object of desire and an object of exchange, valued on
the one hand as a person in her own right, and on the other
considered simply as a relational sign between men. At the
intersection of two incompatible systems, woman appears as the
embodiment of an impossible duality, the locus of an opposition. Lévi-Strauss's contention that woman is both a person
and a sign, a human being and a depersonalized, subjectless
structure, clearly indicates that the discussion of woman's
relationship to language – of woman and/in language – will take
different paths according to whether woman is understood as
being a person or a sign.

As a person, woman is a transcendental being, a consciousness and a voice 'taking her part in the duet'. She is endowed
with individual characteristics which determine her value as a
member of society. Her experience of life is contingent upon her
psychological make-up, her individual circumstances, as well as
society's expectations and limitations linked to age, sex, creed,
and so on. Because a person's perception of events is necessarily
inflected by somatic and psychological characteristics, each
person's experience of life is unique. Nevertheless, since sex is
one of the essential and irreducible differentiating factors
among individuals, women and men, in general, may experience situations in a markedly different manner. For proponents

of the biological argument, sexual differences explain the distinctive features of a feminine or a masculine 'nature'.

It is therefore not surprising that the study of perceptual differences between women and men has elicited the interest of feminist scholars both in the social sciences and in the humanities. In literature, this has led feminist critics to collect and study the works of women authors in order to recover 'a female tradition'. For Elaine Showalter, the existence of separate literary traditions is less a matter of biological differences than the result of differences in the socialization process of the two sexes. 'The female literary tradition comes from the still-evolving relationship between women writers and their society', she tells us, and she adds: 'I am intentionally looking, not at an innate sexual attitude, but at the ways in which the self-awareness of woman writer has translated itself into a literary form in a specific place and time-span' (Showalter 1977, p. 12). Similarly, Gilbert and Gubar suggest that the common thread in the female literary tradition is the search for an emancipated self: 'the striking coherence we noticed in literature by women could be explained by a common, female impulse to struggle free from social and literary confinement through strategic redefinitions of self, art and society' (Gilbert and Gubar 1979, p. xii). For Gilbert and Gubar, as for Showalter, women authors are individuals who react in a collective, sisterly manner to a common social reality. This explains the recurrence of topics, themes, images and metaphors in the literary works of women which was noted by Elaine Showalter (1977, p. 11), and also stated by Gilbert and Gubar:

> Reading the writing of women from Jane Austen and Charlotte Brontë to Emily Dickinson, Virginia Woolf, and Sylvia Plath, we were surprised by the coherence of theme and imagery that we encountered in the works of writers who were often geographically, historically, and psychologically distant from each other. Indeed, even when we studied woman's achievements in radically different genres, we found what began to seem a distinctively female literary tradition.
>
> (Gilbert and Gubar 1979, p. xi)

Feminist critics have tried to understand how social restrictions have shaped women's lives and their relationship to art and literature, and they have then proceeded to validate women's perceptions of life by restoring their writings to public view. By retrieving works written by women and by giving these works the kind of visibility and authority hitherto accorded to men's literary production, feminist critics have established the corpus of a female literary tradition.

Feminist consciousness has given a new ardour and excitement to literary studies. By studying the status of women in literature and the works of women authors, feminist critics have unveiled some of the biases at work in traditional approaches to literature – namely the fact that literary genres, situations and characters have often been defined according to a masculine perspective. Yet an unfortunate consequence of the critics' efforts towards a separate, but equally valid, literary tradition is that they leave unquestioned some of the prejudices which create the authority of tradition in the first place. Among those notions which remain unchallenged are the assumed 'universality' of human experience and the 'reflection' of experience in literary representation. Besides a belief in the possibility and desirability of equality, many feminist critics embrace the learning imparted by traditional humanism and consequently take for granted that, as human beings, we all share basic universal values, and that, although women's and men's experience of the world may be different, we have a common view of experience, a collective understanding of language and literature – in short, that we share an unquestioned 'common sense'.[1]

For Gilbert and Gubar, as for Showalter, there is no doubt that literature reflects life, and that experience of life is translated into literature. Women's alienation from the literary canon is due to the fact that the literary works of male authors reflect chiefly a male view of life which is not necessarily women's experience. To describe, as Gilbert and Gubar have sought to do in *The Madwoman in the Attic*, 'both the experience that generates metaphor and the metaphor that creates experience' (1979, p. xiii) implies a causal relationship between experience and metaphor which simultaneously suggests that life and language are conceived as separate (or separable) entities. When literature is viewed as a representational art whose function is to 'picture' life, what is ignored or pushed aside is the part played by language.

In the last few years, however, critical approaches influenced by structuralism and deconstruction have challenged the view that language is a stable, predictable medium, and have put into question the notion that writing merely 'represents' speech, thought or experience. Language, from a post-structuralist position, is not an empirical object but a structuring process; and questions concerning women and literature will be broached differently according to whether we apprehend language as a stable medium or a continuous process.

Literature may be thought of as a representation of life, but literature can also be viewed as a non-referential linguistic system of communication. Like woman, in Lévi-Strauss's analysis, literature is at the juncture of two systems. If, as Lévi-Strauss suggests, marriage functions like a linguistic system of communication, then a study of marriage as a linguistic operation could help us understand language as a non-referential system. Both the marital vow and the ceremony which enacts it will serve as the working metaphors of this chapter.

In the sentence 'I now pronounce you man and wife', the word 'man' refers to the essence of a male being, and the word 'wife' describes woman, not as a person, in her essence, but as a dependence – that is to say, simply as a relational sign. We are reminded here of Simone de Beauvoir's famous statement: 'She is defined and differentiated with reference to man and not he with reference to her; she is the incidental, the inessential as opposed to the essential. He is the Subject, he is the Absolute – she is the Other' (de Beauvoir 1961, p. xvi). In order to describe both women and men on a par, through equivalent terms whose order need not be fixed, the sentence 'I now pronounce you man and wife' should be changed to either 'I now pronounce you husband and wife', if one wishes to call attention to the social status of the parties, or to 'I now pronounce you man and woman', if one wants to suggest that marriage defines the essence of the two sexes. The choice of words used in the ceremony may not affect the couple's relationship, nor necessarily give an accurate description of the experience of marriage, but it indicates how the marital relationship is viewed or imagined. Because the influence of language can be insidious, the traditional marital pronouncement may help perpetuate sexual discrimination. Whether one prefers the parity of 'husband and wife' or that of 'man and woman', language in this analysis is understood as being simply a tool in the struggle towards equality of the sexes.

While the sentence 'I now pronounce you husband and wife' may not establish or represent a truly egalitarian marriage, it does bring about the social reality of marriage, when spoken by a competent official in the appropriate circumstances. The person who performs the ritual must be someone certified to make such a pronouncement, and the bride and groom need only be individuals legally able to enter into a marital contract. Marriage, like most social interaction, is realized in and through the linguistic medium. Before becoming a social reality, marriage is a verbal deed. The speech act which institutes marriage is preceded by a dialogue where each of the participants is also asked to perform a speech act by answering 'I do' to the question 'Do you take this woman or this man to be your lawful wedded wife or husband?'[2]

For those getting married, the exchange of vows means legal responsibility and supposedly emotional commitment, but, for the linguist, the interaction of the parties, the fact that each in turn occupies the position of speaking subject or addressee, generates a *text*. Utterances have a double aspect: they can be seen as giving us an account of reality, or they can be considered as a discourse, that is to say an enunciation supposing a narrator and a listener or a reader.[3]

As we have seen, the language of the marital vows may be apprehended as a representational medium or as a performative act; literature likewise may be viewed as a mimetic document which represents our concept of reality, or it may be seen primarily as a linguistic construct.[4] Although a specific marital ceremony recalls others and inscribes itself in a series of similar ceremonies, each marriage is a unique performance and denotes only itself. In like manner, a literary work may refer us to others, yet it still retains its specificity. When literature is considered *a priori* as a linguistic construct, it too is a self-referential, dialogical structure. The literary text is the space where writer and reader, narrator and narratee engage in dialogue, and where a specific literary piece enters into the literary system and inscribes itself into a network of intertextual relationships with other literary works.[5]

The performance of the marriage ceremony enacts the formulaic statement of the marital vows. The words 'I' and 'thou' of the marital pronouncement are merely linguistic indicators, signifiers which do not designate specific psychological beings, but depersonalized structural subjects. The participants are speaking subjects, they perform as would characters in a play or a novel, but the lines they speak, whether they acknowledge it or not, have been written by yet another subject, *the subject of enunciation* (Todorov 1972, p. 132). The subject of enunciation is not someone recognizable through biographical or psychological information, not a nameable person. Conceived rather as a strategic position, a structure impervious to individual wishes, it is what Michel Foucault calls the 'author-function' (Foucault 1979, pp. 158–60). Because thinking in terms of a subject of enunciation allows us to delineate the choices available to individual writers and reveal the position they take in established forms of discourses, Julia Kristeva calls it 'the operating consciousness' of signification (1980, p. 131). For her, as for many of her contemporaries, the subject of enunciation is the structure and the space where post-structuralist criticism inscribes political and cultural ideology.[6] Whether in a text written in the first person, or in the third-person realistic novel, or any impersonal form of expository writing, the subject of enunciation delineates the choices available to individual writers in established forms of discourses.

Traditional forms of discourse, be they theoretical, 'realistic', epistolary, confessional or expository, whether written by a woman or a man, are necessarily modulated and codified by our patriarchal cultural values. Thus, as Stephen Heath explains, taking theoretical discourse as an example:

> any answer to the questions posed will be in terms of the identification of a discourse that is finally masculine, not because of some conception of theory as male but because in the last resort any discourse which fails to take account of the problem of sexual difference in its enunciation and address will be, within a patriarchal order, precisely indifferent, a reflection of male domination. It might be added, moreover, as a kind of working rule, that where a discourse appeals directly to an image, to an immediacy of seeing, as a point of

its argument or demonstration, one can be sure that all difference is being elided, that the unity of some accepted vision is being reproduced.

(Heath 1978, p. 53)

When feminist critics focus their interest on women's experience of life and its 'picturing' in literature, what is left unquestioned is whether literature conceived as a representational art is not *per se* a patriarchal form of discourse. What is taken for granted in the study of images and their relation to experience is that the 'picturing' of experience is gender-neutral or free of ideological value.

In the wake of structuralism, however, new attention has been directed to the politics of representation, and particularly to the relationship between language and representation. At the turn of the century, the Swiss linguist Ferdinand de Saussure contested the notion that language was founded on representational characteristics. The words 'woman', '*mujer*', '*Weib*' and '*femme*' have nearly the same meaning, yet their configuration and pronunciation differ greatly, showing that the relationship between concepts, images and words is arbitrary. Words come to have meaning not because of some external exigency but through social consensus. The linguistic system consists of signs, linguistic units which are made up of two interrelated yet asymmetrical parts, a signifier and a signified. Signifiers are the material support of language; they could be described as a series of sounds and/or a network of written letters. For communication to take place, each sound or group of letters is a signifier which needs to be differentiated from all other signifiers in its category. The link between signifier and signified is an arbitrary social convention. For example, the phonetic or visual differences between the infinitive to 'read', the past participle 'read', and the colour 'red' may seem minute, yet these differences put into motion the signifying process which allows us to differentiate among signifiers, to link signifiers to signifieds, and thus understand different concepts. Since there are more signifiers than signifieds, language in the Saussurean viewpoint does not operate according to a system of equivalent exchanges, it is driven rather by an economy of surplus and loss.

In Saussurean linguistics, both reproduction and repetition

participate in a chain of oppositional differences. Thus, for example, when Gertrude Stein writes 'A rose is a rose is a rose . . .', the signifier 'rose' takes on a slightly different meaning or signification according to its place in the series. While the first time the signifier 'rose' appears it may refer only to the flower, its subsequent mentions may evoke a whole gamut of connotations, from botany to poetry to woman. But, aside from its meanings in the referential context of representation, the mere repetition of the signifier 'rose' puts into motion a displacement which ushers in the play of difference – that is, the process of signification. For, whether we assign referential meanings to 'rose' or not, each occurrence of the word modifies the 'rose' that precedes or follows. Finally, from a Saussurean viewpoint, language exists only as the result of an interaction by a subject with the linguistic code. Since language is not a stable object which exists outside its realization by a subject, to speak, read or write means that one is constantly in the process of comparing signifiers in order to give them signification, to have them make sense for oneself as well as for others. The concept of literature as text, as a textual linguistic construct, is founded on the Saussurean understanding of linguistic phenomena as a dynamic relational system of oppositional differences. A *text* is the meeting-place of signifiers, and to read a *text* is to attempt to understand the process of repetition, substitution and displacement of its signifiers.

Traditionally critics have taken a respectful stance towards authors, their presumed intentions, and historical accuracy. The literary *work*, in Roland Barthes's formulation of the traditional position, refers us to a concept of creativity whereby the author guarantees the meaning or the truth of a written piece which is apprehended by the critic as a lasting stable object. The authority of tradition belongs to the tradition which valorizes the concept of authorship. When critics are concerned with authors, influences and filiations, literary genres or problems of periodization, they assume that criticism is an empirical positivistic science, and that literature is its observable and classifiable object of knowledge. The literary *text*, on the other hand, is the result of an interaction: 'it exists only as discourse. . . . In other words, *the text is experienced only in an activity, a production*' (Barthes 1979, p. 75).[7] Because it is the result of a

dialogical process of exchange between reader and writer concerning the signification provided by the materiality of the
linguistic medium, each and every reading is unique, and this in
turn explains the inherently plural character of textual criticism, understood as a post-structuralist activity. Whereas the
literary *work* has an author whose viewpoint and whose intentions need be respected, the literary *text* is fatherless, so to speak,
for it does not privilege the generator or encoder of the message.
In the textual reading process, both the writer's and the reader's
subjectivity are being inscribed simultaneously. Since, for the
textual reader, literature is not a representation of experience
but something that is experienced, from a feminist viewpoint
the question is not whether a literary work has been written by a
woman and reflects her experience of life, or how it compares to
other works by women, but rather how it lends itself to be read
from a feminist position.

In Saussurean linguistics, one enters the system of communication by conforming one's speech (*parole*) – be it by
reading, writing or speaking – to the system of differentiation at
play in one's language (*langue*). One is born into a language, and
must adopt its functioning system in order to produce meaning,
to communicate with others. We may wish to make our language our own, but we must first recognize that we are moulded
into speaking subjects by language and that language shapes
our perceptual world. Like clothes for the androgynous protagonist of Virginia Woolf's *Orlando*, language may serve as a
protective garment or a tool, but, by serving us, language also
transforms us:

> Vain trifles as they seem, clothes have, they say, more
> important offices then merely to keep us warm. They change
> our view of the world and the world's view of us. . . . Thus,
> there is much to support the view that it is clothes that wear us
> and not we them; we may make them take the mould of arm or
> breast; but they would mould our hearts, our brains, our
> tongues to their liking.
>
> (Woolf 1928, pp. 170–1)

Not only are we born into a language which moulds us, but any
knowledge of the world which we experience is itself also
articulated in language. This interdependence between life and

language precludes any order of precedence or causality between experience and metaphor.

The expression of self is also dependent upon oppositional dynamics. Emile Benveniste has argued that, in language, subjectivity can come into being only as the articulation of a dialogical interaction:

> Consciousness of self is only possible if it is experienced by contrast. I use *I* when I am speaking to someone who will be *you* in my address. It is this condition of dialogue that is constitutive of *person*, for it implies that reciprocally *I* becomes *you* in the address of the one who in his turn designates himself as *I*.
>
> (Benveniste 1971, pp. 224–5)

The French psychoanalyst Jacques Lacan has shown that one's entry into language is due to a fundamental alienation resulting from a splitting within the subject (Lacan 1977).[8] The primitive union with the mother is ruptured at the mirror-stage, which is the moment when the child recognizes its reflected image, identifies with it, and becomes aware of being a separate entity from the mother. The moment at which the infant perceives itself as an image, as 'other', is also the moment when the 'I' which does the perceiving is split off from the 'I' which is perceived. Seeing oneself as other determines an everlasting frustration and vain attempts at making one's 'I' and one's imago coincide, as well as a desire for oneself (sameness) under the guise of otherness. The splitting of the subject and the separation from the mother allow for the eruption of desire, determine the need for intersubjective communication, and force the child's inscription in the oedipal triangle. The Oedipus complex is the fundamental structure of the field of psychoanalysis, for it explains the development of the subject as well as the orientation of human desire. In the Oedipus complex the threat of castration acts as the deterrent to incest; it is not surprising, therefore, that for Lévi-Strauss the Oedipus complex stands as the universal organizing principle of social systems.

The mirror-stage is the initial step in the process of an individual's integration in the social system; it marks the child's entrance into the symbolic order which is the realm of what

Lacan calls the Law-of-the-Father or Name-of-the-Father. The relevance of these terms is explained by Jane Gallop as follows:

> The Name-of-the-Father . . . is a powerful Lacanian term, actually a Lacanian displacement of what Freud bequeathed him/us, the Oedipal Father, absolute primal Father. Whereas Freud's Oedipal Father might be taken for a real, biological father, Lacan's Name-of-the-Father operates explicitly in the register of language. The Name-of-the-Father: the patronym, patriarchal law, patrilineal identity, language as our inscription into patriarchy. The Name-of-the-Father is the fact of the attribution of paternity by law, by language. Paternity cannot be perceived, proven, known with certainty: it must be instituted by judgment of the mother's word. . . . Any suspicion of the mother's infidelity betrays the Name-of-the-Father as the arbitrary imposition it is.
>
> (Gallop 1982, p. 47)

In order to disclose the arbitrariness of patriarchal hegemony, feminist critics engage in a dialogical opposition to traditional models and values. In this respect, a textual approach to literature guided by feminist concerns can be an effective political tool. When a textual reader steadfastly ignores an author's presumed intentions or the assumed meaning of a literary work, it is a serious act of insubordination, for it puts into question the authority of authors, that is to say the propriety of paternity. By refusing to abide by the rules of a critical contract which privileges the author, the textual reader joins the ranks of the disloyal and the unfaithful. In the marital contract, the wife's fidelity or the mother's word guarantees paternal origin and hegemony. Betrayal of authorial trust therefore implies denial of patriarchal rule. As expressed by Jane Gallop:

> Infidelity then is a feminist practice of undermining the Name-of-the-Father. The unfaithful reading strays from the author, the authorized, produces that which does not hold as a reproduction, as a representation. Infidelity is *not* outside the system of marriage, the symbolic, patriarchy, but hollows it out, ruins it, from within.
>
> (Gallop 1982, p. 48)

When the child, after the mirror-stage, enters the symbolic order which allows for intersubjective communication, she or he discovers that language itself has a symbolic value. In *Beyond the Pleasure Principle*, Freud describes the behaviour of a child who, although deeply attached to his mother, never cried when she left him. Instead he would hide his toys while letting out a long-drawn-out 'o-o-o-o', which recalled the German word *fort* meaning 'gone'. Freud's observation that the child was indeed playing 'gone' with his toys was confirmed when he saw him throw a reel tied with a string over the side of his crib, uttering 'o-o-o-o' when it was out of his sight, and hailing its reappearance when he pulled it up with a joyful *da* which means 'there'. For Freud, the child's game was a

> great cultural achievement – the instinctual renunciation [that is, the renunciation of instinctual satisfaction] which he had made in allowing his mother to go away without protesting. He compensated himself for this, as it were, by himself staging the disappearance and return of the objects within his reach.
>
> (Freud 1959, p. 34)

While Freud directs his attention to the symbolic function of play, for Lacan this scene discloses the symbolic function of language. The child's verbalizations and game-playing enact his frustrated desire for his mother and his anticipated pleasure at her eventual return. Symbolically, language stands in lieu of the absent mother and is equivalent to her death: 'the symbol manifests itself first of all as the murder of the thing, and this death constitutes in the subject the eternalization of his desire' (Lacan 1977, p. 104).

The symbolic order – that is, the order of the Name-of-the-Father, the order of language which allows intersubjective communication – conveys the very values of the social system which it reflects, supports and encompasses. When we become intelligible, we do so by adopting the values upon which communication is predicated. Because 'language as symbolic function constitutes itself at the cost of repressing instinctual drive and continuous relation to the mother' (Kristeva 1980, p. 136), the French linguist Julia Kristeva posits the existence of another order, an order which does not refute the symbolic order but is anterior to it, and which she associates with the maternal aspects of language. This order, which she calls 'semiotic', is not a separate entity from the symbolic; on the contrary, it is the system which supports symbolic coherence. The semiotic and symbolic orders function in a dialogical relationship

> which places the semiotic *inside* the symbolic as a condition of the symbolic, while positing the symbolic as a condition of the semiotic and founded on its repression. Now it happens that the Name-of-the-Father, in order to establish itself, needs the repression of the mother. It needs this otherness in order to reassure itself about its unity and identity, but is unwittingly affected by this otherness that is working within it.
>
> (Féral 1978, p. 10)[9]

In the symbolic order, most elements of the linguistic system, such as syntax, pronunciation, signs and nomination, have been established and fixed. Yet, as the infant's first attempts at communication show, there is an order of linguistic phenomena which, while not clearly intelligible, still has significance. Although these sounds are seemingly meaningless, the unintelligible verbalizations produced by infants do show that human speech cannot be circumscribed to an established network of signification. Instinctual sounds and rhythms which resist meaning stand in opposition to the symbolic order, and they unsettle and subvert the expected normative forms of discourse codified by our linguistic practices – that is to say, authorized in the Name-of-the-Father. For Kristeva, although women have a privileged relationship to birth, gestation and the body as a place of origin, the territory of the maternal is not a space confined to, or defined by, biological characteristics; it is the position a subject, any subject, can assume towards the symbolic order.

From an empirical viewpoint, the body is a concrete, observable object; but, viewed within a sign system, the body is a social signifier. While sex is an anatomical fact, sexuality is culturally devised; it is the manner in which society fictionalizes its relationship to sex and creates gender roles. Sexuality, as Serge Leclaire points out, 'is a fact of discourse which takes into account anatomical determination' (Leclaire 1979, p. 44). Since in a post-structuralist world there is no place that is conceivably outside culture and safe from its ideology, feminism cannot be construed as a separate system of perceptions and values, but can only be conceived as a position one assumes in relation to the cultural construct of sexuality.

Julia Kristeva has demonstrated that, in the writings of avant-garde authors such as Mallarmé, Lautréamont and Céline, recurrences of morphemes and phonemes, or ruptures in a network of signifiers, set up a dynamic and subversive signifying process which undermines our concepts of representation and rhetorical expression. The works of these male avant-garde writers stand in opposition to the coherent, 'meaningful', logical discourse of culture in the Name-of-the-Father. The disconcerting discourse of the avant-garde with its breaks and dislocations reveals the cracks in the social and cultural façade of the subject resulting from the subject's attempt to 're-ally itself with a phase anterior to the constitution of the unitary subject, a discourse which is always on the verge of shattering the subject and which seems to be the prerogative of artists and women' (Féral 1978, p. 13). Similarly, Hélène Cixous holds the works of a man, the contemporary French novelist and playwright Jean Genet, as representative of 'feminine writing': 'Thus, under the name of Jean Genet, what is inscribed in the movement of a text which divides itself, breaks itself into bits, regroups itself, is an abundant, maternal, pederastic feminity' (Marks and de Courtivron 1981, p. 98). For the psychoanalyst Luce Irigaray, *mimicry* – that is, the playful reproducing of a discourse – undermines the privileged position of the first or original discourse and initiates a displacement through repetition which allows for the emergence of the repressed (Irigaray 1985a, 1985b).[10] Whether written by a woman or by a man, a linguistic intervention which ruptures accepted (acceptable) discursive practices reverts us to the constitution of the social subject which is predicated on the repression of the maternal. Through disruption of the symbolic function of language, we are able to give expression to the repressed, or to detect traces of repression, but in so doing we are, even if only momentarily, in breach of the Law-of-the-Father.

Thinking in terms of binary opposition always implies the subordination of the second element to the first, and reversing the order of the pairing only repeats the system which was at work in the initial opposition. By opposing man to woman or woman to man, whatever the order or the privilege accorded to one of the terms, one is still caught in the system of western philosophical logic whereby one is obliged to search for a truth that is a single, non-equivocal answer. When Lévi-Strauss describes woman as partaking simultaneously in two incompatible systems, he implies that her duality stands in opposition to unity and logical coherence, thereby betraying that he is speaking from within the patriarchal discourse of western philosophical thought. As the philosopher Jacques Derrida has shown, in the discourse of western metaphysics, womanhood occupies the place of non-truth (Derrida 1979).[11] From a Derridian position, the feminist endeavour cannot be conceived in terms of male or female, feminine or masculine; it can only be thought of beyond such polarities as a kind of sexual plurality. In an interview conducted by Christie V. McDonald, Derrida imagines the (im)possibility and the seductiveness of such a sexuality:

What if we were to reach, what if we were to approach here (for one does not arrive at this as one would at a determined location) the area of a relationship to the other where the code of sexual marks would no longer be discriminating? The relationship would not be a-sexual, far from it, but would be sexual otherwise: beyond the binary difference that governs the decorum of all codes, beyond the opposition feminine/masculine, beyond bisexuality as well, beyond homosexuality and heterosexuality which come to the same thing. As I dream of saving the chance that this question offers I would like to believe in the multiplicity of sexually marked voices. . . . Of course, it is not impossible that desire for a sexuality without number can still protect us, like a dream, from an implacable destiny which immures everything for life in the figure 2. And should this merciless closure arrest desire at the wall of opposition, we would struggle in vain: there will never be but two sexes, neither one more nor one less. Tragedy would leave this strange sense, a contingent one finally, that we must affirm and learn to love instead of dreaming of the innumerable. . . . But where would the 'dream' of the innumerable come from, if it is indeed a dream? Does the dream itself not prove that what is dreamt of must be there in order for it to provide the dream?

(Derrida and McDonald 1982, p. 76)

Derrida's dream of a plural sexuality beyond the gender principle would, of course, explode the fabric of our society which we now conceive within the terms of the restricted economy of exchange provided by heterosexual marriage and the family unit.

In our society, marriage is the privileged locus for the interaction of the two sexes; it is the agency that reflects and regulates our attitude towards sexuality. Since one of the functions of marriage is to assure the future of our society through reproduction, it requires that the individuals involved be of opposite sex. Marriage produces a single social unit wherein differences among individuals are seemingly dissolved under one name, the name of the father. Thus, whether one views marriage as the blissful coming together of equal voices speaking in unison, or as the site of an ongoing dialogue between individuals continuously affirming their differences, we cannot escape the structure it imposes, the patriarchal society it sustains.

Whether viewed as the place which can allow for equality, or conceived as an agonistic setting for the expression of difference, marriage may also serve as an allegory of our feminist critical practices. While the egalitarian argument in feminist criticism calls for equal representation in literature of women's and men's experience of life, post-structuralist feminism challenges representation itself as already a patriarchal paradigm, thus positing the existence of a different discursive practice.

By proceeding from a consideration of woman as person to woman as sign, this chapter moved from sisters to wife to mother, and the question of woman's relationship to language shifted from woman *and* language to woman *in* language, replacing conjunctional bondage by spatial enclosure. Although it may be impossible, in the end, to escape the hegemony of patriarchal structures, none the less, by unveiling the prejudices at work in our cultural artefacts, we impugn the universality of the man-made models provided to us, and allow for the possibility of sidestepping and subverting their power. Feminist criticism thereby affirms and gives voice to our Otherness.

Notes

1 For a discussion of the concept of 'common sense' and its relationship to literature, see Belsey (1980), ch. 1.

2 Austin remarked that when we utter 'I do' in a marital ceremony 'we are *doing* something – namely, marrying, rather than *reporting* something, namely *that* we are marrying' (Austin 1975, p. 13). For further study of speech-act theory, see Searle (1969).

3 While viewing marriage as a speech act has allowed us to apprehend language as a performative rather than simply a descriptive medium, speech-act theory itself, however, as the debate between John Searle and Jacques Derrida shows (Derrida and Searle 1977), is rooted in an empirical concept of language.

4 The application of linguistic concepts and speech-act theory to literature is explored by Pratt (1977).

5 For further discussion of the dialogical aspect of literature, see Kristeva (1980).

6 The question of language, Marxism and ideology is studied in Coward and Ellis (1971).

7 For further discussion of the reading process, see Todorov (1980).

8 For a helpful guide to Lacan's work, see Muller and Richardson (1982).

9 The article by Josette Féral (1978) provides an excellent discussion of the works of Julia Kristeva and Luce Irigaray on the question of language.

10 See Luce Irigaray (1985a and 1985b) for her discussion of woman's status in western thought and language, and the manner in which her own writing practice challenges the phallocentrism inherent in the discourse of psychoanalysis and philosophy.

11 For a clear and succinct presentation of Jacques Derrida's work and the question of language, see Norris (1982).

References

Austin, J. L. (1975) *How to do Things with Words*. Cambridge, Mass.: Harvard University Press.

Barthes, Roland (1979) 'From Work to Text'. In Josué V. Harari (ed.), *Perspectives in Post-Structuralist Criticism*. Ithaca, NY: Cornell University Press.

Beauvoir, Simone de (1961) *The Second Sex*. New York: Bantam.

Belsey, Catherine (1980) *Critical Practice*. New Accents. London and New York: Methuen.

Benveniste, Emile (1971) *Problems in General Linguistics*, trans. Mary Elizabeth Meek. Coral Gables, Fla.: University of Miami Press.

Cixous, Hélène (1981) 'Castration or Decapitation?', trans. Annette Kuhn, *Signs*, 7, 1 (Autumn).

Coward, Rosalind, and Ellis, John (1971) *Language and Materialism: Developments in Semiology and the Theory of the Subject*. London and Boston, Mass.: Routledge & Kegan Paul.

Derrida, Jacques (1979) *Spurs: Nietzsche's Style*, trans. Barbara Harlow. Chicago, Ill.: University of Chicago Press.

Derrida, Jacques, and McDonald, Christie V. (1982) 'Choreographies', *Diacritics: A Review of Contemporary Criticism* (Summer).

Derrida, Jacques, and Searle, John R. (1977) *Glyph*, 1 and 2.

Féral, Josette (1978) 'Antigone or *The Irony of the Tribe*', trans. Alice Jardine and Tom Gora, *Diacritics: A Review of Contemporary Criticism*, 8, 3 (Fall), pp. 2–14.

Foucault, Michel (1979) 'What is an Author?' In Josué V. Harari (ed.), *Perspectives in Post-Structuralist Criticism*. Ithaca, NY: Cornell University Press.

Freud, Sigmund (1959) *Beyond the Pleasure Principle*. New York: Bantam.

Gallop, Jane (1982) *The Daughter's Seduction: Feminism and Psychoanalysis*. Ithaca, NY: Cornell University Press.

Gilbert, Sandra M., and Gubar, Susan (1979) *The Madwoman in the Attic: The Woman Writer and the Nineteenth-Century Literary Imagination*. New Haven, Conn., and London: Yale University Press.

Heath, Stephen (1978) 'Difference', *Screen* (Autumn).

Irigaray, Luce (1985a) *Speculum of the Other Woman*. Ithaca, NY: Cornell University Press.

Irigaray, Luce (1985b) *This Sex which is not One*. Ithaca, NY: Cornell University Press.

Kristeva, Julia (1980) 'Word, Dialogue and Novel'. In Leon S. Roudiez (ed.), *Desire in Language: A Semiotic Approach to Literature and Art*. New York: Columbia University Press.

Lacan, Jacques (1977) *Ecrits: A Selection*. London: Tavistock.

Leclaire, Serge (1979) 'Sexuality: A Fact of Discourse', interview by Helene Klibbe. In George Stambolian and Elaine Marks (eds), *Homosexualities and French Literature: Cultural Contexts/Critical Texts*. Ithaca, NY, and London: Cornell University Press.

Lévi-Strauss, Claude (1969) *The Elementary Structures of Kinship*, trans. James Harle Bell, John Richard von Sturmer and Rodney Needham. Rev. edn. Boston, Mass.: Beacon Press.

Marks, Elaine, and Courtivron, Isabelle de (1981) *New French Feminisms: An Anthology*. New York: Schocken Books.

Muller, John P., and Richardson, William J. (1982) *Lacan and Language: A Reader's Guide to 'Ecrits'*. New York: International Universities Press.

Norris, Christopher (1982) *Deconstruction: Theory and Practice*. New Accents. London and New York: Methuen.

Pratt, Mary Louise (1977) *Toward a Speech Act Theory of Literary Discourse*. Bloomington, Ind.: Indiana University Press.

Searle, John R. (1969) *Speech Acts: An Essay in the Philosophy of Language*. Cambridge: Cambridge University Press.

Showalter, Elaine (1977) *A Literature of their Own: British Women Novelists from Brontë to Lessing*. Princeton, NJ: Princeton University Press.

Todorov, Tzvetan (1972) 'Language and Literature'. In Richard Macksey and Eugenio Donato (eds), *The Structuralist Controversy: The Languages of Criticism and the Sciences of Man*. Baltimore, Md, and London: Johns Hopkins University Press.

Todorov, Tzvetan (1980) 'Reading as Construction'. In Susan R. Suleiman and Inge Crosman (eds), *The Reader in the Text: Essays and Audience and Interpretation*. Princeton, NJ: Princeton University Press.

Woolf, Virginia (1928) *Orlando: A Biography*. London: Hogarth Press.

4
Inscribing femininity:
French theories
of the feminine
ANN ROSALIND JONES

French theories of femininity, using Derridian deconstruction and Lacanian psychoanalysis, centre on language as a means through which men have shored up their claim to a unified identity and relegated women to the negative pole of binary oppositions that justify masculine supremacy: subject/object, culture/nature, law/chaos, man/woman. Phallocentrism – this structuring of man as the central reference point of thought, and of the phallus as the symbol of sociocultural authority – is the target of Franco-feminist criticism.

Ann Rosalind Jones traces, through the leading ideas of four writers, the forms this critique has taken. Julia Kristeva posits the concept of the semiotic, a rhythmic free play she relates to mother-infant communication, and looks for in modernist writers. Luce Irigaray emphasizes *différence*, a totality of women's characteristics defined positively against masculine norms, and imagines a specifically feminine language, a *parler femme*. Hélène Cixous celebrates women's sexual capacities, including motherhood, and calls for an *écriture féminine* through which women will bring their bodily energies and previously unimagined unconscious into view. Finally, Monique Wittig rejects this emphasis on *différence*, arguing that women must be understood not in contrast to man but in historical terms as subjected to oppression.

Evaluating the possibilities for criticism that these theories of *féminité* suggest, Jones cautions that 'Every belief about "what women are" raises political as well as literary problems', and questions whether the critique of phallocentrism is yet freed from the metaphysical framework it seeks to dismantle.

A feminine text cannot fail to be
more than subversive. It is volcanic;
as it is written it brings about an
upheaval of the old property crust,
carrier of masculine investments;
there's no other way. There's no room
for her if she's not a he? If she's a
her/she, it's in order to smash everything,
to shatter the framework of institutions,
to blow up the law, to break up the 'truth'
with laughter.

(Hélène Cixous, 'The Laugh of the Medusa')

The context

The most widely exported French theories of women's writing
since the 1970s have a common source: Frenchwomen's responses to Derridian deconstruction and to Lacan's structuralist version of Freud.[1] For both of these philosophical and
psychoanalytic interrogations of culture, language is a central
concern. Derrida argues that the discourse of western
metaphysics has been based on the construction of a fantasized
sovereign subject, an idealized version of 'man'. From the
beginning of philosophy, men have set themselves up as the
central reference point of an epistemology built on a set of
hierarchical oppositions in which 'man' (white, Graeco-
Roman, ruling class) always occupies the privileged position:
self/other, subject/object, presence/absence, law/chaos, man/
woman. Deconstruction takes as its task the exposure and
dismantling of the terms and the logic through which these
claims have been made. French theorizing of the feminine
emphasizes the extent to which the masculine subject has
relegated woman to the negative pole of his hierarchies, asso-
ciating her with all the categories of 'not-man' that shore up his
claim to centrality and his right to power. The portmanteau
term for this male-dominated ('humanist') metaphysics is
'phallocentrism' – the primacy of the phallus, of men's word
as law, of men as the origin of meaning.

Hélène Cixous, one of the most prolific writers involved in
French thinking about the feminine, maps out the binary

oppositions that structure the phallocentric system as follows:

Where is she?
Activity/passivity,
Sun/Moon,
Culture Nature,
Day/Night,
Father/Mother,
Head/Heart,
Intelligible/sensitive,
Logos/Pathos.

Form, convex, step, advance, seed, progress.
Matter, concave, ground – which supports the step, receptacle.

Man
———
Woman

Always the same metaphor: we follow it, it transports us, in all of its forms, wherever a discourse is organized. The same thread, or double tress leads us, whether we are reading or speaking, through literature, philosophy, criticism, centuries of representation, of reflection.

(Cixous 1975a, p. 96)

She suggests the psychic force of this longstanding structure of thought when she writes:

Men and women are caught up in a network of millennial cultural determinations of a complexity that is practically unanalyzable: we can no more talk about 'woman' than about 'man' without getting caught up in an ideological theater where the multiplication of representations, images, reflections, myths, identifications constantly transforms, deforms, alters each person's imaginary order and in advance renders all conceptualization null and void.

(p. 96)

Lacanian psychoanalysis, extending Freud's exposure of the unconscious conflicts at work in any supposedly sovereign subject, intersects with certain deconstructive insights in its theory of the gendered speaking subject. For Lacan too the unified human subject is always a myth. A child's sense of identity results from the internalization of outer views of her/himself, first at the infantile mirror-stage, when, as an ill-coordinated bundle of drives and wayward motor skills, s/he invents a self based on her/his reflection in an actual mirror or in the mirror of others' eyes, and again at the point of language acquisition (the entry into the symbolic order), which provides a unifying verbal term for what is still in fact an internally split and shifting speaker. One says 'I' as language allows or forces one to say it, according to a fiction of selfhood built into the first-person singular and the rules of syntax.

But this 'I' position is not equally accessible to boys and to girls. Lacan defines language, the symbolic order, as the world of public discourses, which the child enters only as a result of culturally enforced separation from her/his mother and his – but not her – identification with the Father, the male in-family representative of culture. Thus Lacanian theory reserves the 'I' position for men. Women, because they lack the phallus, the positive symbol of gender, self-possession and worldly authority around which language is organized, occupy a negative position in language. Moreover, because masculine desire dominates speech and posits woman as an idealized fantasy-fulfilment for the incurable emotional lack caused by the separation from the mother, Lacan can say 'Woman does not exist' (Mitchell and Rose 1982, pp. 48–50). Following Freud's definition of all sexual desire as masculine (that is, active), Lacan also argues that woman can enter into the symbolic life of the unconscious only to the extent that she internalizes male desire (phallic libido) – that is, to the extent that she imagines herself as men imagine her (Lacan 1975, p. 90). In a psycholinguistic world structured by father–son resemblance and rivalry and by the primacy of masculine logic, woman is a gap or a silence, the invisible and unheard sex.

Différence, féminité and écriture féminine

Luce Irigaray, originally a member of Lacan's Ecole Freud-ienne and since 1977 one of its most vocal critics, argues against his conclusions about women. If women-as-subjects are outsiders to language, if they have lacked a position from which to counter or derail male-centred conceptions of both sexes, she shows, this is the consequence not of inevitable family arrangements but of millennia of cultural subordination of women's bodies and their sexuality to the needs and fantasies of men. Irigaray's book *Speculum de l'autre femme* (1974) is an analysis of the suppression of the feminine from Platonic idealism through Hegel to Freud and Lévi-Strauss: woman has been defined as irrational, the Other (a negativity to be transcended), an imperfect man (a man without a penis), an object of exchange among men. Phallocentric concepts and their historical consequences can be transformed, Irigaray argues, only when women find ways to assert their specificity as women, their *différence* from men and men's systems of representation. In contrast to male sexuality, focused on the penis, Irigaray locates women's sexuality in the totality of the female body – including, for example the two lips of the vulva – which she defines as a diffuse erotic field affecting women's *jouissance* (sexual pleasure)[2] as it subtends feminine psychic processes and responses to the discourses of the outer (masculine) world:

> Woman's desire most likely does not speak the same language as men's desire, and it probably has been covered over by the logic that has dominated the West since the Greeks. . . . *Woman has sex organs just about everywhere.* . . . The geography of her pleasure is much more diversified, more multiple in its differences, more complex, more subtle, than is imagined – in an imaginary centered a bit too much on one and the same.
>
> 'She' is indefinitely other in herself. That is undoubtedly the reason she is called temperamental, incomprehensible, perturbed, capricious – not to mention her language in which 'she' goes off in all directions and in which 'he' is unable to discern the coherence of any meaning. Contradictory words seem a little crazy to the logic of reason, and inaudible for him who listens with ready-made grids, a code prepared in advance.
>
> (Irigaray 1977a, pp. 101–3)

Irigaray moves from women's bodies to their being-in-the-world, emphasizing tactile/corporeal sensitivities, multiple focused perception and woman-to-woman relatedness; and these 'feminine' characteristics are proposed, in varying forms, throughout French theorizing of the feminine. The basis for such discussions, however, remains women's exclusion from the symbolic – that is, their absence as subjects from the powerful discourses of philosophy and psychoanalysis.

What are the sites of resistance or liberation in this phallocentric universe? One is writing. If women have been entrapped in the symbolic order, they will mark their escape from it by producing texts that challenge and move beyond the Law-of-the Father. Cixous suggested the urgency of this undertaking in a 1976 article:

> Everything turns on the Word: everything is the Word and only the Word. . . we must take culture at its word, as it takes us into its word, into its tongue. . . . No political reflection can dispense with reflection on language, with work on language. For as soon as we exist, we are born into language and language speaks (to) us, dictates its law . . . ; even at the moment of uttering a sentence . . . we are already seized by a certain kind of masculine desire.
>
> (Cixous 1976b, pp. 44–5)

With a lyricism typical of her own *écriture féminine* (feminine practice/process of writing), she writes in her manifesto 'The Laugh of the Medusa':

> I shall speak about women's writing: about what it will do. Woman must write her self: must write about women and bring women to writing, from which they have been driven away as violently as from their bodies. . . . Woman must put herself into the text – as into the world and into history – by her own movement. . . . Her libido is cosmic, just as her unconscious is worldwide. Her writing can only keep going, without ever inscribing or discerning limits. . . . She lets the other language speak – the language of 1,000 tongues which knows neither enclosure nor death.
>
> (Cixous 1975a, pp. 245, 259–60)

Julia Kristeva, one of the pro-modernist *Tel Quel* circle in the 1970s, takes a position less woman-centred than that of Cixous. She studies male avant-garde writers (such as Mallarmé, Lautréamont and Céline) who, she argues, have access to a pre-linguistic erotic energy she calls the 'semiotic', which sets the bodily rhythms of poetry against the linear structures and codified representations of the symbolic. Kristeva derives the semiotic from infants' pre-oedipal fusion with their mothers, from the polymorphous bodily pleasures and rhythmic play of mother–infant communication, censored or harshly redirected by paternal (social) discourse. When the traces of these early delights, this psychosomatic *jouissance*, are channelled from the unconscious and set against official literary modes, the iron grip of the symbolic is broken (Kristeva 1974a, 1975). Although the semiotic is equally accessible to men and women, Kristeva argues that women's psychosocial position enforces their outsiders' status:

> if logical unity is paranoid and homosexual [directed by men to men], the feminine demand . . . will never find a *proper* symbolic, will at best be enacted as a moment inherent in rejection, in the process of ruptures, of rhythmic breaks. Insofar as she has a specificity of her own, a woman finds it in asociality, in the violation of communal conventions, in a sort of a-symbolic singularity.
>
> (Kristeva 1977a, p. 12)

Kristeva sees maternity as a conceptual challenge to phallogocentrism (Kristeva 1977b): gestation and nurturance break down the oppositions between self and other, subject and object, inside and outside. To the extent that any activity resists the symbolic (or, in the case of semiotic signifying, occupies it in hit-and-run fashion), it is revolutionary. Women's strategy should be neither to adopt masculine modes of power nor to flee encounters with the symbolic, but to assume 'a *negative* function: reject everything finite, definite, structured, loaded with meaning, in the existing state of society. Such an attitude puts women on the side of the explosion of social codes: with revolutionary movements' (Kristeva 1974b, p. 166).

In contrast to Kristeva, Irigaray focuses on a sexually specific relationship between women and language. To speak as a woman (*parler femme*, in her shorthand) is to reproduce the doubleness, contiguity and fluidity of women's sexual morphology and the multi-centred libidinal energy that arises from them. Irigaray also argues that women's psychic position emerges from the complexities of the mother–daughter bond. She writes a monologue in the voice of a daughter attempting to rework her link with her mother in *Et l'une ne bouge pas sans l'autre* ('And One Doesn't Stir without the Other'), a text to which her model of how a woman's speech should be 'heard' (interpreted) could serve as a literary-critical guide:

> One must listen to her differently in order to hear an 'other meaning' which is constantly in the process of weaving itself, at the same time ceaselessly embracing words and yet casting them off to avoid becoming fixed, immobilized. . . . Her statements are never identical to anything. Their distinguishing feature is contiguity. They touch (*upon*).
>
> (Irigaray 1977a, p. 103)

In the text, the daughter-speaker separates from the mother through reproaches but also draws her into a listener's complicity; resentment, nostalgia and the desire for a restorative fusion are suggested by terse but polyvalent images of the body (icy milk, a shared mouth) and the movement of short *je/tu* (I/you) passages towards the suggestion of a newly positive symbiosis: 'And what I wanted from you, Mother, was this: that in giving me life, you still remain alive' (Irigaray 1979, p. 67).

Taken as a whole, Irigaray's shift from philosophic and psychoanalytic deconstruction to short, experimental prose texts demonstrates one way that a theory of *féminité* leads to a particular practice of writing: her fictional texts put into action her critique of phallocentric language and her positing of a *parler femme* analogous to female sexual morphology. As early as *Speculum de l'autre femme*, in fact, she was adjusting her style to indicate her opposition to the authoritative subject/object positions of standard syntax: she suppressed verbs, posed questions rather than writing assertions, used telegraphic and exclamatory phrases. Her punning titles suggest that the multi-layered perception she attributes to women can also be teased out of language as it stands. For example, *Ce Sexe qui n'en est pas un*, the title of a 1977 collection of her essays, looks at first like a misogynist dismissal of women: 'this sex which isn't a sex'. But it also carries the anti-phallocentric charge of 'this sex which isn't *one*' – that is, unified, phallic, merely single. And the spoken quality of her writing, her use of energetic voices calling upon

clearly defined audiences, dramatizes the intersubjective 'contiguity' she sees as one aspect of *féminité*: her sarcastic challenges
to 'Vous les messieurs psychanalystes' in a review of Lacanian
research (Irigaray 1977c), the seductive appeal to the other and
the same woman in the monologue 'Quand nos lèvres se
parlent' ('When Our Lips Speak Together') (Irigaray 1977b).
Irigaray's conception of feminine subjectivity leads to a set of
stylistic and formal tendencies widely recognized in *l'écriture
féminine*: double or multiple voices, broken syntax, repetitive or
cumulative rather than linear structure, open endings.

Cixous, a prolific practitioner of the *écriture féminine* she was
among the first to call for, has the most ambitious and explicit
programme for it. Rejecting Freudian and Lacanian theories of
woman as lack, she calls for an assertion of the female body as
plenitude, as a positive force, the source simultaneously of
multiple physical capacities (gestation, birth, lactation) and of
liberatory texts. She concentrates on an erotics of writing, to be
derived from a feminine unconscious shaped by female bodily
drives:

> Write your self. Your body must be heard. Only then will the
> immense resources of the unconscious spring forth. . . .
>
>   To write. An act which will not only 'realize' the decen-
> sored relation of woman to her sexuality, to her womanly
> being, giving her access to her native strength; it will give her
> back her goods, her pleasures, her organs, her immense
> bodily territories which have been kept under seal.
>
> (Cixous 1975a, p. 250)

Her own writing, she explains, proceeds from a kind of ego loss
followed by attentiveness to the rhythms and images of her
unconscious, which she fleshes out into an ongoing text-as-
process (Cixous 1984, pp. 154–5). Metaphors of abundant
maternity – composition as childbirth, ink as milk – accompany
her portraits of woman as writer:

> She is giving birth. With the strength of a lioness. Of a plant.
> Of a cosmogony. Of a woman. . . . A desire for text! Confu-
> sion! What possesses her? A child! Paper! Intoxications! I'm
> overflowing! My breasts overflow! Milk. Ink. The moment of
> suckling. And I? I too am hungry. The taste of milk, of ink!
>
> (Cixous 1977, p. 37)

Cixous has produced over twenty texts since the mid-sixties. They range from studies of the breakdown of language and logic in Lewis Carroll and James Joyce through recitations by man-oppressed speakers, manifestos for feminine writing, lyrical celebrations of the evolution of a woman's subjectivity and, recently, collage-like representations of collaboration among women, such as *Vivre l'orange* (1979) and *With, ou l'art de l'innocence* (1981). *Vivre l'orange* is a poetic essay dramatizing and reflecting upon Cixous's discovery of a Brazilian poet and novelist, Clarice Lispector. Its multiple modes typify Cixous's invocations of feminine subjectivity – in this case, her belief that women have a pre-conceptual, non-appropriative openness to people and to objects, to the other within and outside them. She breaks down contradictions by juxtaposing meditation and narrative, literal and fantastic images, past and present, concrete detail and incantatory flow:

> A woman's voice came to me from far away, like a voice from a birth-town, it brought me insights that I once had, intimate insights, naïve and knowing, ancient and fresh like the yellow and violet color of freshias [sic] rediscovered, this voice was unknown to me, it reached me on the twelfth of October 1978, this voice was not searching for me, it was writing to no one, to all women, to writing, in a foreign tongue, I do not speak it but my heart understands it, and its silent words in all the veins of my life have translated themselves into mad blood, into joy-blood.
>
> (Cixous 1979, p. 10)

Any critical approach to *l'écriture féminine* must come to terms with Cixous's theory and strategies for inscribing a feminine unconscious.

Counter-views and counter-genres: Monique Wittig and *Questions féministes*

This summary has been intended to suggest that varying theories of *différence* produce diverse approaches to what is defined as a liberatory text. Kristeva's analyses focus on the dialectic between the explosive energies of the semiotic and the structures of official discourse, whatever the gender of the writer; a critical model based on her investigations of the semiotic could be applied to most modernist texts. She begins with a psychobiography of the writer, relates it to his statements about textuality and the erotic if any are to be had, and analyses his raids against the symbolic accordingly, as in the case of Céline (Kristeva 1980). In contrast, Irigaray and Cixous construct fictional texts to exemplify how women's bodily impulses and psychosomatic specificity might deform and transform language. Their writing itself is designed as an anti-phallocentric demonstration.

The biological underpinnings and hypothetical connections between the body and the psyche in Cixous's and Irigaray's positions, however, leave them open to attack, and theories of femininity have their critics as well as their adherents in France. Monique Wittig, a writer/theorist who has been associated with the materialist feminist journal *Questions féministes* throughout its vicissitudes since 1977, totally rejects *néo-féminité* because of its emphasis on *différence*. From a materialist/Marxist point of view, she argues, attempts to define a feminine subjectivity in contrast to phallocentric views of women founder upon masculine/feminine oppositions rather than moving beyond them. In such an analysis, the privileging of the masculine side of such hierarchies may be questioned, but masculine fantasies of centrality still remain the central point of reference. Wittig calls instead for a politically motivated deconstruction of the term 'woman' itself, through a historical analysis of the moves through which men have mystified women's biological potentials into a supposedly unchanging female 'nature' – which, she points out, the celebrants of *féminité* glorify rather than call into question:

> Our first task . . . is to dissociate 'women' (the class within which we fight) and 'woman', the myth. For 'woman' . . . is only an imaginary formation, while 'women' is the product of a social relationship. . . . Furthermore, we have to destroy the myth inside and outside ourselves.
>
> (Wittig 1981, pp. 50–1)

Because lesbians occupy a sociosexual position outside the man/woman dyad, Wittig concludes that a lesbian is not a woman: 'Lesbian is the only concept I know of which is beyond the categories of sex (woman and man), because the designated subject is *not* a woman, either economically, or politically, or ideologically' (p. 53). Her goal is to work towards a new subjectivity by destroying the material and conceptual stranglehold of heterosexuality, a process that must begin with the recognition of women's socio-economic oppression and that can offer them a newly critical view of language:

> When we find that women are the objects of oppression . . . we become subjects, in the sense of cognitive subjects. The movement back and forth between the conceptual reality and the material reality of oppression . . . is accomplished through language. Through language we can move into levels of reality with different dimensions: it is like being able to move from the second dimension into the third.
>
> (Wittig 1979, p. 74)

To Wittig, language is both a mode of oppression and a medium through which it can be countered. She sees language not so much as a mode of bodily expression, but more as a means of conceptual clarity and discursive innovation. Her fictional texts illustrate her conviction that women must take over the literature of the past, remake it according to a perception of women as a historical group, and move on to revised and new representations and terminologies. Wittig rejects Kristeva's negativity (the outsider's stance toward the symbolic), Irigaray's interiorized model of femininity, and Cixous's faith in the speech of the womanly unconscious. She carries out instead a deliberate appropriation of male-derived genres: the schoolgirls' anti-patriarchal *Bildungsroman*, *L'Opoponax*; the lesbian epic, *Les Guérillères*; the regendering of masculine celebration of the female body, *Le Corps lesbien*; the utopian women's history implied in the old and new words defined in *Brouillon pour un dictionnaire des amantes (Lesbian People's Material for a Dictionary)* (Wenzel 1981). An early passage in *Les Guérillères* carries out a characteristic Wittigian critique of the emphasis on the female body as a site of *différence*; against this corporeal fixation, Wittig asserts the group identity that must catalyse the transformation of society and of its languages:

> They say that at the point they have reached they must examine the principle that has guided them. They say it is not

for them to exhaust their strength in symbols. They say
henceforth what they are is not subject to compromise. They
say they must now stop exalting the vulva. . . . They say that
any symbol that exalts the fragmented body must
disappear. . . . They, the women, the integrity of their body
their first principle, advance marching together into another
world.

(Wittig 1969, p. 72)

(The 'they' of the English translation obscures the '*elles*', the
feminine plural that designates the female tribal companions
who speak throughout the text.) Wittig shares other
Frenchwomen's high estimation of fantasy and revised myth.
But she bases her writing not upon a theory of the individual
female body but upon a desire for a plural, social body, a lesbian
body politic.

Franco-feminist criticism: can there be one?

Kristeva, Cixous and Irigaray all concede, though less emphatically than Wittig, the need for practical political action by
women. But the realm of psycho-literary experiment remains
central to their thinking. For Kristeva, transgression of the
symbolic on the printed page has seemed identical to political
resistance (Kristeva 1969, p. 65). Cixous insists that transformations of subjectivity must precede social transformation;
in fact, she rejects feminism as a movement too much like men's,
a search for power that imitates rather than transcends the
phallogocentric order (Cixous 1976a, p. 23). Irigaray remarks,
'For a woman to arrive at the point where she can enjoy her
pleasure as a woman, a long detour via the analysis of the
various systems that oppress her is certainly necessary' (Irigaray 1977a, p. 105); but in her early 1980s publications she gave
priority to the transcription of new versions of *parler femme*.

For the feminist critic who thinks of her work as a more or less
direct form of political action, the conceptual framework of
différence and *écriture féminine* present striking difficulties. Even
if she accepts Irigaray's or Cixous's definition of femininity
as a basis for interpretation, how is she to approach the anti-
symbolic, diffuse, libidinally charged texts produced by women
– or, according to Kristeva, by men? Are they accessible to

analysis based on feminist adaptations of the realist, formalist and generic assumptions that they set out explicitly to challenge? Is there any point in applying feminist versions of more recent critical methods to such texts? What is to be gained from psychoanalysing a text whose express purpose is to reveal its writer's unconscious, from aiming the X-ray techniques of structuralism at a text written to overthrow the 'ready-made grids' of binary opposition, or from turning the historicist ideology-critique of Marxism upon futuristic texts written *against* ideology? Franco-feminist criticism resists any easy pluralist assimilation.

Verena Andermatt, a critic highly sympathetic to Cixous and to the kind of texts produced in her seminar at Vincennes (a 'factory of phantasm', in which participants recount and combine their dreams into collaborative texts), points out the absurdity of bringing the logic of the symbolic to an encounter with the semiotic density of *écriture féminine*:

> Cixous' markedly feminine works ... are self-surpassing, flowing, open-ended. Each of the texts generates from a juxtaposition of other writings. In fact, we wager that it is quasi-impossible to write a coherently explicative essay in narrative or structural terms about a process of their origins or 'composition' in ways the texts of Beckett or the new novel have been scrutinized. There simply is no plausible, detectable matrix of form other than the matrix itself.
>
> (Andermatt 1979, p. 43)

Andermatt is probably responding here to Cixous's warning about the gap between literary-critical generalization and the idiosyncrasy of feminine writing:

> It is impossible to *define* a feminine practice of writing, ... for this practice can never be theorized, enclosed, encoded – which doesn't mean that it doesn't exist. But it will always surpass the discourse that regulates the phallocentric system; it does and will take place in areas other than those subordinated to philosophical/theoretical domination. It will be conceived of only by subjects who are breakers of automatisms, by peripheral figures that no authority can ever subjugate.
>
> (Cixous 1975a, p. 253)

Josette Féral, in a more positive Cixousian vein, suggests that a feminist critical mode properly adapted to *l'écriture féminine* would have to be sought:

> in alignment with the disordering, deviation and derailing of any prior discourse that obliterates the sexual determinants of speech, in order to interrogate that discourse about its own conditions of production: the functioning of its grammar, its tropes, laws and syntactic rules, its image systems, networks of metaphor and also its silences.
>
> (Féral 1980, p. 46)

That is, such criticism would have to carry out a deconstruction of criticism itself. Gestures in this direction are consistently made by Franco-feminist critics commenting on the theory and practice of feminine writing. Féral herself suggested in an early essay on Irigaray and Kristeva that her discussion would reproduce the open-endedness of the theories she was presenting rather than aim towards a totalizing coherence contrary to them:

> Our presentation will be divided and fragmentary in the image of the woman's body and the theories which attempt to explain her difference. The missing fragment(s) which might be able to reconstitute the lost unity of the feminine body are to be found elsewhere, in research still to be outlined which would strive to fill in the holes in the theory and the silences of psychoanalysis.
>
> (Féral 1978, p. 3)

Silence and incompleteness are no longer accurate descriptions of the ever-increasing production, consumption and critical appreciation of *textes féminins* on both sides of the Atlantic, as commentators such as Christiane Makward point out. She suggests, none the less, that the feminist critic's approach to such writing ideally coincides with feminine attentiveness to its object as described by Cixous in *La Venue à l'écriture*: 'She who observes with a gaze that recognizes, studies, respects, doesn't seize or make marks, but attentively, with a gentle stubbornness, contemplates and reads, caresses, bathes, makes the other radiant' (p. 56) Makward offers Cixous's style as a model of self-effacement before a woman's text, not in religious awe but as the opening of a channel that allows the feminine principle to emerge 'both intuitively and rationally' (Makward 1980, p. 49).

But intuition and rationality may intermesh more problematically than in Makward, or in the semiotic/symbolic texts praised by Kristeva. The tension between the two tendencies is foregrounded by French and American critics. Kristeva herself, for example, imitating the typography of Derrida's *Glas*, arranges an article on the maternal feminine into two columns of print. The left-hand column, heavily inked and broken into short sections, lyrically invokes the pre-cultural maternal body; the right-hand column provides information about the historical circumstances and meanings of motherhood assigned to the Virgin Mary (Kristeva 1977b). Jane Gallop, in a deconstructive rather than celebratory essay on Kristeva's rethinking of motherhood, imitates her on-the-page drama in order to clarify her own two-pronged critique. Gallop sets an analysis of Kristeva's remarks about feminism in one column of print, against another comment on Kristeva's emphasis on maternity, pointing out simultaneously the repression in Kristeva's text and its implicit bias:

the digression has an insistent force that perverts and deforms the sentence. The marginal detail, 'more menacing than a father of the primitive horde', sensationally detracts attention away from the main point of the sentence. That which she chooses 'not to mention' takes over the sentence as if she could not control anything so 'menacing'. The invasion of these mammoth, scary 'Anglo-Saxons' is so complete that at the conclusion of the sentence we find an English word. 'Supermen' appears, not even italicized, in Kristeva's French text.

Is Kristeva's move from the impossible heterosexuality of 'Polylogue' to the impossible maternity of 'L'Héréthique', in other words, is the move from the Lacanian scandal to the maternal scandal progress or regression? This question rejoins the problem of whether the maternal is conservative and imaginary or disruptive and semiotic. And uncomfortable as it is (precisely because it is uncomfortable) we must try to sit on the horns of that dilemma. Of course, heterosexuality is always implied by maternity. Except in the case of the Virgin. . . .

(Gallop 1982, p. 129)

Omissions and biases of other kinds seem inevitable in a theory of femininity that has evolved in close association with modernist European writing dominated by men and that has been formulated by a white intelligentsia within the academy, whose concerns (including its targets) reveal its immersion in a late capitalist culture still permeated by idealist philosophy, a psychoanalytic fixation on the gender structures produced by the nineteenth-century family, and an ambivalent relationship to feminism as a political movement. Certainly, the theories of Kristeva, Irigaray and Cixous are bounded by distinct limits of time and place. It would be a dubious undertaking, at best, to seek out the semiotic in canonical texts of the Middle Ages or of neoclassicism; and the cultural production of Native American or Middle-Eastern women calls for a much less Euro-centred optic (Spivak 1981). Franco-feminist theory is most effective as a basis for interpretation to the extent that it is used *differentially* – to the extent that its diverse strands are put to specific uses.

Franco-feminist criticism: four varieties

Four methods have been evolving in Franco-feminist criticism since the 1970s. The two most generally used are the deconstruction of magisterial texts and traditions, and the attention to silences, to what is repressed or only obliquely suggested in women-authored texts. A second set of explicatory strategies includes the decoding of feminine/semiotic modes of writing and a close reading of the politics of style, in the work of women writers and also, arguably, in men's writing, to the extent that certain male writers' marginality to mainstream sexual and socio-literary conventions leads them to produce 'feminine' writing. Proust and Genet are heroes to many Franco-feminist critics.

Deconstruction

Franco-feminist deconstruction has so far been aimed largely at male-authored texts. An excellent example is Shoshana Felman's study of a short story by Balzac, 'Adieu', and its 1974 reception by two male critics. Balzac's heroine, Stéphanie, is an aphasic madwoman, who thus offers a double challenge to the rationalizing discourse of phallocentrism. Felman poses the problem of how such a double marginality can be represented:

> How can the woman be thought about outside of the Masculine/Feminine framework, *other* than as opposed to man, without being subordinated to a primordial masculine model? How can madness, in a similar way, be conceived of outside its dichotomous opposition to sanity, without being subjugated to reason? How can difference as such be thought out as *non-subordinate* to identity? In other words, how can thought break away from the logic of polar opposition?
>
> (Felman 1975, p. 4)

She then shows that this breakaway fails to occur in 'Adieu': both the hero of the story (Philippe) and its critics reduce the figure of the woman first to a mirror of the masculine and finally to invisibility. Philippe believes that he can cure Stéphanie by forcing her to recognize him, to say his name, to address to *him* the 'adieu' she said as they parted years earlier. Replaying the scene of their separation (a boat crossing the Berezina River during Napoleon's retreat from Russia), Philippe attempts to give Stéphanie back an identity – but a 'specular' identity, one that defines the woman as the mirror of man, 'the glory of her lover', the other half of a man–woman pair. Repeating his name over and over to her, Philippe pushes the therapy forward; but at the moment he seems to succeed (she says 'adieu' again), Stéphanie dies. Felman sums up the hero's position as follows:

> Stéphanie's recovery of her 'reason', the restoration of her femininity as well as of her identity, depends then, in Philippe's eyes, on her specular recognition of *him*, on her *reflection* of his own name and his own identity. If the question of female identity remains in the text unanswered, it is simply because it is never truly asked: in the guise of asking 'She? Who?', Philippe is in fact always asking 'I? Who?'
>
> (Felman 1975, p. 8)

Felman then moves to consider how academic criticism reproduces Philippe's narcissistic effacement of the woman. In the Gallimard edition of Balzac's story, both commentators mention only the second of the three sections of 'Adieu', a flashback to the war scene that explains Stéphanie's madness. Felman comments:

> The 'explication' thus excludes two things: the madness and the woman. Viewed through the eyes of the two critics, *Adieu* becomes a story about the suffering of men in which the real protagonists are none but 'the soldiers of the Grand Army'. The *Preface* indeed makes a great point of praising Balzac for 'the realism, unprecedented in the history of literature, with which the war is here depicted'.
>
> (p. 5)

And she sums up what she has uncovered in a bracingly direct attack on literary criticism as a general practice:

> This supposedly 'objective' reading of what is called Balzac's 'realism' in fact screens out and disguises an ideological pattern of textual amputations. . . . It is in just this manner that the institution of literary criticism pronounces its expert, professional discourse, without even noticing the conspicuousness of its flagrant misogyny. . . . Madness and women turn out to be the two outcasts of the establishment of readability.
>
> (p. 6)

Such an approach, diagnosing the narrative and critical subordination of a female figure to the logic of phallocentrism in one text, can be expanded to a critique of genres and literary modes. Felman's deconstruction of the critics' response to 'Adieu' includes an argument that realism as a mode demands the suppression of whatever stands outside masculine norms. In a study of the genre of the *blason*, the list in praise of women's beauties common in Renaissance love poetry, Nancy Vickers suggests that this fragmentary representation of the female body reveals the poets' attempts to defend themselves against the threat of the female other by reducing her/it to separate, manipulable body parts (Vickers 1981). In a similar vein, Xavière Gauthier points out the masculine self-aggrandizement made possible by the surrealist view of women as childish, close to nature and irrational (Gauthier 1971; Ladimer 1980). The phallocentrism of literary history is brilliantly deconstructed by Domna Stanton in her study of the notion of the *précieuses*, the absurdly punctilious bluestockings who have been stable characters in French seventeenth-century studies. Stanton shows that the *précieuses* were largely the invention of satiric writers attempting to put a stop to women's literary activities. She details the ploys through which writers of comedy presented the learned woman as ridiculously eccentric, phallicly ambitious so sexually suspect, and the shift through which *préciosité* as a style came to be detached from the women who supposedly practised it: 'Preciosity or the précieux has been masculinized and progressively valorized as a poetic tendency, while the female specificity of *la précieuse* [the *précieuse* woman] has been effaced' (Stanton 1981, p. 10). She demonstrates, like Cixous, that

> No field of human enterprise, no system for the production of meaning lacks the magic stamp of men's naming, and literary history is no exception. Our conceptions of genres and schools, methods and readers, first and second-rate texts, these are the ideological creations of the first, not the second, sex.
>
> (p. 107)

Hearing silences

The second approach in Franco-feminist criticism is to listen 'otherwise', to read between the lines for desires or states of mind that cannot be articulated in the social arena and the languages of phallocentrism. Such a method is sometimes likened to a psychoanalyst's attention to the gaps, displacements and indirection in an analysand's speech. Resistance to official discourses, the breaking of taboos and the exploration of homosexual or otherwise anti-patriarchal relationships are often perceived in the interstices of single texts or of collections of texts. Sherry Dranch, for example, deduces Colette's lesbian *jouissance* and her hesitation to celebrate it explicitly from the euphemisms, oblique sexual imagery and silences – 'the clearly stated covertness' – of *The Pure and the Impure*. She spells out her approach as follows:

> Since the unsaid in a literary text is established in contrast to what is said, we can detect the features, the contours, of the unsaid by identifying patterns of ellipses, through a hermeneutic reading of a censored style. Ellipses are the connection . . . between the subliminal style . . . and a forbidden obsession. A subtext, consisting of the clearly stated unsaid, or more precisely of an inter-said (*inter-dit*: forbidden), is indicated through ellipsis and metaphor, and constitutes a unifying matrix for what appears to be a loosely-connected series of stories.
>
> (Dranch 1983, p. 177)

This kind of analysis can be applied to Victorian women's allusions to the erotic, to Proust and to Gide, to any writer who adopts but also permits a reader to see through her/his socially enforced reticence. Dranch concludes that Colette's textual repression is a negative symptom ('a virile and sensual woman's capitulation to silence, to censorship, to the unsaid'), but other critics evaluate silences more positively. A case in point is Marcelle Marini, writing about the novels and films of Marguerite Duras. Duras has declared her preference for the open potential of women's silence over the 'theoretical rattle of men' (Duras 1973, p. 111), and Marini interprets the speechlessness of Duras's heroines as their refusal of a language 'which others wish to impose upon them by violence' (Marini 1977, p. 22), as stages that make possible a moment of memory or repose leading to new life.

One subtext given major emphasis by Franco-feminist critics is the role of the mother in mother–daughter relationships. The foregrounding of the pre-oedipal dimensions of maternity, central in varying ways to Kristeva, Irigaray and Cixous, finds a parallel in many recent studies. Marianne Hirsch, for example, argues against the traditional interpretation of *La Princesse de Clèves* as an account of the coupling of the heroine to her husband and then to the man she loves. Hirsch shifts away from the husband–lover axis to a mother–daughter focus: the heroine's final refusal to marry is a sign of her internalization of her dead mother's distrust of love at court. Hirsch's reassessment of the novel is based largely on recent Anglo-American work in object-relations psychology, a very different undertaking from Lacanian psychoanalysis; yet her concern with the troubling maternal substratum of public identity coincides with Frenchwomen's efforts to recover, as Hirsch puts it, 'the early erotic attachment between mother and daughter which remains permanently incorporated into the daughter's psyche' (Hirsch 1981, p. 86). Mother–daughter bonds also interest Ronnie Scharfman in her comparison of two contemporary women's texts, Jean Rhys's *Wide Sargasso Sea* and Simone Schwartz-Bart's *Pluie et vent sur Télumée miracle*. Scharfman uses a historicized version of Lacan's mirror-stage to explain the textual confidence of the second novel. Rhys's Bertha is alienated and speechless in the white male world as a result of her inability to incorporate a sustaining reflection of herself in the eyes of her Creole mother; Schwarz-Bart's Télumée prevails as a result of the positive mirroring of family and racial identity she receives from her ex-slave grandmother, 'a story told and a story-teller, the authority for Télumée's own discourse' (Scharfman 1981, p. 92). In this essay Scharfman works out a promising synthesis of the single mother–child dyad as Kristeva and Irigaray present it and the politically oriented, collective identity towards which Wittig points in her fictions. In addition, alertness to the suppression of the maternal can add depth to historical studies of male-authored texts, as in Coppélia Kahn's study of *King Lear* (Kahn 1982), Stephen Orgel's commentary on *The Tempest* (Orgel 1984) and Louis Montrose's study of power plays in *A Midsummer Night's Dream* (Montrose 1983).

Decoding the feminine semiotic

The third approach, that of feeling out the feminine, anti-symbolic elements in a woman's text, seems potentially a rather nebulous or problematic procedure. If corporeal, libidinal *écriture féminine* moves against the grain of masculine, objectivity-claiming discourse, how is the critic to analyse such writing in abstract metalanguage? And how, if *parler femme* can never be codified, can a reader be confident that a critic has actually heard it? Not surprisingly, the attempt to *écouter femme* leads to some interesting rhetorical and structural moves. The critic often opens with a formula of aural or tactile receptivity, and she invites the reader to participate in a celebration of the text. Cécile Cloutier, for example, begins her commentary on a recent novel by the Québecoise Louky Bersianik as follows:

> To speak of the text and the meanings of *L'Euguélionne* is a difficult task. We must slowly let its form in-form us, its allegory unify us at a deep level. It springs forth, arrives at the end of a long patience, like a sort of semiotic, structuralist world beyond.
>
> (Cloutier 1980, p. 95)

She then does some fairly conventional analysis of the numerological and mythic patterns in the novel, but she also suggests that it requires its reader to identify in simultaneously emotional and political terms with its central figure:

> To read *L'Euguélionne* is also to wander back and forth constantly between the real and the imaginary, and I know of very few books that call for so much adaptation on the part of the reader. The *Euguélionne* is the woman of today, now and in centuries to come. . . . She exists in actuality in the daughter and the mother in all of us. . . . She is the woman of the present who is rising within us, who struggles, who frees herself, who feels delight [*jouit*], who weeps.
>
> (p. 97)

This empathetic approach is adopted with unnerving effect by a male critic, Alain Duault, in a review of Chantal Chawaf's novel *Cercœur*. Duault's appropriation of *féminité* arouses suspicion, particularly when he interrupts his rapturous feeling-through of the novel with transparently self-interested praise for its 'non-aggressive and non-exclusive femininity' and then moves into an irritable critique of the 'euphoric' notion of a feminine unconscious (Duault 1977, p. 286). The critic adopting the empathetic mode must, at the least, expect her/his credentials and motives to be sharply scrutinized.

Another strategy of dealing with feminine writing is to imitate the linguistic play of the writer under discussion rather than to explicate the work in plain critical prose. Verena Conley, for example, reviewing Cixous's contribution to *La Jeune née*, opens with a Cixousian simile and pun ('the text reproduces itself from one volume to another like the starfish, from the amputation of members') and concludes with a pyrotechnical replay of the

neologisms and *doubles entendres* in Cixous's mockery of male
critics in an essay on Joyce: 'this is indeed part of the histeric,
histheoric misstery in its urgent call for missexual writing. . . .
The work will doubtless open a breech in American writing'
(Conley 1977, p. 82). Retracing Irigaray's paths, Carolyn
Burke structures her commentary to parallel Irigaray's
theoretical development: 'To follow her trajectory, this essay
adopts the strategy of first locating her starting points and
defining their intellectual ambiance, then imitating her
progress in search of an ideological space for the *parler femme*'
(Burke 1981, p. 290). Reconstructing deconstruction, Burke
warns, is a particularly futile approach to Irigaray:

> As readers, we are invited not to begin objectively, outside the
> text, but rather, to start inside and work our way out into its
> complex web of textual relations. We recognize our textuality
> while adjusting to the quality of intertextuality that inhabits
> Irigaray's writing. To become the reader of *Ce Sexe qui n'en est
> pas un* is to recognize that we are all implicated in this
> discourse. This realization may then generate a new critical
> attitude: one that rejects the lonely fiction of superiority over
> a text.
>
> (p. 296)

The politics of style

Burke's presentations of Irigaray are admirably clear and
informative, however, and they demonstrate one way through
the dilemma of distancing analysis versus participatory immersion in a text: to examine the writing for its textual politics – that
is, to draw out the connections between its grammatical,
figurative and structural patterns and the theory of femininity
underlying it. The writer may, of course, have a thoroughly
phallocentric version of the feminine; an analysis of the
lexical and syntactic performances supporting such an attitude
is carried out by Kristeva in her study of Céline (Kristeva 1980).
Whether applied to women-authored or men-authored texts,
however, Franco-feminist 'close reading' departs from the
'neutral' rhetorical explication of New Criticism and from
structuralism's 'scientific' enumeration of binary oppositions.
Burke's presentation of her translation of Irigaray's 'When Our

Lips Speak Together' typifies the Franco-feminist approach. She writes an empathetic introduction: 'drawn into the process of discovery by the text, the reader is provoked into an almost physical realization of the difficulties involved in trying to speak "otherwise" through the old language' (Burke 1980, p. 8). She then limits her commentary to brief footnotes relating Irigaray's puns, neologisms and collapsing of conventional oppositions to her theoretical essays. Familiar literary-critical terms may appear in such analyses, but they are consistently linked to the deconstructive or utopian purposes of the text.

Wittig's work is directly accessible to this kind of reading. Hélène Wenzel, for example, explains Wittig's revisionary use of pronouns as a technique for affirming the female collectivity in each of her texts. In *L'Opoponax*, the neuter *on* (one) alternates with *ils* (they, masculine), referring to the mixed-sex group of schoolchildren among whom the heroine, Catherine Legrand, explores the world. Wittig eventually adds *nous* (us) to emphasize the shared subjectivity acquired by Catherine and Valerie Borge, the other half of the lesbian couple through which Catherine finally comes to say *je* (I) in the last sentence of the book. Wenzel comments on these shifts: 'Any sense of rigid gender or number is thus eliminated, creating a quasi-utopic "free zone" in which these children may grow up outside the confines of socialized, rigidified sexual difference' (Wenzel 1981, p. 277). In *Les Guérillères*, Wittig mostly avoids words for woman (*la femme, les femmes*), repeating instead the feminine plural *elles* – in order, Wenzel explains, 'to designate the collective female protagonist, thus emphasizing women as an historical and social class, rather than woman as an immutable feminine essence'.

Two more elusive tendencies in *l'écriture féminine*, silence and the verbalization of the 'delirium' of the unconscious, are analysed by Christiane Makward in a study of Duras and Cixous. She points to 'the reticence or systematic braking of signification' in Duras's use of paradox and repetition, and in her minimalist dialogues, built on single words and short-stopped clauses. Analogues in Duras's films include outcries or music rather than speech; empty settings; a blank or a dark screen (Makward 1978). Makward also unravels the polymorphous play of meanings condensed by Cixous into, for example, the title of her novel *LA*: the word recalls the sixth note of the musical scale, a faraway space, the repeated syllable of infant babble (as in 'echolalia'), the feminine pronoun and definite article in French, triumphantly asserted against Lacan's formulation for the suppression of women through language: '*La* femme n'existe pas.' Makward also points out the dizzying variety of opposed registers in Cixous's prose, which mixes liturgical, surrealist, free-associative and philosophically abstract styles without privileging any one of them. And she shows that Cixous incorporates words and phrases from the journals of one of Lacan's patients, the Aimée whom he diagnosed as a curable paranoid psychotic. Cixous, needless to say, refuses to be 'cured'. Makward ends with the suggestion, not at all surprising in the context of Cixous's programme for a systematic 'derangement' of language, that Duras's speechless Procne has been transformed into the wildly singing Philomel, in a typically Cixousian revision of myth.

At times, Franco-feminist explication goes beyond linking the details of a text to its theoretical premisses, in order to take a stand within the debate over *féminité*. Critics opposing Wittig to Cixous, for example, base their arguments on the political implications of style. Diane Griffin Crowder attacks Cixous's use of metaphor, arguing that the parallels she draws between women's writing and their bodily outpourings (blood, milk) imply that biological maternity defines women. In support she quotes Cixous in 'The Laugh of the Medusa':

> We're not going to repress something so simple as the desire for life. Oral drive, anal drive, vocal drive – all these drives are our strengths, and among them is the gestation drive – just like the desire to live self from within, a desire for the swollen belly, for language, for blood.
>
> (Crowder 1983, p. 139)

Crowder's objection is that by treating the body in such a symbolic way, as cosmic force, as an 'immense astral space', Cixous unwittingly suggests that it needs such rhetorical embellishments. In contrast, Wittig's refusal to treat the female body metaphorically, as in the limbs, muscles, organs and secretions she lists so concretely in *Le Corps lesbien*, results in a more totalizing and positive representation. A counter-argument would need to be made in equally precise stylistic and structural terms. One might say that Wittig's anatomical details objectify the body in another way by stressing visualizable parts rather than the energies and capacities of the body in action – to which a Wittig supporter could answer that the narrative voice carries out an affectionate synthesis or reuniting of the fragments. In any case, the terms of the debate would remain the fit (or the misfit) between the theses underlying the texts and the linguistic devices they deploy.

If criticism is judged for its interpretative value, for its capacity to reveal something unpredictable or otherwise invisible in a text, reading feminine writing according to its own manifestos may not be entirely satisfying. The manifestos, on the other hand, might lead to revealing readings of *other* texts. The critic convinced by Irigaray's definition of the diffuse, multi-focused sensibility arising from feminine libido, for example, may see similar symptoms in the writing of George Eliot (Jacobus 1981) or Virginia Woolf. One can, in fact, be usefully alerted to the symptoms, while also believing that they are overdetermined – that is, produced by a range of sociocultural conditions in addition to psychosomatic gender. If *différence* is taken as a repertoire of verbal possibilities, their intersection in men and women writers and their effects on readers seem promising fields of investigation (Frémont 1979; DuPlessis 1980).

None the less, feminist critics of any persuasion need to examine closely the premises of any account of femininity. Every belief about 'what women are' raises political as well as aesthetic problems, and Franco-feminist theory, given its assertions about pre-verbal and unconscious activity that must finally remain conjectural, is no exception. The practice of women's writing is out in the open, for all to see; its basis in the body and the id is less certain. I have raised elsewhere the political objection that theories of *féminité* remain fixated within the metaphysical and psychoanalytic frameworks they attempt to dislodge (Jones 1981, 1984). Irigaray and Cixous often seem to be describing women's subjectivity on the basis of biological and psychic traits that might have enormously different effects in different social situations (Plaza 1978; Brown and Adams 1979). Kristeva hits *écriture féminine* above and below the belt, questioning its 'theological' dimensions and dismissing much of it as warmed-over Romanticism and manic-depressive narcissism (Kristeva 1981, p. 25). Without making deprecatory psychoanalytic diagnoses, feminists may still doubt the efficacy of privileging changes in subjectivity over changes in economic and political systems; is this not dangling a semiotic carrot in front of a mare still harnessed into phallocentric social practices? French and Anglo-American feminists have pointed out the risk of paralysis inherent in cultural modes that glorify marginal discourses – silence, hysteria, delirium – and thus leave official structures intact (Clément 1975; Richman 1980; Bowlby 1983). Claims for the emergence of a new feminine language can be called into question as well. Can a *parler femme* really escape the boundaries of discourse as we know them, or will it, rather, extend the sayable through increasingly familiar or assimilable techniques (Makward 1980)? And might the search for feminine writing lead to the imposition of a single aesthetic upon what should in theory remain a multiplicity of women's discourses (McClelland 1983)?

There is no easy way through these questions – although the fact that they are so widely raised suggests that feminist criticism is in no danger of being taken over by a united Franco-feminist front. In fact, two strands of Franco-feminist criticism should guarantee its resistance to any monolithic position. Committed to deconstructing the certainties of phallocentrism, such criticism would contradict its own purposes by erecting a new table of commandments; committed to listening otherwise, its practitioners are more likely to hear than to suppress the debates and the sceptical voices contributing to its elaboration. The Anglo-American reception of Kristeva, Irigaray and Cixous, as of Wittig in her different way, already suggests that French theory has led to productive doubt as well as enthusiastic acceptance in countries with such different political and intellectual traditions. Our political pragmatism, empiricism and search for a women's literary history are already intersecting in provocative ways with French interrogations of the politics of discourse, the processes of the unconscious and the outlines of a future *à la féminine*. Feminist investigations of textual politics must take place in more languages than one – or even two.

Notes

1   Two good overviews of the intellectual and political climate of woman-oriented theories in France as of 1978 are Elaine Marks, 'Women and literature in France', and Carolyn Burke, 'Report from Paris: women's writing and the women's movement', *Signs*, 3, 4 (1978). A more recent summary, clarifying debates and splits, is Danièle Steward, 'The women's movement in France', *Signs*, 6, 2 (1980). See also Dorothy Kaufmann-McCall, 'Politics of difference: the women's movement in France from May 1968 to Mitterand', *Signs*, 9, 2 (1983).

2   *Jouissance* is a word rich in connotations and, by now, the catalyst of a critical mini-industry. 'Pleasure' is the simplest translation. The noun comes from the verb *jouir*, to enjoy, to revel in without fear of the cost; also, to have an orgasm. Stephen Heath's Translator's Note to a collection of essays by Roland Barthes, *Image–Music–Text*, includes the following:

> English lacks a word able to carry the range of meaning in the term *jouissance* which includes enjoyment in the sense of a legal or social possession (enjoy certain rights, enjoy a privilege), pleasure, and, crucially, the pleasure of sexual climax. The problem would be less acute were it not that *jouissance* is specifically contrasted to *plaisir* by Barthes in his *Le Plaisir du texte*: on the one hand a pleasure (*plaisir*) linked to cultural enjoyment and identity, to the cultural enjoyment of identity, to a homogenizing movement of the ego; on the other a radically violent pleasure (*jouissance*) which shatters – dissipates, loses – that cultural identity, that ego.
>
> (Heath 1977, p. 9)

A note in *New French Feminisms*, an anthology of French writings that will be very useful to English-language readers, defines the *féminité*-linked appropriation of the term as follows:

> This pleasure, when attributed to a woman, is considered to be a different order from the pleasure that is represented within the male libidinal economy often described in terms of the capitalist gain and profit motive. Women's jouissance carries with it the notion of fluidity, diffusion, duration. It is a kind of potlatch in the

world of orgasms, a giving, expending, dispensing of pleasure
without concern about ends or closure.

(Marks and de Courtivron 1980, p. 36)

See also, for remarks on the ineffability of the term, Gallop (1984).

References

Dates for French-authored texts refer to their first publication in
French. Page numbers refer to the English translation if one is cited.

Andermatt, Verena (1979) 'Hélène Cixous and the Uncovery of a
Feminine Language', *Women and Literature*, 7, 1, pp. 40–8.

Bowlby, Rachel (1983) 'The Feminine Female', *Social Text*, 7,
pp. 54–68.

Brown, Beverly, and Adams, Parveen (1979) 'The Feminine Body and
Feminist Politics', *m/f*, 3, pp. 33–7.

Burke, Carolyn (1980) Introduction and translation of Luce Irigaray,
'Quand nos lèvres se parlent' ('When Our Lips Speak Together'),
Signs, 6, 1, pp. 69–79.

Burke, Carolyn (1981) 'Irigaray through the Looking Glass', *Feminist
Studies*, 7, 1, pp. 288–306.

Cixous, Hélène (1975a) 'Le Rire de la Méduse', *L'Arc*, 61. Trans. as
'The Laugh of the Medusa' in Marks and de Courtivron (1980),
pp. 245–64.

Cixous, Hélène (1975b) 'Sorties'. In *La Jeune née*. Paris: Union Générale d'Editions, 10/18. In Marks and de Courtivron (1980), pp. 90–8.

Cixous, Hélène (1976a) Interview with Christiane Makward (in
French), *Sub-stance*, 13, pp. 19–37.

Cixous, Hélène (1976b) 'Le Sexe ou la tête?', *Les Cahiers du GRIF*, 13,
pp. 5–15. Trans. as 'Castration or Decapitation?' by Annette Kuhn,
Signs, 7, 1 (1981), pp. 36–55.

Cixous, Hélène (1977) *La Venue à l'écriture*, with Annie Leclerc and
Madeleine Gagnon. Paris: Union Générale d'Editions, 10/18.

Cixous, Hélène (1979) *Vivre l'orange: to live the orange*, with an English
text by Cixous based on the translation by Ann Liddle and Sarah
Cornell. Paris: des femmes.

Cixous, Hélène (1981) *With, ou l'art de l'innocence*. Paris: Des femmes.

Cixous, Hélène (1984) 'An Exchange with Hélène Cixous'. In Verena
Andermatt Conley, *Hélène Cixous*, pp. 129–61. Lincoln, Neb., and
London: University of Nebraska Press.

Clément, Catherine (1975) 'Enclave/Esclave', *L'Arc*, 61. In Marks and
de Courtivron (1980), pp. 130–6.

Cloutier, Cécile (1980) '*L'Euguélionne*: texte et significations', *Revue de
l'Université d'Ottawa*, 50, 1, pp. 95–8.

Conley, Verena (1977) 'Missexual Misstery', *Diacritics*, 7, 2, pp. 70–82.

Crowder, Diane Griffin (1983) 'Amazons and Mothers: Monique Wittig, Hélène Cixous and Theories of Women's Writing', *Contemporary Literature*, 24, 2, pp. 114–43.

Dranch, Sherry A. (1983) 'Reading through the Veiled Text: Colette's *The Pure and the Impure*', *Contemporary Literature*, 24, 2, pp. 176–89.

Duault, Alain (1977) 'La Chant', *Critique*, 33, pp. 280–7.

DuPlessis, Rachel Blau (1980) 'For the Etruscans: Sexual Difference and Artistic Production – The Debate over a Female Aesthetic'. In Hester Eisenstein and Alice Jardine (eds), *The Future of Difference: Papers from the Barnard College Women's Center Conference*, I. Boston, Mass.: G. K. Hall.

Duras, Marguerite (1973) Interview in Suzanne Horer and Jeanne Socquet (eds), *La Création étouffée*. Paris: Horay. In Marks and de Courtivron (1980) p. 111.

Felman, Shoshana (1975) 'Women and Madness: The Critical Phallacy', *Diacritics*, 5, 4, pp. 2–10.

Féral, Josette (1978) 'Antigone or *The Irony of the Tribe*', trans. Alice Jardine and Tom Gora, *Diacritics*, 8, 3, pp. 2–14.

Féral, Josette (1980) 'Du texte au sujet: conditions pour une écriture et un discours au féminin', *Revue de l'Université d'Ottawa*, 50, 1, pp. 39–46.

Frémont, Gabrielle (1979) 'Casse-texte', *Etudes littéraires*, 12, 3, pp. 315–30.

Gallop, Jane (1982) *The Daughter's Seduction: Feminism and Psychoanalysis*. Ithaca, NY: Cornell University Press.

Gallop, Jane (1984) 'Beyond the Jouissance Principle', *Representations*, 7, pp. 110–15.

Gauthier, Xavière (1971) *Surréalisme et sexualité*. Paris: Gallimard.

Heath, Stephen (1977) Translator's Note to Roland Barthes, *Image-Music-Text*, pp. 7–11. New York: Hill & Wang.

Hirsch, Marianne (1981) 'A Mother's Discourse: Incorporation and Repetition in *La Princesse de Clèves*', *Yale French Studies*, 62, pp. 67–87.

Irigaray, Luce (1974) *Speculum de l'autre femme*. Paris: Minuit. Trans. as *Speculum of the Other Woman* by Gillian Gill. Ithaca, NY: Cornell University Press, 1985.

Irigaray, Luce (1977a) 'Ce Sexe qui n'en est pas un'. In *Ce Sexe qui n'en est pas un*. Paris: Minuit. Trans. as *This Sex Which Is Not One* by Catherine Porter. Ithaca, NY: Cornell University Press, 1985.

Irigaray, Luce (1977b) 'Quand nos lèvres se parlent'. In *Ce Sexe qui n'en est pas un*. Trans. as 'When Our Lips Speak Together' by Carolyn Burke, *Signs*, 6, 1 (1980), 69–79.

Irigaray, Luce (1977c) 'La Misère de la psychanalyse', *Critique*, 33, 365, pp. 879–903.

Irigaray, Luce (1979) *Et l'une ne bouge pas sans l'autre*. Paris: Minuit. Trans. as 'And One Doesn't Stir without the Other' by Hélène Wenzel, *Signs*, 7, 1 (1981), pp. 56–67.

Jacobus, Mary (1981) 'The Question of Language: Men of Maxims and *The Mill on the Floss*', *Critical Inquiry*, 8, 2, pp. 207–22.

Jones, Ann Rosalind (1981) 'Writing the Body: Toward an Understanding of *l'écriture féminine*', *Feminist Studies*, 7, 2, pp. 247–63.

Jones, Ann Rosalind (1984) 'Julia Kristeva on Femininity: The Limits of a Semiotic Politics', *Feminist Review*, 18, pp. 56–73.

Kahn, Coppélia (1982) 'Excavating Those "Dim Minoan Regions": Maternal Subtexts in Patriarchal Literature', *Diacritics*, 12, 2, pp. 32–41.

Kristeva, Julia (1969) 'Word, Dialogue and Novel'. In *Semeiotike*, pp. 143–73. Paris: Seuil. Trans. in Leon S. Roudiez (ed.), *Desire in Language: A Semiotic Approach to Literature and Art*. New York: Columbia University Press, 1980. Oxford: Blackwell, 1981.

Kristeva, Julia (1974a) *La Révolution du langage poétique*. Paris: Seuil. Trans. as *Revolution in Poetic Language* by Margaret Waller. New York: Columbia University Press, 1984.

Kristeva, Julia (1974b) 'Oscillation du "pouvoir" au "refus"', interview with Xavière Gauthier, *Tel Quel*, 58, pp. 98–102. In Marks and de Courtivron (1980), pp. 165–7.

Kristeva, Julia (1975) 'D'une identité à l'autre', *Tel Quel*, 62. Trans. as 'From One Identity to an Other' in Leon S. Roudiez (ed.), *Desire in Language*, pp. 124–47. New York: Columbia University Press, 1980. Oxford: Blackwell, 1981.

Kristeva, Julia (1977a) From *Polylogue*, quoted by Féral (1978).

Kristeva, Julia (1977b) 'Héréthique de l'amour', *Tel Quel*, 74, pp. 30–49.

Kristeva, Julia (1980) *Pouvoirs de l'horreur: essai sur l'abjection*. Paris: Seuil. Trans. as *Powers of Horror* by Leon Roudiez. New York: Columbia University Press, 1982.

Kristeva, Julia (1981) 'Le Temps de femmes', *34/44: Cahiers de recherche des sciences de textes et documents*, 5. Trans. as 'Women's Time' by Alice Jardine and Harry Blake, *Signs*, 7, 1 (1981), pp. 13–35.

Lacan, Jacques (1975) *Encore: Le Séminaire XX, 1972–4*, p. 90. Paris: Seuil.

Ladimer, Bethany (1980) 'Madness and the Irrational in the Work of André Breton', *Feminist Studies*, 6, 1, pp. 175–95.

McClelland, Jane (1983) 'Now that the Muse is Writing: *Ecriture féminine* and Contemporary French Women's Poetry', *Contemporary Literature*, 24, 2, pp. 159–72.

Makward, Christiane (1978) 'Structures du silence/du délire: Marguerite Duras/Hélène Cixous', *Poétique*, 35, pp. 314–24.

Makward, Christiane (1980) 'Nouveau regard sur la critique féministe en France', *Revue de l'Université d'Ottawa*, 50, 1, pp. 47–54.

Marini, Marcelle (1977) *Territoires du féminin: avec Marguerite Duras*. Paris: Minuit.

Marks, Elaine, and Courtivron, Isabelle de (1980) *New French Feminisms*. Amherst, Mass.: University of Massachusetts Press. Brighton: Harvester.

Mitchell, Juliet, and Rose, Jacqueline (eds) (1982) *Feminine Sexuality: Jacques Lacan and the 'école freudienne'*. 'Introduction II' by Jacqueline Rose, pp. 27–57. New York and London: Norton.

Montrose, Louis Adrian (1983) ' "Shaping Fantasies:" Figurations of Gender and Power in Elizabethan Culture', *Representations*, 1, 2, pp. 61–94.

Orgel, Stephen (1984) 'Prospero's Wife', *Representations*, 8, pp. 1–3.

Plaza, Monique (1978) 'Phallomorphic Power and the Psychology of Woman', trans. Miriam David and Jill Hodges, *Ideology and Consciousness*, 4, pp. 5–36.

Richman, Michèle (1980) 'Sex and Signs: The Language of French Feminist Criticism', *Language and Style*, 13, 4, pp. 62–80.

Scharfman, Ronnie (1981) 'Mirroring and Mothering in Simone Schwartz-Bart's *Pluie et vent sur Télumée Miracle* and Jean Rhys' *Wide Sargasso Sea*', *Yale French Studies*, 62, pp. 88–106.

Spivak, Gayatri (1981) 'French Feminism in an International Frame', *Yale French Studies*, 62, pp. 154–84.

Stanton, Domna (1981) 'The Fiction of *Préciosité* and the Fear of Women', *Yale French Studies*, 62, pp. 107–34.

Vickers, Nancy (1981) 'Diana Described: Scattered Woman and Scattered Rhyme', *Critical Inquiry*, 8, 2, pp. 265–79.

Wenzel, Hélène (1981) 'The Text as Body/Politics: An Appreciation of Monique Wittig's Writings in Context', *Feminist Studies*, 7, 2, pp. 264–87.

Wittig, Monique (1969) *Les Guérillères*. Paris: Minuit. Trans. David Le Vay. New York: Avon, 1973.

Wittig, Monique (1979) 'One is not Born a Woman', talk given at the Second Sex Conference, New York Institute for the Humanities (Fall).

Wittig, Monique (1980) 'La Pensée straight', *Questions féministes*, 7, pp. 45–53. Trans. as 'The Straight Mind,' *Feminist Issues*, 1, 1 (1980), pp. 103–11.

Wittig, Monique (1981) 'One is not Born a Woman', *Feminist Issues*, 1, 2 (1981), pp. 47–54.

5
Mind mother:
psychoanalysis and feminism
JUDITH KEGAN GARDINER

According to Judith Kegan Gardiner, psychoanalysis is useful for feminists because it purports to tell us what gender means – that is, how persons become psychologically feminine or masculine. Freud claimed that the father-dominated Oedipus complex originated this binary division, but more recent English and American psychoanalytic theory pushes gender asymmetries back to the mother-dominated pre-oedipal period of a child's life. Gardiner shows how feminist critics use psychoanalytic concepts to analyse gendered subjects in relation to the texts they write and read – through authors' projections, characters' motives, readers' responses, and other structures latent in texts.

She begins with feminist applications of some basic Freudian concepts: the unconscious, the infantile origin of adult emotion, and the symbolic expression of unconscious wishes in art. After surveying some other psychological approaches (derived from Jung and Piaget), she turns to post-Freudian theories: ego psychology and identity theory, transference phenomena, new theories about narcissism, and 'object relations'. She concludes with the explicitly feminist reformulations of psychoanalytic theory by Dorothy Dinnerstein, Nancy Chodorow and Adrienne Rich. Their insights into mothering and its effects on female personality, she suggests, offer models of the ways women writing and reading enter into texts in order to use them in a process of self-definition.

*

Psychoanalytic literary criticism privileges two basic analogies. First, 'mind': the literary text can be understood as the human mind is understood. Second, 'mother': all relationships, including literary ones between persons and texts, reverberate with the strong emotions engendered by and associated with one's childhood family ties. For the feminist literary critic, the words 'mind mother' evoke the contradictions of women's experience in patriarchal cultures, cultures like ours that define 'mind' as male and immaterial and mother as mindless mat(t)er whose responsibility is total and whose authority is denied.

This chapter outlines some ways in which feminist literary critics interpret psychoanalytic concepts. Within a cultural context, psychoanalysis aims to understand individuals by uncovering desires hidden deep within our minds and revealing their connections with the conscious surface. This approach to minds applies to texts as well. Although we may think of the cumulative collective of readers as an interpretative community, most literary texts are written by a single person and read singly by individuals, and literary critics, while interested in periods and genres, usually consider individual works of art to be their special subject. Most of what we regard as literature, as distinct from the other written information that surrounds us, revolves around human character and emotion. Thus, while recognizing that texts are socially situated and constructed, as people are, psychoanalytic critics insist on their unique and personal dimensions.

To comprehend individuals, psychoanalysis suggests more general patterns of development, and the most fundamental division in its system is that of gender. Moreover, psychoanalysis purports to tell us what gender means – that is, how persons become psychologically 'feminine' or 'masculine'. Freud claimed that the father-dominated Oedipus complex originated this binary division, but more recent English and American psychoanalytic theory pushes gender asymmetries back to the mother-dominated pre-oedipal period of a child's life. Using these concepts, psychoanalytic feminist critics analyse gendered subjects in their relationships to the literary texts they write and read and in which they appear as characters. This chapter begins with feminist applications of Freud's ideas and moves to alternative psychologies and to post-Freudian analysis; it concludes with explicitly feminist reformulations of psychoanalytic theory, especially those focusing on the primacy of the mother–daughter bond in female development. At every step, it discusses the psychology first, then the literary applications, in part because this is often chronologically accurate, but more emphatically because literary criticism is the goal and purpose of our enterprise.

Before beginning this survey, it may be necessary to defend the very idea of a female subject. According to some popular intellectual histories like those of Michel Foucault, 'man' has only existed for the last 200 years. That is, the concept of each person as an autonomous, unified, coherent individual is a relatively recent one, and this concept has even more recently been attacked by the post-modernist notion that minds are intrinsically split, fragmented and self-alienated. Juliet Mitchell backs this view with the authority of the French psychoanalyst Jacques Lacan:

> Humanism believes that man is at the center of his own history and of himself; he is a subject more or less in control of his own actions. . . . The matter and manner of all Lacan's work challenges this notion of the human subject: there is none such.
>
> (Mitchell 1982, p. 4)

Operating on the homology between the mind and the text, many literary critics have ceased to look for the unifying themes of works and instead explore their contradictions and ruptures. However, this homology implicitly assumes that both minds and texts are male. Early in this century, feminist writers like Dorothy Richardson, Virginia Woolf and Gertrude Stein also challenged the concept of a unified self. Their approach differed from that of the male mainstream. Instead of cracking the self into self-pitying pieces, they attempted to melt it into a female choral and collective voice. Today's women too may feel that the old unified subject was never a female subject, and women may therefore find little advantage in the current project of dismantling it. Moreover, although some feminist critics work to overthrow the old fathers' authority, others, who fear that this rebellion chiefly benefits the sons, may prefer to support the authority of foremothering women, in an effort to build women's community.

Freud

All psychoanalytic criticism starts with Freud's theories. For a literary critic, three interrelated categories are crucial: the unconscious; the sexual origin of human motivation in repressed infantile incestuous desires; and the symbolic manifestation of unconscious wishes in dreams, jokes, errors and art. According to Freud, we each harbour an unconscious mind that operates by rules more primitive than those of consciousness. Our earliest childhood desires and fantasies, primarily sexual in origin, remain permanently lodged in our unconscious minds. These desires are so frightening and guilt-producing that they are repressed and kept from consciousness. As the young child develops, its libidinal drives attach themselves to oral, then anal, then genital areas of the body. The child's earliest attachments to its parents have permanent and far-reaching consequences. The little boy desires to possess his mother absolutely, regarding his father as a hostile rival. To resolve the fear that his father will punish him with castration, he represses both his desire for his mother and his hostility towards his father. Instead, he identifies with his father, with his father's social power and his possession of women. The child's repressed desires never age; disguised like Mardi Gras mummers, they disrupt adult consciousness with their imperious demands. In every night's dreams, the mechanisms of condensation and displacement mask a carnival of symbolically gratified wishes that slip past the censorious superego. Literary works similarly disguise and gratify unconscious desires, but, by contrast with dreams, their artful and conscious defences can delight many people besides their authors.

Freud's basic concepts, which assume a male paradigm, are broadly accepted as they apply to men. However, his specific notions about female development are much more controversial. These ideas are sparse among Freud's total writings, late, and sometimes contradictory. They include the idea that, until oedipal differentiation, 'the little girl is a little man' and also the opposing idea that a woman's biology is her destiny (Freud 1933, p. 118). According to Freud, girls' femininity forms through a more difficult and tortuous process than boys' masculinity. When the girl discovers she lacks a penis, she resents her inferior anatomical equipment and resents her mother for making her inferior. She wants a baby to substitute for a penis, and she turns to her father and later to other men as love objects, although she never completely relinquishes her earliest erotic attachment to her mother. As a result of this developmental history, women have weak superegos and deficient moral sense; typically, even normally, they are masochistic, narcissistic and passive, competitively hostile towards other women and envious of men (Freud 1925, 1931, 1933).

Feminist psychoanalytic critics usually accept Freud's morphology of mental functioning. They may either reject his ideas about women or accept them provisionally as accurate portraits of the ways in which patriarchal social relations damage women psychologically. One current locus for feminist redress is the Freudian *œuvre* itself, analysed as literature. Particularly in his early case histories, Freud's words dominated those of his hysterical female patients. The French analyst Marie Balmary thinks psychoanalysis went bad when Freud ceased believing his patients (Balmary 1982). He decided they merely fantasized sexual assaults by male relatives; thus he reassigned disturbing sexual desires to female children rather than male adults. Other feminists dramatize Freud's case histories, casting the female patients as leading ladies: 'Anna O' invented the 'talking cure' that Freud developed as free association, and Dora broke off her analysis with Freud because she felt he colluded in a sexual bargain exchanging her between her father and her father's mistress's husband (Freud 1905; Gallop 1982, pp. 132–50; Hertz 1983).

Often the feminist psychoanalytic critic relies on orthodox Freudian conceptions about the unconscious, sexuality, fantasies and defences to solve specifically feminist literary problems. Chief of these problems are the roles that gender plays in authors' projections, in characters' motivations, in readers' responses and in the latent structures of literary texts. Meredith Skura (1981) suggests that the critic may treat a literary work as the analyst treats a case history, another verbal text that reveals its speaker, or as the author's wish-fulfilling fantasy or symbolic dream. Or the critic may take the entire psychoanalytic process, with its transference and counter-transference between patient and analyst, as a model for the interactions among author, reader and text. One traditional psychoanalytic approach explains persistent themes in an author's work with reference to the author's biography, especially the traumatic conflicts of the author's childhood. Feminist critics may analyse how Keats's or Dickens's childhood affected his portraits of women, although more frequently they prefer women writers. For example, Ellen Moers links Mary Shelley's creation of Frankenstein's monster to fears about monstrous childbirth engendered by her own mother's death in bearing her and by her stressful experiences as an outcast's daughter, teenage mother and illegitimate wife – to 'the motif of revulsion against newborn life, and the drama of guilt, dread, and flight surrounding birth and its consequences' (Moers 1977, p. 142).

Another traditional approach interprets female literary characters, chiefly in plays and novels, as though they were human beings. This approach presumes that good authors create characters who act like real people in their overt behaviour and also in the slips, dreams, and so on, that imply unconscious life. Prolific as a goddess, Shakespeare attracts psychoanalytic feminist character critics. One scholar may see Desdemona as a strong, sexually self-assured woman who speaks for her own rights, where another points to the repressed and baffled anger she sings in the 'Willow' song. A third believes Desdemona encourages her maid Emilia to express the aggression she dares not, and a fourth traces Desdemona's fatal paralysis to ambivalent idealization of Othello as a father figure.

That approach which analyses a whole text as a projection of authorial fantasies is an expansion of character criticism. To cite another example from Shakespeare, a fifth *Othello* scholar might explain Desdemona as one of a series of tragic heroines that assuage Shakespeare's anxiety about female sexuality through spiritualizing idealization. None the less, the drama expresses that anxiety by equating intercourse and death in the scene in which Othello kills Desdemona on their nuptial bed. Such dramatization allows viewers, too, to re-enact and hence master threatening unconscious material, comforted as the Venetian patriarchs reimpose control.

The feminist Shakespearians, then, exemplify a group of critics who use complementary psychoanalytic and other approaches (see Lenz, Greene and Neely 1980; Greene and Swift 1981, 1982; Schwartz and Kahn 1980). They show Shakespeare's world as a grand dream-like construction, inhabited by men and women with gendered psychologies. They question structure and language in the plays as well as character and plot. And they interrogate the absent as well as the present. Why do so many characters have dead mothers or no mothers at all? Why does the man who is 'not of woman born' and whose wife and children have been destroyed emerge as the invulnerable hero of *Macbeth*?

Of course, Shakespeare did not create his plays from unmediated fantasies. He transformed conventional sources in the literary genres of his period, and these genres affect the plays' psychological shapes. For example, one recurrent pattern in his plays is that husbands who destroy their brides later idealize them. In each instance, Shakespeare condemns the man's misogyny and exonerates the woman's virtue. But Shakespeare alters the pattern to fit the genres of each play. Othello understands that Desdemona is chaste only after he has murdered her, whereas in the comedy *Much Ado about Nothing* and the romance of *The Winter's Tale* the women are not really dead, and so their husbands can renew their marriages. Thus a comedy presents a wish-fulfilment fantasy, while a tragedy, rolling relentlessly towards the major characters' deaths, expresses similar unconscious material in scenes like nightmares. Some critics evaluate Shakespeare's sexism by comparing his plays with their conventional sources or analogues. In such comparisons he usually fares well. For instance, suspected wives are truly unfaithful in Renaissance domestic tragedies other than *Othello*, and Shakespeare's *Taming of the Shrew* gives Kate a psychologically more credible role and treats her less vindictively than his sources do (Bean 1980; Boose 1982). However, evaluative criticism does not depend solely on source study, but strives for a broader reading of the way an author typically treats female characters in comparison with male ones. For example, scholars argue over the extent to which Shakespeare empowers his transvestite heroines or reins them into submissive marriages (Dusinberre 1975; Jardine 1983).

Aldous Huxley doubted if *Brave New World*'s somatized souls could comprehend Shakespearian passion, but he assumed we readers understood Shakespeare as he did. Much traditional psychoanalytic criticism assumes that minds have always been as they are now, that psychoanalytic laws are permanent and timeless. From this perspective, all people who were once babies fear engulfment, and it is part of the human condition to rebel against powerful and prohibiting father figures. In contrast, feminist critics, who assume that minds are socially constructed, postulate historical and cultural variations in people's psychologies. As critics bring history, politics and psychoanalysis into their literary criticism, they open up new areas for feminist analysis as well. For example, a Marlowe hero's 'aspiring mind' may reflect European imperialism's outward thrust, and an Elizabethan courtier may charge his love lyrics with anxieties about political success (Greenblatt 1980; Marotti 1982). A feminist critic might read these Renaissance texts looking for distinctive alignments of 'manhood' and 'womanhood', of narcissistic investment and sexual desire in the period. The 'aspiring mind' may accompany Protestant reinforcement of patriarchy as well as imperialism, and the Elizabethan court lady's interpretation of honour may be different from her sonneteer's.

We need to deconstruct the label 'patriarchy' to understand how fathers and daughters felt about one another at different times and how economic relations affected those feelings. Lear rages at his daughters' 'filial ingratitude' and at the unforeseen psychological consequences of his own economic dependency. As Lillian Rubin demonstrates through interviews with contemporary Americans, economic and psychological dependencies are closely linked (Rubin 1983). Whole genres of literature exist, like the women's courtship novel, to justify what are essentially economic arrangements as emotional choices, providing a rich field for feminist psychoanalytic critics. Jane Austen opens *Pride and Prejudice* with the famous sentence: 'It is a truth universally acknowledged, that a single man in possession of a good fortune must be in want of a wife.' Much of the novel's wit consists in showing that men and women have different investments in this 'universal' acknowledgement. Often critics have been less sensitive than Austen about what is 'universally acknowledged', using the canonical texts to prove that past minds worked just like ours. *Hamlet* is made to prove again the debilitating power of the Oedipus complex. However, texts that fit our preconceptions less well may encourage our historical/ psychological imaginations more. If we cannot decide whether Shakespeare's sonnets are heterosexual or homosexual, perhaps we can question the historical adequacy of these polarized categories.

The psychology of oppression

When a feminist critic looks into a woman writer's mind, she often sees anger and self-doubt. Some critics extend this approach to the generalization that what unifies women's writing is the psychology of oppression, the psychology of women living under patriarchy. Virginia Woolf chastized Charlotte Brontë's intrusive anger, an anger that Woolf felt distracted Brontë from her story and 'deformed and twisted' its expression. But Woolf imagined an angry tale of her own, that of Shakespeare's talented sister who was seduced, abandoned and driven to suicide: 'who shall measure the heat and violence of the poet's heart when caught and tangled in a woman's body?' (Woolf 1957, pp. 72, 50). More recently, Sandra Gilbert and Susan Gubar describe nineteenth-century women writers as enraged 'madwomen' whispering their secrets from patriarchal attics. Gilbert and Gubar open their study by asking whether the pen is a 'metaphorical penis'. In so far as both men and women thought it was, women writers felt themselves to be freaks. Alienated and derogated, expected to nurture others while not being nurtured themselves, these writers developed a language of madness, confinement, anorexia and disease, and they produced 'literary works that are in some sense palimpsestic, works whose surface designs conceal or obscure deeper, less accessible (and less socially acceptable) levels of meaning' (Gilbert and Gubar 1979, pp. 3, 73). To express and deny their rage at these social double-binds, they paired their docile heroines with negative doubles – wild, sexy, crazy women. Rochester's first wife in Brontë's *Jane Eyre* is the prototype of such a madwoman, but mad, rebellious eyes gleam, too, from inside Emily Dickinson's virginal and decorous New England persona.

Creative as are her protective strategies, the 'madwoman' author is a victim. As many feminist critics illustrate, social victimization has broad psychological consequences. Studies of rape and incest in literature may take this cast, for example, by showing Lolita as the abused child whose attacker claims he is only giving her what she wants. Feminist analyses of pornography, too, blame male needs to humiliate women and wonder why some women like to comply (Lederer 1980; Lesage 1981). Similarly, feminist media critics explore images in film, television or popular literature that cater specifically to male projections or female fantasies. Some critics, like Patricia Meyer Spacks (1975), accept Freud's portrait of women and find narcissism, passivity and masochism native to 'the female imagination'. However, others believe women can imagine freer lives than those we have known. In science-fiction stories written by men, Pamela Sargent notes, all-female societies may seek vengeance against men, whereas all-female cultures imagined by women ignore men and co-operate peacefully among themselves (Sargent 1974).

Heterosexuality monopolizes western love lyrics and novels of courtship and adultery. For some feminist critics, women's heterosexuality is another psychological consequence of growing up under patriarchy, a consequence neither inevitable nor desirable (Rich 1980). They cite Freud's account of girls' strained progress towards heterosexuality as evidence that it is a restrictive disposition forced upon women by society. From this perspective, romantic literature warps women's minds; fairytales like 'Cinderella' and 'Snow White' encourage female passivity; and the pernicious giants like Dante, Milton, Goethe and Yeats discourage full female humanity.

Although Freud acknowledges that the heterosexual is made, not born, his prejudice against 'perversion' renders his theories inadequate to explain lesbian literature. Psychologies of victimized, colonized or 'muted' people may sometimes clarify writing by lesbians, as they may writing by women of colour or by working-class women (Showalter 1982). However, psychologies of victimization underestimate a group's strengths and minimize creative variations among its members. Toni Morrison's *The Bluest Eye* demonstrates how white ideals of physical beauty destroy a black girl's mind, but her *Sula* shows black women who both harm and sustain one another (see Spillers 1983).

Jung and Piaget

Orthodox psychoanalysts call their discipline 'depth psychology', but psychologies other than Freud's also claim to understand human nature deeply. Because he makes each person's bisexuality a central tenet of his philosophy, Carl Jung's ideas have attracted some feminists. Jung believes that each person needs to incorporate aspects of the opposite sex into his or her personality, that the woman's 'animus' and the man's 'anima' help them achieve wholeness. Rachel Blau DuPlessis describes the mythological Psyche as a representation of the integrated female self:

> She is wholeness in the female, of female male and child; she is the woman with parents inside her and she is the parents, a woman who, of her own powers, carries the little female self inward swaddled . . . carries a box, empty, the child has been born, she steals from death – this is psyche, the hera.
>
> (DuPlessis 1979, p. 87)

Jung thought a collective, transpersonal unconscious stocked the contents of each individual's unconscious mind. Cross-culturally, certain archetypes reappeared in myths and legends, dramatizing our deepest hopes and fears and our human desire for psychological growth. Presiding over these archetypes is the original Great Mother, goddess of life and death, mother of beasts and cities (Neumann 1955). Some feminist critics approve Jung's attention to 'masculine' and 'feminine' aspects of people and cultures, although others believe Jung reinforces stereotyped notions of gender. Annis Pratt (1981) uses Jungian categories while differentiating female plots in fiction from male ones. She follows the female hero and discovers that her quest differs from that of the archetypal male hero. Instead of venturing out into the world, she journeys within the self, finding restoration in the green world of nature. A male companion helps her, but he is neither the object of her search nor her reward for accomplishing it. Thus, once again, feminist critics find that writing by women is neither the same as nor opposite to men's writing, but differently structured, presumably because of women's different psyches and social experiences.

Of course, critics must know the theories that affect their subjects, whether they believe them to be true or not. For example, the prophetic Doris Lessing assimilates ideas from Freud, Laing and the Sufi mystics. In her novel *Memoirs of a Survivor*, Jungian typology determines the plot, the impersonal characterization and the metaphoric imagery; it also explains the otherwise mysterious ending. Lessing calls this novel an 'autobiography' because it is the story of every immature soul trying to hatch itself into history. The novel's end is a Jungian vision; a renewed primal family follows the female 'Shining One' through the unfolded gates to the new era, trailed by an archetypal procession of children of all races and the Great Mother's lion mascot.

Jean Piaget believed that children's mental structures developed in an invariant sequence of distinctive stages. Although his cognitive psychology is very different from both Freud's psychoanalysis and Jung's gendered mysticism, Piaget's views seem sufficiently compelling for some theorists, like Lawrence Kohlberg, to wish to integrate his insights about mental growth into those of depth psychology, particularly in the field of moral development. Carol Gilligan (1982) challenges the masculinist bias of these moral-development theories. Although she assaults Freud's notion that women are morally inferior to men, she accepts his hypothesis that female morality develops differently from male morality. Gilligan interviewed women about decisions concerning abortion and concluded that women typically develop different moral languages and decision-making styles from those of men. Whereas male theoreticians posit abstract rights as the highest stage of morality and then fault women for failing to achieve this stage, women refuse to abstract any act from its concrete causes and results. Gilligan hears in her informants' voices an ethic of responsibility, nurturance and interdependence, quite unlike the male ethic of autonomous individual entitlement. Sara Ruddick, too, believes that women develop a distinctive morality, which she sees as related to maternal practice. She defines a cognitive style of 'maternal thinking' – holistic, open-ended and field-dependent – and a concomitant ethic of 'preservative love' (Ruddick 1980).

Some contemporary novels by women seem to accept a new double standard that differentiates morality by gender. The old double standard judged a man's honour by his deeds but a woman's only by her chaste not-doing. The new double standard still tests men's courage and commitment in the world, while censoring women, not for sexual liberty, but for failures of maternal responsibility. In such fiction, the values of responsibility, nurturance and interdependence become psychologically charged in quite complex ways. For example, Margaret Drabble's fiction is overtly concerned with the moral issue of responsibility, and it is densely populated with mothers – wonderful, all-giving mothers; gentle neurotics; and horribly rejecting ones. In *Jerusalem the Golden*, Clara's mother is mean and puritanical. When Clara returns from a clandestine sexual jaunt, she learns that her mother is dying and leaving her free. Is it Clara's matricidal wish that destroys her mother or Drabble's fantasy of being a good mother to her character?

Post-Freudian psychoanalysis

In the decades since Freud's death, psychoanalysis has developed new concerns that have enriched literary criticism. As we have seen, the central Freudian ideas are related: the sexual origin of human emotion, the repression of infantile impulses in patterns different for the two sexes, and the symbolic expression of unconscious wishes in art and in everyday life interlock in a variety of ways. Because of the interdependence of its conceptual system and because of Freud's authority, new psychoanalytic ideas tend to be assimilated into the old framework, and some old ones, like the universal Oedipus complex and penis envy, resist displacement. The controversial French analyst Jacques Lacan claims to preserve the true revolutionary and subversive Freud against conservative adaptations by American and English psychoanalysis. To reject Lacan's theories, his followers believe, is to dodge harsh truths – for example, that the 'phallus' is the only 'signifier'. Even more than Freud's concepts, Lacan's are linked by internal logic so that the whole justifies its constituent parts and cannot be refuted, especially not by empirical data, whose relevance they reject. However,

Lacan's highly influential theories have inspired some brilliant feminist critical readings.

Of many post-Freudian developments in psychoanalysis, four are especially significant to feminist criticism. All four arise from the understanding that early social interactions in the family, rather than biology alone, shape psychological structures. These developments are ego psychology and identity theory; transference and counter-transference phenomena; new theories of narcissism; and the 'object relations' school's stress on pre-oedipal relations between mothers and children.

Post-war ego psychologists shifted their emphasis from instinctual drives to the social adaptations of the growing self. Erik Erikson, a leading figure of this school, popularized two extremely influential concepts: life stages and identity. Erikson expanded Freud's oral, anal and genital stages in two ways: he extended the notion of life stages past childhood, and he discussed the social accomplishments of each stage. Thus, according to Erikson, the child learns to relate to its bodily pleasures and frustrations through its interactions with others. In the Freudian oral stage, the child learns to trust its nurturing human environment. Each developmental stage presents its own crisis or problem, the successful resolution of which enables the next stage. Like Freud, Erikson implies a male paradigm and briefly treats female development as its variant. None the less, his outline of life stages can illuminate certain genres of fiction – for example, the current spate of novels about women's 'midlife crises' (Erikson 1950).

The second major Eriksonian concept is that of identity, which includes biological make-up, infantile identifications, social roles and mature self-image. The concept of 'identity' is related to that of life stages in that, although identity grows throughout a person's life, it consolidates at a specific stage – that of the adolescent identity crisis (Erikson 1959). The traditional *Bildungsroman* chronicles a young man's identity crisis and its resolution in a known social world. Feminist critics find that the female novel of development has its own concerns – apprenticeship to social constraint or sudden awakening – that do not fit a linear male model of steady progress (Abel, Hirsch and Langland 1983). Some scholars see women's quests for identity as the dominant theme of women's fiction. Those feminists who analyse the stages of man's life in literature know that they study the distinctively male, not a generic humanity. Thus in *Man's Estate* Coppélia Kahn traces the changes in Shakespeare's depiction of male characters as he himself ages. Callow Adonis remains trapped in adolescent narcissism, whereas Romeo matures through sexual love and leaves his gang of competitive boyfriends. The jealous husbands of the later tragedies suffer because they cannot control those they love, but the fathers in the final romances learn to preserve their family lines by letting their daughters go (Kahn 1981).

Both identity theory and transference phenomena provide models for readers' responses to literary texts. Norman Holland sometimes seeks a text's unity by defining the unifying 'identity theme' of its author's personality; sometimes he demonstrates that readers reconstruct texts to echo their own distinctive 'identity themes' (Holland 1978). Other critics derive models of reader response from the analytic transference, in which the patient projects emotions on to the analyst that have to do with the patient's past. Scholars like Stanley Fish propose themselves as exemplary readers (Fish 1980), while others like Holland report the case histories of their students. Both stances preserve the critic's authority over the text and over its less expert readers. Whereas these theorists emphasize the idiosyncratic nature of individual reader responses, feminist reader-response critics investigate the decisive role that gender plays in shaping women's responses to literature (Flynn 1983; Kolodny 1980).

Analysing audiences involves sociological methodology as well as psychological theory. For popular literature, audience analysis is also analysis of genre. Critics survey buyers of supermarket romances, asking how their fictions please or fail them (Radway 1984). Conversely, critics may deduce from the content of a genre its psychological appeal to a specific category of readers (Modleski 1982). For example, gothic thrillers may safely express female fears about houses, entrapment and heterosexuality (Holland and Sherman 1977). In popular romances, apparently harsh older men ultimately enfold spunky heroines in tender passion. Is the romance reader an addicted fool, sublimating her dissatisfaction with men, marriage and lost career opportunities on to silly plots that strengthen her dependence on the patriarchal order? Or is she actively escaping her housewife role by defending her private pleasures?

The same controversy appears in feminist film criticism. Some scholars argue that camera, narrative and male characters fetishize the female spectacle and negate the female spectator. Linda Williams claims that women tend to turn away from the mutilated female victims in horror films. When the woman looks, however, she recognizes herself not only in the passive heroine but also in the monster, the object of our horrified gaze but also the rebel against proprieties (Williams 1984). Other film critics try to locate positions from which feminist film-makers can question the dominant visual order and from which female viewers can reappropriate their own visual pleasure (Mulvey 1975). This reappropriation is complicated by the convention that associates women with excessive self-regard. In film, as in literature and life, women are accustomed to seeing themselves being seen, to valuing themselves according to others' evaluations of their appearance, and then to being devalued for this 'narcissism'.

Recently, psychoanalysts have advanced exciting new theories about narcissism. According to Freud, every normal infant passes through a stage of primary narcissism, in which its mobile, unitary libido is attached to the child's own body. Then the libido transfers its energies to other people. Some people, like male homosexuals and women, regress to perverse narcissism (Freud 1914). In contrast to this view, Heinz Kohut suggests that the self develops along two parallel tracks: the first is Freud's line of libidinal investments; the second, not discussed by Freud, fosters ego values and ideals, feelings of self-esteem and the formation of a self-image (Kohut 1971). In this formulation, the child first experiences itself as merged with its mother and harbours notions of magical omnipotence. Optimally, its mirroring adult caretaker responds to its real needs, letting the child know that these needs are valid and the child good. Some infants who are inadequately mirrored may become narcissistic adults with a defective thermostat of self-esteem. Such narcissists may be arrogant and grandiose, reacting to slight criticism with overwhelming rage. Or they may be depressed, feeling that they are worthless unless they merge with some powerful idealized person or ideology. Through transference, the analyst can help them by mirroring them as their mothers should have done when they were infants. The other major new theorist about narcissistic personalities, Otto Kernberg, disputes Kohut's double-track hypothesis (Kernberg 1975). Neither of these theorists discusses gender differences in narcissism.

In literature, each sex accuses the other of excessive vanity, a belief that seems related to different ways in which men and women build their self-esteem. Freud believes female narcissism is normal. In contrast, Virginia Woolf flees the shadow that a giant phallic 'I' casts over everything men write, although she also blames women for puffing men: 'women have served all these centuries as looking-glasses possessing the magic and delicious power of reflecting the figure of man at twice its natural size' (Woolf 1957, p. 35). The philosopher Sandra Bartky defines female narcissism as an infatuation with an inferiorized body and suggests that the social identification of a woman with her body affects her self-image (Bartky 1979). John Berger (1972) exposes the way women are trained to watch themselves being observed and so to think of themselves as objects. This analysis explains many images of women in the visual arts, advertising, film and literature. Literary texts reveal a distinctively male narcissism; for example, in *The Man Who Loved Children* Christina Stead implies that 'Uncle Sam' Pollit's genial and expansive male egotism reflects America's patronizing imperialism toward the 'childlike' Third World. Narcissism may have differing meanings in male and female texts, since men and women construct their self-images with varying degrees of attachment to differing body images. Charlotte Brontë and George Eliot, for instance, make their characters' physical beauty or plainness a matter of intimate importance. Perhaps, too, the sexes develop self-esteem differently.

As post-modernist literature becomes increasingly self-referential, critics will focus more on literary self-presentation. Already many critics cherish past literary works like *Tristram Shandy* that demonstrate precocious textual self-consciousness, and the future history of modernism may well describe dual male and female traditions of self-presentation in the interior monologues of Dorothy Richardson and James Joyce, or in the egotisms of Gertrude Stein and D. H. Lawrence, or in the self-deprecating strategies of Virginia Woolf and T. S. Eliot.

Object-relations theory

The theory of narcissism is one branch of the broader psycho-analytic area of object-relations theory, other branches of which have led to the most significant feminist revisions of psychoanalysis. Object-relations theory explains how the child becomes a person. It stresses the construction of the self in social relationships rather than through instinctual drives. In this terminology, 'objects' include everything that the self perceives as not itself. That is, the maternal object is not the mother but the child's mental representation of its mother. For our pur-poses, three ideas of the object-relations school are particularly important: pre-oedipal primacy, the separation–individuation process and the transitional space. Whereas Freud saw the oedipal stage at ages 3–6 as forming the child's character, the object-relations theorists stress the first three years in the child's life, believing that the self forms in infancy, principally through its relationships with its primary caretaker, usually the mother. As a result, the child's relationship with its mother is of crucial importance, and fathers play a very secondary role (Fairbairn 1952). D. W. Winnicott, a paediatrician and child analyst, emphasizes the active role of the 'good enough mother' in helping her child achieve a sense of self. The 'good enough' mother is the normal mother who both gratifies and inhibits her children, who loves them and mirrors them so that they develop reasonably well. This assignment of a positive role for mothers marks a great improvement over the tendency to polarize mothers into perfectly nurturant ideals or schizophrenogenic witches who are responsible for all patient pathology.

According to the object-relations school, the child's primary task in its first years is achieving separation–individuation. This is a dual process by which the child becomes psychologi-cally separate from its mother and simultaneously develops its own sense of self. The theory assumes that babies at first cannot distinguish themselves from their surrounding environments, including their mothers, and that they must establish ego and body boundaries and learn to perceive other people as truly other, not subject to their magical destructive control. They must also learn to perceive themselves as the agents of their actions, separate persons who can feel coherent while experiencing both positive and negative feelings about themselves and others. Margaret Mahler (1979) claims that girls have a more difficult time separating and individuating from their mothers than boys do.

Before the toddler fully distinguishes itself from its not-self, it may become especially attached to a 'transitional object' like a teddy bear or blanket. The child may also indulge in imaginative play in a privileged 'transitional space' before it has clearly defined boundaries between the real and the not-real (Winnicott 1971). Play in the transitional space suggests dramatic play on the bare boards of the stage. So far critics have not used this concept to explore gender differences in literary or dramatic representations. However, psychological studies of children's imaginative play differentiate girls' typical play themes and roles from boys'. Erikson describes girls defending 'inner spaces' made of blocks, while boys build tall towers and knock them down again (Erikson 1965). Another study states that girls playing games maintain game boundaries and solace other players rather than losing themselves in rapt involvement (Sutton-Smith 1971, p. 104).

By attending chiefly to the first few years of life, the object-relations school focuses on a period that orthodox psychoanalysis considers pre-gendered. According to the Freudian scheme, children of both sexes progress similarly through oral, anal and phallic stages of libidinal attachment, and the little girl remains a 'little man' until she discovers she has been 'castrated'. Although the object-relations theorists do not deny this model, their emphasis on the child's mother profoundly differs from the Freudian emphasis on oedipal conflict with the father.

Feminist psychoanalytic theories

Current feminist revisions of psychoanalytic theory use the insights of the object-relations school to account for the different experiences of boys and girls and thus for the growth of children into masculine and feminine persons. They accept the primacy of the mother–infant bond in child development but see it as

affecting boys and girls differently. Thus they reject both biological explanations of natural or essential gender differences
and gender-free descriptions of early childhood. Instead, they
claim that gender differences have social causes that start very
early in child development (see Miller 1976; Person 1980).

From the beginning of his work, Freud battled against those
who rejected his controversial ideas, such as the sexual aeti-
ology of neurosis. He attacked philistines, prudes and
religious ideologues. He also attacked feminists who futilely
protested against their inferiority. Feminist psychoanalysts
from Karen Horney on criticized Freud's masculinist bias and
saw in male power, not penises, the reason why women envied
men.

While traditional Freudian analysts developed ego psychology and object-relations theory, preparing the way for new
ideas about gender, empirical psychologists observed children
and disproved several of Freud's theories, especially about
female sexuality and gender acquisition (see Maccoby and
Jacklin 1974). The Money and Ehrhard (1972) studies of
inadvertent transsexuals showed that anatomy was not destiny,
since early acculturation could contradict it. Social differentiation begins at birth, according to studies that show adults
varying their behaviour to the same babies depending on
whether they are told the children are boys or girls (Oakley
1981, p. 96). Children establish their gender identity much
earlier than Freud predicted. Between 18 months and 3 years of
age, boys know they are male like their fathers and girls that
they are female like their mothers, and this knowledge is not
dependent on seeing others' naked bodies or understanding
their anatomies but grows from the parents' labelling and the
child's cognitive schematizing (Bem 1983). Moreover, girls
want babies very early, and women seem to enjoy babies as
babies, not as penis substitutes. Current studies of female
sexuality also deny Freud's contention that a normal girl must
turn from an active 'phallic' interest in her clitoris to mature,
passive feminine fulfilment through vaginal orgasms experienced during heterosexual intercourse. These observations
undercut Freud's concept of inevitable female penis envy.
Although many analysts agree that their female patients fantasize having penises, the doctors now reject penis envy as the

unanalysable bedrock of female psychology. Instead, they explain that penis envy may symbolize earlier experiences of abandonment and loss, narcissistic injury, or envy at greater male social privilege. Thus Freud was mistaken about the formation of female gender identity and about the formation of the desire to mother. Freud underestimated the pre-oedipal period, though in one late essay on female sexuality he acknowledged its archaeological importance in the psyche as analogous to that of the Minoan culture buried deep beneath Greek civilization's more obvious splendours (see Blum 1977; Fliegel 1982).

Although feminist revisions of psychoanalytic theory are diverse, they agree not only that the infant's relationship with its mother determines much of its sense of self but also that this relationship is inevitably gendered from the very beginning; this developmental difference accounts for typical variants in male and female sexuality, psyche and personality. Gender asymmetry develops from a social fact – the fact that in all known societies women tend young children as well as bear them. The theories so far formulated assume traditional families in which mothers are mostly present and fathers mostly absent from young children's lives; they have not yet examined the effects of new, less sex-typed forms of childrearing. According to Dorothy Dinnerstein (1976), the fact of female mothering means that both boys and girls learn to associate women as a class with infancy's powerful irrational needs and fears. Children fantasize a perfectly responsive mother, and adults criticize women for not being that person (see Contratto and Chodorow 1982). Children also project against women their earliest rage at life's frustrating realities. Repressed male fear of women accounts for western men's endemic aggression, misogyny and technological folly, though girls learn they may some day share maternal power, and therefore they fear it less than boys do.

Because the boy's first caretaker and love object is female, he must struggle to define himself as separate from her, as *not* like mother, in order to achieve a sense of himself as male. He must repress his earliest attachment and fight its engulfing intimacy. Later, trying to become like father offers him the prospect of emotional distance and rational control, but only at the cost of denying internalized 'feminine' aspects of himself. By continuing to desire mother, he preserves heterosexuality while investing it with misogyny. Such attitudes may create the double standard and obsessive male concern with female sexual behaviour. At some historical periods, this obsession dominates literature, as in the male 'honour' duels to control women's bodies in the literature of the Spanish Golden Age. However, we need a more historically specific psychoanalytic theory to explain why such concerns appear so unevenly in literary genres and cultures and why male sexual honour is glorified by fading feudal classes.

Nancy Chodorow explains the cycle whereby women wish to be mothers and succeed at their role. She believes that societies ensure an adequate supply of child-tenders by encouraging all women to be empathic and nurturant. Moreover, because men are socialized to be aggressive, non-empathetic and affectively repressed, intimate relations between men and women will always disappoint women, who crave more intimacy than men can provide. Women therefore seek this intimacy by re-creating with their babies the symbiotic bonds they first enjoyed with their mothers. As symbiotic mothers, they will perpetuate the cycle by distancing their sons while intimately merging with their daughters. As a result, the 'masculine sense of self' is separate; the 'feminine sense of self remains connected to others in the world' (Chodorow 1978, p. 169). For Chodorow, as for Freud, a woman's desire for a baby is to some extent compensatory to her dissatisfaction with heterosexual relations. None the less, she assumes that affectively homo-erotic women will turn to men sexually. Despite this belief, lesbian theorists note that Chodorow's theory undercuts some heterosexist assumptions by stressing women's primary bonds with other women and women's difficulties with men (see Stimpson 1982). Adrienne Rich celebrates the power of mother love and sees all women as originally and potentially lesbian because all women first love another woman. She also describes lesbian relationships as invested with the intensity and ambivalence of the mother–daughter bond.

Dinnerstein, Chodorow and Rich describe gender differences in terms that imply women are nicer than men. Empathy, responsibility and interdependence seem preferable to defensive aggression, destructive rage against women and nature, and a compulsion for control. However, other feminists evaluate the same characteristics in terms of female disadvantage. For Jane Flax (1978) and Jessica Benjamin (1980), women's fluid ego boundaries are a weakness. They see women's chief problems as achieving independence, separation from others and autonomous individual identities. Gender-polarized childhood experiences affect sexual desire too. Benjamin contends that the male value of rational control shapes male and female sexual desire as well as male personality. Domination is not a nasty additive to nice eroticism but its essence, for, in patriarchies, domination and submission constitute erotic excitement.

The theories of Dinnerstein, Chodorow and Rich, augmented by numerous recent studies on mothering, have been enormously influential on literary critics (see Hirsch 1981b). By providing a comprehensive and relatively simple explanation for differences between male and female personalities as they are structured in modern western culture, these theories offer to account for differences in literature written by women and by men. If women have more flexible, less rigid ego boundaries than men; define themselves through relationships, especially intense and ambivalent mother–daughter bonds; experience difficulties with autonomy, independence and heterosexuality; and feel morally responsible to a human network rather than to an abstract code of rights, then their writing should reflect these qualities.

Of course, despite its current popularity, difference need not be the only model for investigating gender in writing. One might argue that, whether or not women and men differ, their writing does not, because literature transcends gender. Conversely, one might suggest that, although women and men do not differ significantly, their writings do, because literary conventions reflect ideology as much as social reality. Or, to pick a more popular view among feminist critics, one might claim that writing differs according to the 'feminine' or 'masculine' components of writers' psyches, structures not dependent on biological sex, so that George Eliot may be said to be a more 'masculine' author than Jean Genet. For the present, it may be simpler to describe writing by women and by men, male and female characters in literature, and men's and women's literary responses, and investigate which attributes pile up under each heading rather than assuming we already know the attributes and can redistribute them. One reason some feminist critics prefer psychoanalytic gender theories based on mother–daughter bonding to those based on phallic lack is that such theories permit them to disregard difference altogether. Theories of interdependence among women allow theoretical independence from men and break with past theories that define the female by deviations from the male.

Mother-based theories encourage critics to investigate relationships among women. Scholars explore these relationships both outside and inside texts' fluid margins. Elaine Showalter, Ellen Moers, and others, trace a literary history in which women writers create a community of influence that transcends nations and generations (Showalter 1977). The new focus on relationships among women challenges traditional views of women authors, revising, for example, the portrait of Emily Dickinson as a neurotic recluse who poured her broken-hearted love for a married minister into her fragile verse. Current feminist readers concentrate, rather, on her strong and sustaining friendships with other women, especially her sister-in-law, and interpret the mysterious 'he's' in her verse neither as God nor as lost lover but as her own creative power, conceptualized as male (see Juhasz 1983; Rich 1979, pp. 157–83). Feminist historians support psychoanalytic theories about women's relationships; Carroll Smith-Rosenberg's often cited study (1975) of nineteenth-century American women documents a 'female sphere' of intense intimacy and interdependence that was estranged from the male public sphere.

Within literary texts too, where critics previously read overt plots concerning courtship, marriage or adultery, some now discover crucial subtexts built around relationships among women. Nina Auerbach studies communities of women in fiction (Auerbach 1978); Elizabeth Abel, women's friendships. As a consequence of women's flexible ego boundaries, female friends define themselves and one another: 'through the intimacy which is knowledge, friendship becomes a vehicle of self-definition for women, clarifying identity through relation to an other who embodies and reflects an essential aspect of the self' (Abel 1981, p. 16). In Toni Morrison's *Sula*, for instance, the conventional Nel needs her self-affirming friendship with the wild Sula, a woman who carelessly sleeps with Nel's husband but who appreciates Nel as an equal, as the husband cannot.

The emotional priority of bonds between women is also the focus of Marianne Hirsch's essay on *La Princesse de Clèves*. The princess rebuffs sexual love in order to remain faithful to her mother's deathbed injunction, a warning against men that ultimately sends the princess to a convent with her integrity and ties with women intact (Hirsch 1981a). Nancy Miller reads the novel's ending not as a defeat but as a triumphal fantasy of female power, the power to withdraw from the traditional plot of love and marriage (Miller 1981). One might read the literature of seduced and abandoned women in the same way, since such women can control their lives verbally while appearing socially dependent and compliant; lamenting a man after he has gone may be easier than conforming to his wishes when he is present.

Critics find the merging identities and blurred boundaries, which are attributed to women's relationships, in all aspects of writing by women. French critics of *écriture féminine* attribute women's 'fluid' styles to the blood, milk and joyful flow of women's bodies. Fluidity may describe the genres of women's writing as well as their themes, styles, characters and structures. A recent anthology claims that women's autobiographies are typically less goal-oriented than men's, more attuned to social contexts and inner reveries than to outer accomplishments (Jelinek 1980).

Moreover, the line between women's novels, autobiographies and journals is often a thin one. Instead of judging it from the outside, the feminist literary critic may enter her text. Rachel Brownstein (1982) claims we want to become the heroines we read. For the writer-critic, these connections are even more direct. Alice Walker poses as Zora Neale Hurston's 'niece' to place a headstone on her great predecessor's unmarked grave, feeling the pain of Hurston's disparagement as 'so direct a threat to one's own existence' (Walker 1979, p. 313).

Inside merges with outside: the psychology of women determines women's relationships with their texts as well as the relationships among female authors and characters. I think women writers often use their texts, particularly those focused on female heroes, as part of a self-defining process involving empathetic identifications with those characters. Thus, even if the author creates the character as a narcissistic, idealized projection of herself, she must shape it in accordance with literary conventions, social facts and her self-distancing aesthetic judgement. Like a daughter, the character thus acquires a 'life of her own', a limited autonomy. I believe the author often defines herself through the text while creating her female hero in a process analogous with learning to be a mother, that is, learning to experience oneself simultaneously as a well-nurtured child and as one's own nurturing parent, and, at the same time, learning that one's creation is separate from one's self (Gardiner 1982).

Drawing on her experience as Margaret Fuller's biographer, Bell Gale Chevigny comes to similar conclusions. 'Women writing about women will symbolically reflect their internalized relations with their mothers and in some measure re-create them', she claims. Although Chevigny thus speaks as a writing 'daughter', she indicates that she mothers her book as well, until it 'takes its first steps and leaves home for the dangerous outer world'. 'In the biographical process I describe, there is a stage in which author and subject in effect become *surrogate mothers* in that they offer one another "maternal" nurture' in a 'fantasy of reciprocity' in which 'both "mothers" are engaged in struggle; but nurture not an infant, but a girl or woman; and for both, nurture is a sanctioning of their autonomy' (Chevigny 1983, pp. 80, 92, 95–6).

I think that woman readers undergo an analogous process in empathetically identifying with female characters, particularly those that are close extensions of their authors. Despite this intimacy, the female reader does not remain completely immersed in the text; she may dip more deeply into empathetic identification or bob up as she reads, breaking her connection to reflect about the work. At times both writer and reader may relate to the text as though it were a person with whom one might be merged empathetically or from whom one might be separated and individuated. Through such identifications, women writers intimately unite with female readers and so foster each other's self-awareness through their texts.

Psychoanalytic mother–daughter theory has been exciting

and fruitful for feminist critics, but it has increased their tendency to focus solely on texts by and about women. In the future, we must integrate the male-domination model of women's experience with the maternal-bonding model. Moreover, we must expand psychoanalytic feminist criticism so that it can clarify how gender works everywhere in literature – in texts by both men and women; in books about identity, work and politics as well as those concerning love, marriage and the family; and in both popular communal forms and élite self-referential meditations. We must also develop an ability to read women's sexuality in its historical context and women's self-presentations outside of pejorative comparisons with male norms. As we learn to look for them, too, we may well find buried 'maternal' and paternal subtexts in works by men, relationships that challenge our exclusive focus on male autonomy, individuality and difference.

Mind mother.

The injunction to 'mind mother' is fallacious in so far as it suggests that all women are to be considered exclusively in their psychological roles as mothers. None the less, it may be a usefully provocative demand. As daughters and sons, we automatically resent such a demand, a response we need to understand if female texts are ever to have communal weight without merely imitating patriarchal authority. One positive response is to reverse the demand and remind ourselves that mothers are all persons who resent being treated only through our needs. When she is so treated, mother minds. But objection may give way to resentful obedience. As we reassess the literary canon, we must continue to struggle against old patterns lest 'mother' mind them submissively. We can do this, in part, by extending, rather than reifying, traditionally positive female values: when given a baby or a text to tend, even the male 'mother' can learn to mind it. And, most important, we will continue that vital activity of women thinking, an activity we might call, intransitively, 'mother minds'.

Note

For their comments, suggestions and references, I should like to thank the editors of this volume and Richard Gardiner, Annette Hollander,

Leah Marcus, Erica Rosenfeld and Linda Williams. The notation '(see
. . .)' cites a reference that is not the direct source of the preceding
statement. I regret that this chapter necessarily omits many valuable
studies.

References

I have roughly coded the entries below into works of literary criticism
(L); psychology, psychoanlytic theory or works with a psychoanalytic perspective (P); and explicitly feminist studies (F). Thus a
piece of feminist, psychoanalytic literary criticism is labeled FPL. A
few entries do not fit any of these categories; they are not coded by
letter.

Abel, Elizabeth (1981) '(E)Merging Identities: The Dynamics of
    Female Friendship in Contemporary Fiction by Women', *Signs*, 6, 3,
    pp. 413–35. Response by Gardiner with reply by Abel. FPL.
Abel, Elizabeth, Hirsch, Marianne, and Langland, Elizabeth (eds)
    (1983) *The Voyage In: Fictions of Female Development.* Hanover, NH,
    and London: University Press of New England. Anthology of critical
    essays. FL, some FPL.
Auerbach, Nina (1978) *Communities of Women: An Idea in Fiction.*
    Cambridge, Mass., and London: Harvard University Press. FL.
Balmary, Marie (1982) *Psychoanalyzing Psychoanalysis: Freud and the
    Hidden Fault of the Father* (1979), trans. Ned Lukacher. Baltimore,
    Md, and London: Johns Hopkins University Press. FP.
Bartky, Sandra Lee (1979) 'On Psychological Oppression'. In Sharon
    Bishop and Marjorie Weinzsweig (eds), *Philosophy and Women*,
    pp. 33–41. Belmont, Cal.: Wadsworth. F.
Bean, John C. (1980) 'Comic Structure and the Humanizing of Kate in
    The Taming of the Shrew'. In Lenz, Greene and Neely (1980),
    pp.   65–78. FL.
Bem, Sandra Lipsitz (1983) 'Gender Schema Theory and its Implica-
    tions for Child Development: Raising Gender-Aschematic Children
    in a Gender-Schematic Society', *Signs*, 8, 4, pp. 598–616. FP.
Benjamin, Jessica (1980) 'The Bonds of Love: Rational Violence and
    Erotic Domination'. In Hester Eisenstein and Alice Jardine (eds),
    The Future of Difference, pp. 41–70. Boston, Mass.: G. K. Hall. FP.
Berger, John (1972) *Ways of Seeing.* Harmondsworth: Penguin. Art and
    culture criticism; originally BBC lectures.
Blum, Harold (1977) *Female Psychology: Contemporary Psychoanalytic
    Views.* New York: International Universities Press. Collection of
    essays revising Freud. P, some FP.
Boose, Lynda (1982) 'The Misogynistic Fantasy of Jacobean Drama

and Shakespeare's Expose of it in *Othello*', unpublished conference paper. FL.

Brownstein, Rachel M. (1982) *Becoming a Heroine: Reading about Women in Novels*. New York: Viking. FL.

Chevigny, Bell Gale (1983) 'Daughters Writing: Toward a Theory of Women's Biography', *Feminist Studies*, 9, 1, pp. 79–102. Biographer of Margaret Fuller. FPL.

Chodorow, Nancy (1978) *The Reproduction of Mothering: Psychoanalysis and the Sociology of Gender*. Berkeley, Cal: University of California Press. Highly influential. FP.

Contratto, Susan, and Chodorow, Nancy (1982) 'The Fantasy of the Perfect Mother'. In Barrie Thorne and Marilyn Yalom (eds), *Rethinking the Family: Some Feminist Questions*, pp. 54–75. New York: Longman. Questions certain uses of mother-based theories. FP.

Dinnerstein, Dorothy (1976) *The Mermaid and the Minotaur: Sexual Arrangements and Human Malaise*. New York: Harper & Row. Influential cultural criticism. FP.

DuPlessis, Rachel Blau (1979) 'Psyche, or Wholeness', *Massachusetts Review*, 20, 1, pp. 77–96. FPL.

Dusinberre, Juliet (1975) *Shakespeare and the Nature of Women*. London: Macmillan. New York: Barnes & Noble. FL.

Erikson, Erik H. (1950) *Childhood and Society*. New York: Norton. P.

Erikson, Erik H. (1959) *Identity and the Life Cycle*. New York: Norton. P.

Erikson, Erik H. (1965) 'Womanhood and the Inner Space'. In Robert Jay Lifton (ed.), *The Woman in America*, pp. 1–26. Boston, Mass.: Houghton Mifflin. P.

Fairbairn, W. R. D. (1952) *An Object-Relations Theory of the Personality*. New York: Basic Books. P.

Fish, Stanley (1980) *Is There a Text in This Class? The Authority of Interpretive Communities*. Cambridge, Mass.: Harvard University Press. L.

Flax, Jane (1978) 'The Conflict Between Nurturance and Autonomy in Mother–Daughter Relationships and Within Feminism', *Feminist Studies*, 4, 2, pp. 171–89. FP.

Fliegel, Zenia Odes (1982) 'Half a Century Later: Current Status of Freud's Controversial Views on Women', *Psychoanalytic Review*, 69, 1, pp. 7–28. Full bibliography. FP.

Flynn, Elizabeth A. (1983) 'Gender and Reading', *College English*, 45, 3, pp. 236–52. Small empirical study. FL.

Freud, Sigmund (1905) 'Fragment of an Analysis of a Case of Hysteria'. In Freud (1951–73), 8, pp. 3–122. Study of Dora. P.

Freud, Sigmund (1914) 'On Narcissism: An Introduction'. In Freud (1951–73), 14, pp. 69–102. P.

Freud, Sigmund (1925) 'Some Psychical Consequences of the Anatomical Distinction between the Sexes'. In Freud (1951–73), 19, pp. 243–58. P.

Freud, Sigmund (1931) 'Female Sexuality'. In Freud (1951–73), 21, pp. 223–43. P.

Freud, Sigmund (1933) *New Introductory Lectures on Psychoanalysis*. In Freud (1951–73), vol. 22, pp. 3–182. P.

Freud, Sigmund (1951–73) *The Standard Edition of the Complete Psychological Works of Sigmund Freud*, trans. and ed. James Strachey. London: Hogarth Press. P.

Gallop, Jane (1982) *The Daughter's Seduction: Feminism and Psychoanalysis*. Ithaca, NY: Cornell University Press. Uses Lacan. FPL.

Gardiner, Judith Kegan (1982) 'On Female Identity and Writing by Women'. In Elizabeth Abel (ed.), *Writing and Sexual Difference*, pp. 177–92. Chicago, Ill., and London: University of Chicago Press. FPL.

Gilbert, Sandra M., and Gubar, Susan (1979) *The Madwoman in the Attic: The Woman Writer and the Nineteenth-Century Imagination*. New Haven, Conn., and London: Yale University Press. Highly influential study. FPL.

Gilligan, Carol (1982) *In a Different Voice: Psychological Theory and Women's Development*. Cambridge, Mass., and London: Harvard University Press. FP.

Greenblatt, Stephen (1980) *Renaissance Self-Fashioning: From More to Shakespeare*. Chicago, Ill., and London: University of Chicago Press. L.

Greene, Gayle, and Swift, Carolyn Ruth (eds) (1981) (1982) *Feminist Criticism of Shakespeare*. Special editions of *Women's Studies*, 9, 1–2. Anthology of essays. FL, some FLP.

Hertz, Neil (ed.) (1983) 'A Fine Romance: Freud and Dora', *Diacritics* (special edition) (Spring). Includes Cixous's 'Portrait of Dora' and Dora bibliography. FP.

Hirsch, Marianne (1981a) 'A Mother's Discourse: Incorporation and Repetition in *La Princesse de Clèves*', *Yale French Studies*, special issue on 'Feminist Readings: French Texts/American Contexts', 62, pp. 67–87. FPL.

Hirsch, Marianne (1981b) 'Mothers and Daughters: Review Essay', *Signs*, 7, 1, pp. 200–22. FL, FP.

Holland, Norman N. (1978) 'Human Identity', *Critical Inquiry*, 5, 3, pp. 451–69. PL.

Holland, Norman N., and Sherman, Leona F. (1977) 'Gothic Possibilities', *New Literary History*, 8, pp. 279–94. FPL.

Horney, Karen (1967) *Feminine Psychology*. New York: Norton. FP.

Jardine, Alice (1983) *Still Harping on Daughters*. Brighton: Harvester. New York: Barnes & Noble. FL.

Jelinek, Estelle C. (ed.) (1980) *Women's Autobiographies*. Bloomington, Ind., and London: Indiana University Press. Anthology of critical studies. FL, some FLP.

Juhasz, Suzanne (ed.) (1983) *Feminist Critics Read Emily Dickinson*. Bloomington, Ind., and London: Indiana University Press. Anthology of critical studies. FL, some FLP.

Jung, Carl G. (1959) *The Basic Writings of C. G. Jung*, ed. Violet Staub de Laszlo. New York: Modern Library. P.

Kahn, Coppélia (1981) *Man's Estate: Masculine Identity in Shakespeare*. Berkeley, Cal.: University of California Press. FPL.

Kernberg, Otto F. (1975) *Borderline Conditions and Pathological Narcissism*. New York: Jason Aronson. P.

Kohlberg, Lawrence (1981) *The Philosophy of Moral Development*. San Francisco, Cal.: Harper & Row. P.

Kohut, Heinz (1971) *The Analysis of the Self: A Systematic Approach to Psychoanalytic Treatment of Narcissistic Personality Disorders*. New York: International Universities Press. P.

Kolodny, Annette, (1980) 'A Map for Rereading: or, Gender and the Interpretation of Literary Texts', *New Literary History*, 11, 3 (Spring), pp. 451–67. FL.

Lederer, Laura (ed.) (1980) *Take Back the Night: Women on Pornography*. New York: William Morrow. F.

Lenz, Carolyn Ruth Swift, Greene, Gayle, and Neely, Carol Thomas (eds) (1980) *The Woman's Part: Feminist Criticism of Shakespeare*. Urbana, Ill.: University of Illinois Press. Collection of critical essays. FL, some FPL.

Lesage, Julia (ed.) (1981) 'Women and Pornography', *Jump Cut*, 26, pp. 46–60. Several essays on film; includes bibliography by Gina Marchetti. FL, some FPL.

Maccoby, Eleanor, and Jacklin, Carol (1974) *The Psychology of Sex Differences*. Stanford, Cal.: Stanford University Press. Surveys psychological literature. FP.

Mahler, Margaret S. (1979) *Separation–Individuation*. New York: Jason Aronson. P.

Marotti, Arthur (1982) '"Love is not Love": Elizabethan Sonnet Sequences and the Social Order', *ELH*, 49, 2, pp. 396–428. L.

Miller, Jean Baker (1976) *Toward a New Psychology of Women*. Boston, Mass.: Beacon Press. FP.

Miller, Nancy, K. (1981) 'Emphasis Added: Plots and Plausibilities in Women's Fiction', *PMLA*, 96, 1, pp. 36–48. FPL.

Mitchell, Juliet (1982) 'Introduction I'. In Juliet Mitchell and Jacqueline Rose (eds), *Feminine Sexuality: Jacques Lacan and the 'école freudienne'*, trans. Jacqueline Rose, pp. 1–26. New York and London: Norton. FP.

Modleski, Tania (1982) *Loving with a Vengeance: Mass-Produced Fantasies for Women*. Hamden, Conn.: Archon Books. FPL.

Moers, Ellen (1977) *Literary Women: The Great Writers*. Garden City, NY: Anchor Press/Doubleday. FL.

Money, John, and Ehrhardt, Anke (1972) *Man and Woman, Boy and Girl*. Baltimore, Md: Johns Hopkins University Press. P.

Mulvey, Laura (1975) 'Visual Pleasure and Narrative Cinema', *Screen*, 16, pp. 6–27. FPL.

Neumann, Erich (1955) *The Great Mother: An Analysis of the Archetype*, trans. Ralph Manheim. Princeton, NJ: Princeton University Press. P.

Oakley, Ann (1981) *Subject Women*. New York: Pantheon Books. Sociology and psychology. FP.

Person, Ethyl Spector (1980) 'Sexuality as the Mainstay of Identity: Psychoanalytic Perspectives', *Signs*, 5, 4, pp. 605–30. FP.

Piaget, Jean (1965) *The Moral Judgment of the Child* (1932). New York: Free Press. P.

Pratt, Annis (1981) *Archetypal Patterns in Women's Fiction*, with Barbara White, Andrea Loewenstein and Mary Wyer. Bloomington, Ind.: Indiana University Press. FPL.

Radway, Janice A. (1984) *Reading the Romance: Women, Patriarchy and Popular Literature*. Chapel Hill, NC: University of North Carolina Press. Uses interviews. FL.

Rich, Adrienne (1976) *Of Woman Born*. New York: Norton. Influential feminist treatment of the institution of motherhood. F, FP, some FL.

Rich, Adrienne (1979) *On Lies, Secrets, and Silence: Selected Prose 1966– 1978*. New York: Norton, Essays, some on literature; exposition of radical lesbian feminism. F, some FL.

Rich, Adrienne (1980) 'Compulsory Heterosexuality and Lesbian Existence', *Signs*, 5, 4, pp. 631–60. FP.

Rubin, Lillian B. (1983) *Intimate Strangers: Men and Women Together*. New York: Harper & Row. Social psychology and sociology. FP.

Ruddick, Sara (1980) 'Maternal Thinking', *Feminist Studies*, 6, 2, pp. 342–67. Philosophical approach. F.

Sargent, Pamela (ed.) (1974) *Women of Wonder: Science Fiction Stories by Women about Women*, pp. xlix–liv. New York: Random House. F.

Schwartz, Murray M., and Kahn, Coppélia (eds) (1980) *Representing Shakespeare: New Psychoanalytic Essays*. Baltimore, Md: Johns Hopkins University Press. Critical anthology. PL, some FPL.

Showalter, Elaine (1977) *A Literature of their Own: British Women Novelists from Brontë to Lessing*. Princeton, NJ: Princeton University Press. FL.

Showalter, Elaine (1982) 'Feminist Criticism in the Wilderness'. In Elizabeth Abel (ed.), *Writing and Sexual Difference*, pp. 9–35. Chicago, Ill., and London: University of Chicago Press.

Skura, Meredith Anne (1981) *The Literary Use of the Psychoanalytic Process*. New Haven, Conn.: Yale University Press. PL.

Smith-Rosenberg, Carroll (1975) 'The Female World of Love and Ritual: Relations between Women in Nineteenth-Century America', *Signs*, 1, 1, pp. 1–29. Highly influential; contends that women lived in an intimate, conflict-free sphere with one another. F.

Spacks, Patricia Meyer (1975) *The Female Imagination*. New York: Knopf. L.

Spillers, Hortense J. (1983) 'A Hateful Passion, A Lost Love', *Feminist Studies*, 9, 2, pp. 293–323. On women characters by American black women writers. FL.

Stimpson, Catharine R. (1982) 'Zero Degree Deviancy: The Lesbian Novel in English'. In Elizabeth Abel (ed.), *Writing and Sexual Difference*, pp. 243–59. Chicago, Ill., and London: University of Chicago Press. FPL.

Sutton-Smith, Brian (1971) 'Boundaries'. In R. E. Herron and Brian Sutton-Smith (eds), *Child's Play*. New York and London: Wiley. P.

Walker, Alice (ed.) (1979) *I Love Myself When I Am Laughing . . . And Then Again When I Am Looking Mean And Impressive: A Zora Neale Hurston Reader*. Old Westbury, NY: Feminist Press. FL.

Williams, Linda (1984) 'When the Woman Looks'. In Mary Ann Doane, Patricia Mellencamp and Linda Williams (eds), *Re-Vision: Essays in Feminist Film Criticism*, pp. 83–99. Los Angeles, Cal: American Film Institute. Film criticism. FPL.

Winnicott, D. W. (1965) *The Family and Individual Development*. New York: Basic Books. P.

Winnicott, D. W. (1971) *Playing and Reality*. New York: Basic Books. P.

Woolf, Virginia (1957) *A Room of One's Own* (1929). New York and London: Harcourt Brace Jovanovich. Start reading feminist criticism here. FL.

6

Pandora's box: subjectivity, class and sexuality in socialist feminist criticism

CORA KAPLAN

Cora Kaplan points to a split in feminist criticism, between liberal humanists, who take psychosexual experience as more meaningful for women than social oppression, and socialist feminists, who foreground social and economic elements in texts and view fantasy and desire as anarchic and regressive. While liberal humanists fail to interrogate the idea of a unified female subject as ideology, she says, socialist feminists tend to stigmatize the literary representation of feeling as bourgeois. Exploring the origins of this split in Rousseau and Wollstonecraft, Kaplan argues for a criticism which can come to grips with the relationship between female subjectivity and class identity – which deals with the unconscious processes of subjective identity as, at the same time, structures through which class is lived and understood.

*

Feminist criticism, as its name implies, is criticism with a Cause, engaged criticism. But the critical model presented to us so far is merely engaged to be married. It is about to contract what can only be a *mésalliance* with bourgeois modes of thought and the critical categories they inform. To be effective, feminist criticism cannot become simply bourgeois criticism in drag. It must be ideological and moral criticism; it must be revolutionary.

(Lillian Robinson, 'Dwelling in Decencies' (1978))

The 'Marriage' of marxism and feminism has been like the marriage of husband and wife depicted in English common law: marxism and feminism are one, and that is marxism . . . we need a healthier marriage or we need a divorce.

(Heidi Hartmann, 'The Unhappy Marriage of
Marxism and Feminism' (1981))

I

In spite of the attraction of matrimonial metaphor, reports of feminist nuptials with either mild-mannered bourgeois criticism or macho mustachioed Marxism have been greatly exaggerated. Neither liberal feminist criticism decorously draped in traditional humanism, nor her red-ragged rebellious sister, socialist feminist criticism, has yet found a place within androcentric literary criticism, which wishes to embrace feminism through a legitimate public alliance. Nor can feminist criticism today be plausibly evoked as a young deb looking for protection or, even more problematically, as a male 'mole' in transvestite masquerade. Feminist criticism now marks out a broad area of literary studies, eclectic, original and provocative. Independent still, through a combination of choice and default, it has come of age without giving up its name. Yet Lillian Robinson's astute pessimistic prediction is worth remembering. With maturity, the most visible, well-defined and extensive tendency within feminist criticism has undoubtedly bought into the white, middle-class, heterosexist values of traditional literary criticism, and threatens to settle down on her own in its cultural suburbs. For, as I see it, the present danger is not that feminist criticism will enter an unequal dependent alliance with any of the varieties of male-centred criticism. It does not need to, for it has produced an all too persuasive autonomous analysis which is in many ways radical in its discussion of gender, but implicitly conservative in its assumptions about social hierarchy and female subjectivity, the Pandora's box for all feminist theory.

This reactionary effect must be interrogated and resisted from within feminism and in relation to the wider socialist feminist project. For, without the class and race perspectives which socialist feminist critics bring to the analysis both of the literary texts and of their conditions of production, liberal feminist criticism, with its emphasis on the unified female subject, will unintentionally reproduce the ideological values of mass-market romance. In that fictional landscape the other structuring relations of society fade and disappear, leaving us with the naked drama of sexual difference as the only scenario that matters. Mass-market romance tends to represent sexual difference as natural and fixed – a constant, transhistorical femininity in libidinized struggle with an equally 'given' universal masculinity. Even where class difference divides lovers, it is there as narrative backdrop or minor stumbling-block to the inevitable heterosexual resolution. Without overstraining the comparison, a feminist literary criticism which privileges gender in isolation from other forms of social determination offers us a similarly partial reading of the role played by sexual difference in literary discourse, a reading bled dry of its most troubling and contradictory meanings.

The appropriation of modern critical theory – semiotic with an emphasis on the psychoanalytic – can be of great use in arguing against concepts of natural, essential and unified identity: against a static femininity and masculinity. But these theories about the production of meaning in culture must engage fully with the effects of other systems of difference than the sexual, or they too will produce no more than an anti-humanist avant-garde version of romance. Masculinity and femininity do not appear in cultural discourse, any more than they do in mental life, as pure binary forms at play. They are always, already, ordered and broken up through other social and cultural terms, other categories of difference. Our fantasies of sexual transgression as much as our obedience to sexual regulation are expressed through these structuring hierarchies. Class and race ideologies are, conversely, steeped in and spoken through the language of sexual differentiation. Class and race meanings are not metaphors for the sexual, or vice versa. It is better, though not exact, to see them as reciprocally constituting each other through a kind of narrative invocation, a set of associative terms in a chain of meaning. To understand how gender and class – to take two categories only – are articulated together transforms our analysis of each of them.

The literary text too often figures in feminist criticism as a gripping spectacle in which sexual difference appears somewhat abstracted from the muddy social world in which it is elsewhere embedded. Yet novels, poetry and drama are, on the contrary, peculiarly rich discourses in which the fused languages of class, race and gender are both produced and re-represented through the incorporation of other discourses. The focus of feminist analysis ought to be on that heterogeneity within the literary, on the intimate relation there expressed between all the categories that order social and psychic meaning. This does not imply an attention to content only or primarily, but also entails a consideration of the linguistic processes of the text as they construct and position subjectivity within these terms.

For without doubt literary texts do centre the individual as object and subject of their discourse. Literature has been a traditional space for the exploration of gender relations and sexual difference, and one in which women themselves have been formidably present. The problem for socialist feminists is not the focus on the individual that is special to the literary, but rather the romantic theory of the subject so firmly entrenched within the discourse. Humanist feminist criticism does not object to the idea of an immanent, transcendent subject but only to the exclusion of women from these definitions which it takes as an accurate account of subjectivity rather than as a historically constructed ideology. The repair and reconstitution of female subjectivity through a rereading of literature becomes, therefore, a major part, often unacknowledged, of its critical project. Psychoanalytic and semiotically oriented feminist criticism has argued well against this aspect of feminist humanism, emphasizing the important structural relation between writing and sexuality in the construction of the subject. But both tendencies have been correctly criticized from a socialist feminist position for the neglect of class and race as factors in their analysis. If feminist criticism is to make a central contribution to the understanding of sexual difference, instead of serving as a conservative refuge from its more disturbing social and psychic implications, the inclusion of class and race must transform its terms and objectives.

II

The critique of feminist humanism needs more historical explication than it has so far received. Its sources are complex, and are rooted in that moment almost 200 years ago when modern feminism and Romantic cultural theory emerged as separate but linked responses to the transforming events of the French Revolution. In the heat and light of the revolutionary decade 1790–1800, social, political and aesthetic ideas already maturing underwent a kind of forced ripening. As the progressive British intelligentsia contemplated the immediate possibility of social change, their thoughts turned urgently to the present capacity of subjects to exercise republican freedoms – to rule themselves as well as each other if the corrupt structures of aristocratic privilege were to be suddenly razed. Both feminism as set out in its most influential text, Mary Wollstonecraft's *A Vindication of the Rights of Woman* (1792), and Romanticism as argued most forcefully in Wordsworth's introduction to *Lyrical Ballads* (1800) stood in intimate, dynamic and contradictory relationship to democratic politics. In all three discourses the social and psychic character of the individual was centred and elaborated. The public and private implications of sexual difference as well as of the imagination and its products were both strongly linked to the optimistic, speculative construction of a virtuous citizen subject for a brave new egalitarian world. Theories of reading and writing – Wollstonecraft's and Jane Austen's as well as those of male Romantic authors – were explicitly related to contemporary politics as expressed in debate by such figures as Tom Paine, Edmund Burke and William Godwin.

The new categories of independent subjectivity, however, were marked from the beginning by exclusions of gender, race and class. Jean-Jacques Rousseau, writing in the 1750s, specifically exempted women from his definition; Thomas Jefferson, some twenty years later, excluded blacks. Far from being invisible ideological aspects of the new subject, these exclusions occasioned debate and polemic on both sides of the Atlantic. The autonomy of inner life, the dynamic psyche whose moral triumph was to be the foundation of republican government, was considered absolutely essential as an element of progressive political thought.

However, as the concept of the inner self and the moral psyche was used to denigrate whole classes, races and genders, late nineteenth-century socialism began to de-emphasize the political importance of the psychic self, and redefine political morality and the adequate citizen subject in primarily social terms. Because of this shift in emphasis, a collective moralism has developed in socialist thought which, instead of criticizing the reactionary interpretation of psychic life, stigmatizes sensibility itself, interpreting the excess of feeling as regressive, bourgeois and non-political.

Needless to say, this strand of socialist thought poses a problem for feminism, which has favoured three main strategies to deal with it. In the first, women's psychic life is seen as being essentially identical to men's, but distorted through vicious and systematic patriarchal inscription. In this view, which is effectively Wollstonecraft's, social reform would prevent women from becoming regressively obsessed with sexuality and feeling. The second strategy wholly vindicates women's psyche, but sees it as quite separate from men's, often in direct opposition. This is frequently the terrain on which radical feminism defends female sexuality as independent and virtuous between women, but degrading in a heterosexual context. It is certainly a radical reworking of essentialist sexual ideology, shifting the ground from glib assertions of gender complementarity to the logic of separatism. The third strategy has been to refuse the issue's relevance altogether – to see any focus on psychic difference as itself an ideological one.

Instead of choosing any one of these options, socialist feminist criticism must come to grips with the relationship between female subjectivity and class identity. This project, even in its present early stages, poses major problems for the tendency. While socialist feminists have been deeply concerned with the social construction of femininity and sexual difference, they have been uneasy about integrating social and political determinations with an analysis of the psychic ordering of gender. Within socialist feminism, a fierce and unresolved debate continues about the value of using psychoanalytic theory, because of the supposedly ahistorical character of its paradigms. For those who are hostile to psychoanalysis, the meaning of mental life, fantasy and desire – those obsessive themes of the novel and poetry for the last two centuries – seems particularly intractable to interpretation. They are reluctant to grant much autonomy to the psychic level, and often most attentive to feeling expressed in the work of non-bourgeois writers, which can more easily be read as political statement. Socialist feminism still finds unlocated, unsocialized psychic expression in women's writing hard to discuss in non-moralizing terms.

On the other hand, for liberal humanism, feminist versions included, the possibility of a unified self and an integrated consciousness that can transcend material circumstance is represented as the fulfilment of desire, the happy closure at the end of the story. The psychic fragmentation expressed through female characters in women's writing is seen as the most important sign of their sexual subordination, more interesting and ultimately more meaningful than their social oppression. As a result, the struggle for an integrated female subjectivity in nineteenth-century texts is never interrogated as ideology or fantasy, but seen as a demand that can actually be met, if not in 1848, then later.

In contrast, socialist feminist criticism tends to foreground the social and economic elements of the narrative and socialize what it can of its psychic portions. Women's anger and anguish, it is assumed, should be amenable to repair through social change. A positive emphasis on the psychic level is viewed as a valorization of the anarchic and regressive, a way of returning women to their subordinate ideological place within the dominant culture, as unreasoning social beings. Psychoanalytic theory, which is by and large morally neutral about the desires expressed by the psyche, is criticized as a confirmation and justification of them.

Thus semiotic or psychoanalytic perspectives have yet to be integrated with social, economic and political analysis. Critics tend to privilege one element or the other, even when they acknowledge the importance of both and the need to relate them. A comparison of two admirable recent essays on Charlotte Brontë's *Villette*, one by Mary Jacobus and the other by Judith Lowder Newton, both informed by socialist feminist concerns, can illustrate this difficulty.

Jacobus uses the psychoanalytic and linguistic theory of Jacques Lacan to explore the split representations of subjectivity that haunt *Villette*, and calls attention to its anti-realist gothic elements. She relates Brontë's feminized defence of the imagination, and the novel's unreliable narrator-heroine, to the tension between femininity and feminism that reaches back to the eighteenth-century debates of Rousseau and Wollstonecraft. Reading the ruptures and gaps of the text as a psychic narrative, she also places it historically in relationship to nineteenth-century social and political ideas. Yet the social meanings of *Villette* fade and all but disappear before 'the powerful presence of fantasy', which 'energizes *Villette* and satisfies that part of the reader which also desires constantly to reject reality for the sake of an obedient, controllable, narcissistically pleasurable image of self and its relation to the world' (Jacobus 1979, p. 51). In Jacobus's interpretation, the psyche, desire and fantasy stand for repressed, largely positive elements of a forgotten feminism, while the social stands for a daytime world of Victorian social regulation. These social meanings are referred to rather than explored in the essay, a strategy which renders them both static and unproblematically unified. It is as if, in order to examine how *Villette* represents psychic reality, the dynamism of social discourses of gender and identity must be repressed, forming the text's new 'unconscious'.

Judith Lowder Newton's chapter on *Villette* in her impressive study of nineteenth-century British fiction, *Women, Power, and Subversion* (1981), is also concerned with conflicts between the novel's feminism and its evocation of female desire. Her interpretation privileges the social meanings of the novel, its search for a possible *détente* between the dominant ideologies of bourgeois femininity and progressive definitions of female autonomy. For Newton, 'the internalized ideology of women's sphere' includes sexual and romantic longings – which for Jacobus are potentially radical and disruptive of mid-Victorian gender ideologies. The psychic level as Newton describes it is mainly the repository for the worst and most regressive elements of female subjectivity: longing for love, dependency, the material and emotional comfort of fixed class identity. These desires which have 'got inside' are predictably in conflict with the rebellious, autonomy-seeking feminist impulses, whose source is a rational understanding of class and gender subordination. Her reading centres on the realist text, locating meaning in its critique of class society and the constraints of bourgeois femininity.

The quotations and narrative elements cited and explored by Jacobus and Newton are so different that even a reader familiar with *Villette* may find it hard to believe that each critic is reading the same text. The psychic level exists in Newton's interpretation, to be sure, but as a negative discourse, the dead weight of ideology on the mind. For her, the words 'hidden', 'private' and 'longing' are stigmatized, just as they are celebrated by Jacobus. For both critics, female subjectivity is the site where the opposing forces of femininity and feminism clash by night, but they locate these elements in different parts of the text's divided selves. Neither Newton nor Jacobus argues for the utopian possibility of a unified subjectivity. But the *longing* to close the splits that characterize femininity – splits between reason and desire, autonomy and dependent security, psychic and social identity – is evident in the way each critic denies the opposing element.

III

My comments on the difficulties of reading *Villette* from a materialist feminist stance are meant to suggest that there is more at issue in the polarization of social and psychic explanation than the problem of articulating two different forms of explanation. Moral and political questions specific to feminism are at stake as well. In order to understand why female subjectivity is so fraught with *Angst* and difficulty for feminism, we must go back to the first full discussion of the psychological expression of femininity, in Mary Wollstonecroft's *A Vindication of the Rights of Woman*. The briefest look will show that an interest in the psychic life of women as a crucial element in their subordination and liberation is not a modern, post-Freudian preoccupation. On the contrary, its long and fascinating history in 'left' feminist writing starts with Wollstonecraft, who set the terms for a debate that is still in progress. Her writing is central for socialist feminism today, because she based her interest in the emancipation of women as individuals in revolutionary politics.

Like so many eighteenth-century revolutionaries, she saw her own class, the rising bourgeoise, as the vanguard of the revolution, and it was to the women of her own class that she directed her arguments. Her explicit focus on the middle class, and her concentration on the nature of female subjectivity, speaks directly to the source of anxiety within socialist feminism today. For it is at the point when women are released from profound social and economic oppression into greater autonomy and potential political choice that their social and psychic expression becomes an issue, and their literary texts become sites of ambivalence. In their pages, for the last 200 years and more, women characters seemingly more confined by social regulation than women readers today speak as desiring subjects. These texts express the politically 'retrogade' desires for comfort, dependence and love as well as more acceptable demands for autonomy and independence.

It is Mary Wollstonecraft who first offered women this fateful choice between the opposed and moralized bastions of reason and feeling, which continues to determine much feminist thinking. The structures through which she developed her ideas, however, were set for her by her mentor Jean-Jacques Rousseau, whose writing influenced the political and social perspectives of many eighteenth-century English radicals. His ideas were fundamental to her thinking about gender as well as about revolutionary politics. In 1792, that highly charged moment of romantic political optimism between the fall of the Bastille and the Terror when *A Vindication* was written, it must have seemed crucial that Rousseau's crippling judgement of female nature be refuted. How else could women freely and equally participate in the new world being made across the Channel? Rousseau's ideas about subjectivity were already immanent in Wollstonecraft's earlier book *Mary: A Fiction* (1788). Now she set out to challenge directly his offensive description of sexual difference which would leave women in post-revolutionary society exactly where they were in unreformed Britain, 'immured in their families, groping in the dark' (Wollstonecraft 1975a, p. 5).

Rousseau had set the terms of the debate in his *Emile* (1762), which describes the growth and education of the new man, progressive and bourgeois, who would be capable of exercising the republican freedoms of a reformed society. In Book V, Rousseau invents 'Sophie' as a mate for his eponymous hero, and here he outlines his theory of sexual asymmetry as it occurs in nature. In all human beings passion was natural and necessary, but in women it was not controlled by reason, an attribute of the male sex only. Women, therefore, must be subject all their lives, to the most constant and severe restraint, which is that of decorum; it is therefore necessary to accustom them early to such confinement that it may not afterwards cost them too dear. . . . we should teach them above all things to lay a due restraint on themselves.

(Rousseau 1974, p. 332)

To justify this restraint, Rousseau allowed enormous symbolic power to the supposed anarchic, destructive force of untrammelled female desire. As objects of desire Rousseau made women alone responsible for male 'suffering'. If they were free agents of desire, there would be no end to the 'evils' they could cause. Therefore the family, and women's maternal role within it, were, he said, basic to the structure of the new society. Betrayal of the family was thus as subversive as betrayal of the state; adultery in *Emile* is literally equated with treason. Furthermore, in Rousseau's regime of regulation and restraint for bourgeois women, their 'decorum' – the social expression of modesty – would act as an additional safeguard against unbridled, excessive male lust, should its natural guardian, reason, fail. In proscribing the free exercise of female desire, Rousseau disarms a supposed serious threat to the new political as well as social order. To read the fate of a class through the sexual behaviour of its women was not a new political strategy. What is modern in Rousseau's formulation is the harnessing of these sexual ideologies to the fate of a new progressive bourgeoisie, whose individual male members were endowed with radical, autonomous identity.

In many ways, Mary Wollstonecraft, writing thirty years after *Emile*, shared with many others the political vision of her master. Her immediate contemporary Thomas Paine thought Rousseau's work expressed 'a loveliness of sentiment in favour of liberty', and it is in the spirit of Rousseau's celebration of liberty that Wollstonecraft wrote *A Vindication*. Her strategy was to accept Rousseau's description of adult women as suffused in sensuality, but to ascribe this unhappy state of things to culture rather than nature. It was, she thought, the vicious and damaging result of Rousseau's punitive theories of sexual difference and female education when put into practice. Excessive sensuality was for Wollstonecraft, in 1792 at least, as dangerous if not more so than Rousseau had suggested, but she saw the damage and danger first of all to women themselves, whose potential and independence were initially stifled and broken by an apprenticeship to pleasure, which induced psychic and social dependency. Because Wollstonecraft saw pre-pubescent children in their natural state as mentally and emotionally unsexed as well as untainted by corrupting desire, she bitterly refuted Rousseau's description of innate infantile female sexuality. Rather, the debased femininity she describes is constructed through a set of social practices which by constant reinforcement become internalized parts of the self. Her description of this process is acute:

> Every thing they see or hear serves to fix impressions, call forth emotions, and associate ideas, that give a sexual character to the mind. . . . This cruel association of ideas, which every thing conspires to twist into all their habits of thinking, or, to speak with more precision of feeling, receives new force when they begin to act a little for themselves.
>
> (Wollstonecraft 1975a, p. 177)

For Wollstonecraft, female desire was a contagion caught from the projection of male lust, an ensnaring and enslaving infection that made women into dependent and degenerate creatures, who nevertheless had the illusion that they acted independently. An education which changed women from potentially rational autonomous beings into 'insignificant objects of desire' was, moreover, rarely reversible. Once a corrupt subjectivity was constructed, only a most extraordinary individual could transform it, for 'so ductile is the understanding and yet so stubborn, that the association which depends on adventitious circumstances, during the period that the body takes to arrive at maturity, can seldom be disentangled by reason' (p. 116).

What is disturbingly peculiar to *A Vindication* is the undifferentiated and central place that sexuality as passion plays in the corruption and degradation of the female self. The overlapping Enlightenment and Romantic discourses on psychic economy all posed a major division between the rational and the irrational, between sense and sensibility. But they hold sensibility *in men* to be only in part an antisocial sexual drive. Lust for power and the propensity to physical violence were also, for men, negative components of all that lay on the other side of reason.

Thus sensibility in men included a strong positive element too, for the power of the imagination depended on it, and in the 1790s the Romantic aesthetic and the political imagination were closely allied. Sexual passion controlled and mediated by reason, Wordsworth's 'emotion recollected in tranquility', could also be put to productive use in art – by men. The appropriate egalitarian subjects of Wordsworth's art were 'moral sentiments and animal sensations' as they appeared in everyday life (Wordsworth and Coleridge 1971, p. 261). No woman of the time could offer such an artistic manifesto. In women the irrational, the sensible, even the imaginative are all drenched in an overpowering and subordinating sexuality. And in Wollstonecraft's writing, especially in her last, unfinished novel *Maria, or the Wrongs of Woman* (1798), which is considerably less punitive about women's sexuality in general than *A Vindication*, only maternal feeling survives as a positively re-alized element of the passionate side of the psyche. By defending women against Rousseau's denial of their reason, Wollstonecraft unwittingly assents to his negative, eroticized sketch of their emotional lives. At various points in *A Vindication* she interjects a wish that 'after some future revolution in time' women might be able to live out a less narcissistic and harmful sexuality. Until then they must demand an education whose central task is to cultivate their neglected 'understanding'.

It is interesting and somewhat tragic that Wollstonecraft's paradigm of women's psychic economy still profoundly shapes modern feminist consciousness. How often are the maternal, romantic-sexual and intellectual capacity of women presented by feminism as in competition for a fixed psychic space. Men seem to have a roomier and more accommodating psychic home, one which can, as Wordsworth and other Romantics insisted, situate all the varieties of passion and reason in creative tension. This gendered eighteenth-century psychic economy has been out of date for a long time, but its ideological inscription still shadows feminist attitudes towards the mental life of women.

The implications of eighteenth-century theories of subjectivity were important for early feminist ideas about women as readers and writers. In the final pages of *A Vindication*, decrying female sentimentality as one more effect of women's psychic degradation, Wollstonecraft criticizes the sentimental fictions increasingly written by and for women, which were often their only education. 'Novels' encouraged in their mainly young, mainly female audience 'a romantic twist of the mind'. Readers would 'only be taught to look for happiness in love, refine on sensual feelings and adopt metaphysical notions respecting that passion'. At their very worst the 'stale tales' and 'meretricious scenes' would by degrees induce more than passive fantasy. The captive, addicted reader might, while the balance of her mind was disturbed by these erotic evocations, turn fiction into fact and 'plump into actual vice' (p. 183). A reciprocal relationship between the patriarchal socialization of women and the literature that supports and incites them to become 'rakes at heart' is developed in this passage. While Wollstonecraft adds that she would rather women read novels than nothing at all, she sets up a peculiarly gendered and sexualized interaction between women and the narrative imaginative text, one in which women become the ultimately receptive reader easily moved into amoral activity by the fictional representation of sexual intrigue.

The political resonance of these questions about reader response was, at the time, highly charged. An enormous expansion of literacy in general, and of the middle-class reading public in particular, swelled by literate women, made the act of reading in the last quarter of the eighteenth century an important practice through which the common sense and innate virtue of a society of autonomous subject-citizens could be reached and moulded. An uncensored press, cheap and available reading matter and a reading public free to engage with the flood of popular literature, from political broadsheets to sensational fiction, was part of the agenda and strategy of British republicanism. 'It is dangerous', Tom Paine warned the government in the mid-1790s after his own writing had been politically censored, 'to tell a whole people that they shall not read.' Reading was a civil right that supported and illustrated the radical vision of personal independence. Political and sexual conservatives, Jane Austen and Hannah More, as well as the republican and feminist left, saw reading as an active, not a passive function of the self, a critical link between the psychic play of reason and passion and its social expression. New social categories of readers, women of all classes, skilled and unskilled working-class males, are described in this period by contemporaries. Depending on their political sympathies, observers saw these actively literate groups as an optimistic symptom of social and intellectual progress or a dire warning of imminent social decay and threatened rebellion.

Wollstonecraft saw sentiment and the sensual as reinforcing an already dominant, approved and enslaving sexual norm, which led women to choose a subordinate social and subjective place in culture. The damage done by 'vice' and 'adultery', to which sentimental fiction was an incitement, was a blow to women first and to society second. Slavish legitimate sexuality was almost as bad for women in Wollstonecraft's view as unlicensed behaviour. A more liberal regime for women was both the goal and the cure of sentimental and erotic malaise. In *A Vindication* women's subjection is repeatedly compared to all illegitimate hierarchies of power, but especially to existing aristocratic hegemony. At every possible point in her text, Wollstonecraft links the liberation of women from the sensual into the rational literally and symbolically to the egalitarian transformation of the whole society.

'Passionlessness', as Nancy Cott has suggested (Cott 1978), was a strategy adopted both by feminists and by social conservatives. Through the assertion that women were not innately or excessively sexual, that on the contrary their 'feelings' were largely filial and maternal, the imputation of a degraded subjectivity could be resisted. This alternative psychic organization was represented as both strength and weakness in nineteenth-century debates about sexual difference. In these debates, which were conducted across a wide range of public discourses, the absence of an independent, self-generating female sexuality is used by some men and women to argue for women's right to participate equally in an undifferentiated public sphere. It is used by others to argue for the power and value of the separate sphere allotted to women. And it is used more nakedly to support cruder justifications of patriarchal right. The idea of passionlessness as either a natural or a cultural effect acquires no simple ascendancy in Victorian sexual ideology, even as applied to the ruling bourgeoisie.

As either conservative or radical sexual ideology, asexual femininity was a fragile, unstable concept. It was constructed through a permanently threatened transgression, which fictional narrative obsessively documented and punished. It is a gross historical error to infer from the regulatory sexual discourses in the novel the actual 'fate' of Victorian adulteresses, for novels operated through a set of highly punitive conventions in relation to female sexuality that almost certainly did not correspond to lived social relations. However, novels do call attention to the difficulty of fixing such a sexual ideology, precisely because they construct a world in which there is no alternative to it.

IV

One of the central weaknesses of humanist criticism is that it accepts the idea advanced by classical realism that the function of literature is mimetic or realistic representation. The humanist critic identifies with the author's claim that the text represents reality, and acts as a sympathetic reader who will test the authenticity of the claim through the evidence of the text. The Marxist critic, on the other hand, assumes that author and text speak from a position within ideology – that claims about fictional truth and authenticity are, in themselves, to be understood in relation to a particular historical view of culture and art which evolved in the Romantic period. Semiotic and psychoanalytic theories of representation go even further in rejecting the possibility of authentic mimetic art. They see the literary text as a system of signs that constructs meaning rather than reflecting it, inscribing simultaneously the subjectivity of speaker and reader. Fiction by bourgeois women writers is spoken from the position of a class-specific femininity. It constructs us as readers in relation to that subjectivity through the linguistic strategies and processes of the text. It also takes us on a tour, so to speak, of a waxworks of other subjects-in-process – the characters of the text. These fictional characters are there as figures in a dream, as constituent structures of the narrative of the dreamer, not as correct reflections of the socially real.

It is hard for feminism to accept the implications of this virtual refusal of textual realism, if only because literature was one of the few public discourses in which women were allowed to speak themselves, where they were not the imaginary representations of men. None the less, the subjectivity of women of other classes and races and with different sexual orientations can never be 'objectively' or 'authentically' represented in literary texts by the white, heterosexual, middle-class woman writer, however sympathetically she invents or describes such women in her narrative. The nature of fiction and the eccentric relation of female subjectivity itself both to culture and to psychic identity, as understood from a psychoanalytic perspective, defeats that aim. We can, however, learn a great deal from women's writing about the cultural meanings produced from the splitting of women's subjectivity, especially her sexuality, into class and race categories. But before we say more about this way of reading women's writing we need a more precise working definition of 'class'.

Unlike subjectivity, 'class' has been a central category for socialist feminist criticism, but remains somewhat inert within it, if not within socialist feminist theory as a whole. Socialist critics hesitate to identify their own object of study, the literary text, as a central productive site of class meaning, because it seems too far away from 'real' economic and political determinations. The same worry, conversely, can induce a compensatory claim that *all* the material relations of class can be discovered within the discourse; indeed, that they are most fully represented there, because language is itself material. These positions, which I confess I have parodied a little, remain unresolved in current debate, although efforts at *détente* have been made. They indicate the uneasy relationship between the political and the literary in the Marxist critical project, an unease shared by socialist feminists too.

Among socialist historians in the last few years the understanding of the history of class has undergone vigorous reappraisal in response to debates about the changing composition and politics of the working class in modern capitalist societies. In a recent collection of essays, *The Languages of Class*, the British historian of the nineteenth century, Gareth Stedman Jones, proposes some radical approaches to that history which have an immediate relevance for the analysis of representation. First of all, Stedman Jones asks for a more informed and theoretical attention by historians to the linguistic construction of class. '"Class" is a word embedded in language and should be analysed in terms of its linguistic content,' he states. In the second place, 'class' as a concept needs to be unpacked, and its differential construction in discourse recognized and given a certain autonomy:

> because there are different languages of class, one should not proceed upon the assumption that 'class' as an elementary counter of official social description, 'class' as an effect of theoretical discourse about distribution or productive relations, 'class' as the summary of a cluster of culturally signifying practices or 'class' as a species of political or ideological self-definition, share a single reference point in anterior social reality.
>
> (Stedman Jones 1983, pp. 7–8)

While 'anterior social reality' hangs slightly loose in this formulation, the oppressively unitary character of class as a concept is usefully broken down. Class can be seen as defined in different terms at different levels of analysis, as well as being 'made' and 'lived' through a variety of languages at any given point in history.

How can this pulling apart of the languages of class help socialist feminist critics to put class and gender, social and psychic together in a non-reductive way? First of all, these distinctions put a useful space between the economic overview of class – the Marxist or socialist analysis – and the actual rhetoric of class as it appears in a novel. The class language of a nineteenth-century novel is not only or even primarily characterized by reference to the material circumstances of the protagonists, though that may be part of its representation there. The language of class in the novel foregrounds the language of the self, the inner discourse of the subject *as* class language, framing that discourse through the dissonant chorus of class voices that it appropriates and invents. In the novel, class discourse *is* gendered discourse; the positions of 'Emile' and 'Sophie' are given dramatic form. Class is embodied in fiction in a way that it never is either in bourgeois economic discourse or in Marxist economic analysis. In those discourses of class, gender is mystified, presented in ideological form. In fiction, though difference may be presented through sexual ideologies, its immanent, crucial presence in the social relations of class, as well as its psychic effects, is strongly asserted. Fiction refuses the notion of a genderless class subjectivity, and resists any simple reduction of class meaning and class identity to productive forces. This refusal and resistance cannot be written off, or reduced to the humanist ideologies of transcendence which those fictions may also enunciate, for the presence of gendered subjectivity in nineteenth-century fiction is always 'in struggle' with the Romantic ideologies of unified identity.

Within socialist feminist cultural analysis it has been easier to describe the visual or linguistic fusion of class and gender meanings in representation than it has been to assess the role such fusion plays in the construction of either category. Let us assume that in these signifying practices class is powerfully defined through sexual difference, and vice versa, and that these representations are constitutive of certain class meanings, not merely a distorted or mendacious reflection of other languages. 'Class' needs to be read through an ensemble of these languages, often contradictory, as well as in terms of an economic overview. The overpowering presence of gender in some languages of class and its virtual absence in others needs to be related not to a single anterior definition of class reality, but to the heterogeneous and contradictory nature of that reality.

Literature is itself a heterogeneous discourse, which appropriates, contextualizes and comments on other 'languages' of class and gender. This process of intertextuality – the dialogic, as the Russian critic Bakhtin called it (Bakhtin 1981) – undermines the aspirations of the text towards a unifying definition. The language of class in the nineteenth-century novel obsessively inscribes a class system whose divisions and boundaries are at once absolute and impregnable and in constant danger of dissolution. Often in these narratives it is a woman whose class identity is at risk or problematic; the woman and her sexuality are a condensed and displaced representation of the dangerous instabilities of class and gender identity for both sexes. The loss and recuperation of female identity within the story – a favourite lost-and-found theme from *Mansfield Park* to *Tess* – provides an imaginary though temporary solution to the crisis of both femininity and class. Neither category – class or gender – was ever as stable as the ideologies that support them must continually insist. The many-layered, compacted representations of class and gender found in imaginative literature are not generic metaphors, peculiar to fiction, drama and poetry, though in them they are given great scope. They occur in many other nineteenth-century discourses – metonymic, associative tropes which are linked by incomparable similarities, through a threat to identity and status that inheres to both sets of hierarchies, both structures of difference.

The class subjectivity of women and their sexual identity thus became welded together in nineteenth-century discourses and took on new and sinister dimensions of meaning. Ruling groups had traditionally used the sexual and domestic virtue of their women as a way of valorizing their moral authority. By focusing on the issue and image of female sexual conduct, questions about the economic and political integrity of dominant groups could be displaced. When the citizen subject became the crucial integer of political discourse and practice, this type of symbolization, which was always 'about' sexual difference as well as 'about' the political, took on new substantive, material meaning. The moral autonomy of individuals and the moral behaviour of social groups now converged in a political practice and theory – liberal, constitutional and legitimated through an expanding franchise – in which the individual voter was the common denominator of the political. Women, as we have seen, were explicitly excluded from these political practices, but, as we have also seen, attempts to naturalize that exclusion were never wholly successful. Feminism inserted itself into the debate just at the point where theories of innate difference attempted to deny women access to a full political identity. The debate about women's mental life signalled, as I have suggested, a more general anxiety about non-rational, unsocial behaviour. Female subjectivity, or its synecdotal reference, female sexuality, became the displaced and condensed site for the general anxiety about individual behaviour which republican and liberal political philosophy stirred up. It is not too surprising that the morality of the class as a whole was better represented by those who exercised the least political power within it, or that the punishment for female sexual transgression was fictionally represented as the *immediate* loss of social status.

The ways in which class is lived by men and women, like the ways in which sexual difference is lived, are only partly open to voluntary, self-conscious political negotiation. The unconscious processes that construct subjective identity are also the structures through which class is lived and understood, through which political subjection and rebellion are organized. Arguing for the usefulness of psychoanalysis in historical analysis, Sally Alexander emphasizes that its theories do not imply a universal human nature. Rather,

> Subjectivity in this account is neither universal nor ahistorical. First structured through relations of absence and loss, pleasure and unpleasure, difference and division, these are simultaneous with the social naming and placing among kin, community, school, class which are always historically specific.
>
> (Alexander 1984, p. 134)

Literary texts give these simultaneous inscriptions narrative form, pointing towards and opening up the fragmentary nature of social and psychic identity, drawing out the ways in which social meaning is psychically represented. It is this symbolic shaping of class that we should examine in fiction. Literary texts tell us more about the intersection of class and gender than we can learn from duly noting the material circumstances and social constraints of characters and authors.

However mimetic or realistic the aspirations of fiction, it always tells us less about the purely social rituals of a class society organized around the sexual division of labour than about the powerful symbolic force of class and gender in ordering our social and political imagination. The doubled inscription of sexual and social difference is the most common, characteristic trope of nineteenth-century fictions. In these texts, the difference between women is at least as important an element as the difference between the sexes, as a way of representing both class and gender. This salient fact often goes unnoticed in the emphasis of bourgeois criticism on male/female division and opposition. In turn, this emphasis on heterosexual antagonisms and resolutions effaces the punitive construction of alternative femininities in women's writing. If texts by women reveal a 'hidden' sympathy between women, as radical feminist critics often assert, they equally express positive femininity through hostile and denigrating representations of women. Imperilled bourgeois femininity takes meaning in relation to other female identities, and to the feminized identities of other social groups which the novel constructs and dialogizes. The unfavourable symbiosis of reason and passion ascribed to women is also used to characterize both men and women in the labouring classes and in other races and cultures. The line between the primitive and the degraded feminine is a thin one, habitually elided in dominant discourse and practically used to limit the civil and political rights of all three subordinated categories: blacks, women and the working class.

Through that chain of colonial associations, whole cultures became 'feminized', 'blackened' and 'impoverished' – each denigrating construction implying and invoking the others. 'True womanhood' had to be protected from this threatened linguistic contamination, not only from the debased subjectivity and dangerous sexuality of the lower-class prostitute, but from all other similarly inscribed subordinate subjectivities. The difference between men and women in the ruling class had to be written so that a slippage into categories reserved for lesser humanities could be averted. These fragmented definitions of female subjectivity were not only a mode through which the moral virtue of the ruling class was represented in the sexual character of its women; they also shaped, and were shaped by, the ways in which women of the middle and upper classes understood and represented their own being. It led them towards projecting and displacing on to women of lower social standing and women of colour, as well as on to the 'traditionally' corrupt aristocracy, all that was deemed vicious and regressive in women as a sex.

It is deeply troubling to find these projected and displaced representations in the writing of sexual and social radicals, and in the work of feminists from Wollstonecraft to Woolf, as well as in conservative sexual and social discourses. They are especially marked in those texts and writers who accept in whole or in part the description of mental life and libidinal economy of the Enlightenment and the moral value attached to it. In *A Vindication*, working-class women are quite unselfconsciously constructed as prostitutes and dirty-minded servants corrupting bourgeois innocence. Turn the page over and you will also find them positioned in a more radical sense as the most brutalized victims of aristocratic and patriarchal despotism. Note the bestial descriptions of the female poor in Elizabeth Barrett Browning's *Aurora Leigh*. Remember the unhappy, ambivalent and contradictory relationship to black subjectivity, male and female, of many mid-nineteenth-century American feminists and abolitionists. Most distressing of all, because nearer to us in time, think about the contrast between Woolf's public polemical support of working-class women and the contempt with which the feelings and interests of her female servants are treated in her diaries, where they exist as lesser beings. These representations are neither natural nor inevitable. They are the historic effects of determinate social divisions and ideologies worked through psychic structures, worked into sexual and social identity. If they are understood they can be changed.

In Ann Radcliffe's *Mysteries of Udolpho*, one of the most popular of the Enlightenment gothic novels of the 1790s, the heroine, Emily, flees from the sinister importunities of her titled foreign host. The scene is rural Italy, as far away as possible from genteel British society. Emily's flight from the castle is precipitous, and in her terror and haste she forgets her hat. Within the world of the text, Emily's bare head threatens her identity as pure woman, as surely as do the violent, lascivious attentions of her pursuer. Both the narrative and her flight are interrupted while Emily restores her identity by purchasing 'a little straw hat' from a peasant girl. A woman without a hat was, in specular terms, a whore; the contemporary readership understood the necessary pause in the story. They understood too that the hat, passed from peasant to lady, securing the class and sexual status of the latter, was not only a fragment of domestic realism set against gothic fantasy. Hat and flight are part of a. perfectly coherent psychic narrative in which aristocratic seducer, innocent bourgeois victim, peasant girl and straw hat play out the linked meanings of class and sexuality.

Stories of seduction and betrayal, of orphaned, impoverished heroines of uncertain class origin, provided a narrative structure through which the instabilities of class and gender categories were both stabilized and undermined. Across the body and mind of 'woman' as sign, through her multiple representations, bourgeois anxiety about identity is traced and retraced. A favourite plot, of which *Jane Eyre* is now the best-known example, sets the genteel heroine at sexual risk as semi-servant in a grand patriarchal household. This narrative theme allowed the crisis of middle-class femininity to be mapped on to the structural sexual vulnerability of all working-class servants in bourgeois employment. Such dramas were full of condensed meanings in excess of the representation of sexuality and sexual difference. A doubled scenario, in which the ideological and material difference between working-class and bourgeois women is blurred through condensation, it was popular as a plot for melodrama with both 'genteel' and 'vulgar' audiences.

We do not know very much so far about how that fictional narrative of threatened femininity was understood by working-class women, although it appeared in the cheap fiction written for servant girls as well as in popular theatre. Nineteenth-century bourgeois novels like *Jane Eyre* tell us almost nothing about the self-defined subjectivity of the poor, male or female. For, although they are both rich sources for the construction of dominant definitions *of* the inner lives of the working classes, they cannot tell us anything about how even these ideological inscriptions were lived *by* them. For an analysis of the subjectivity of working-class women we need to turn to non-literary sources, to the discourses in which they themselves spoke. That analysis lies outside the project of this paper but is, of course, related to it.

I want to end this chapter with an example of the kind of interpretative integration that I have been demanding of feminist critics. No text has proved more productive of meaning from the critic's point of view than Charlotte Brontë's *Jane Eyre*. I have referred to the condensation of class meanings through the characterization and narrative of its heroine, but now I want to turn to that disturbing didactic moment in volume I, chapter 12, which immediately precedes the entry of Rochester into the text. It is a passage marked out by Virginia Woolf in *A Room of One's Own*, where it is used to illustrate the negative effect of anger and inequality on the female literary imagination. Prefaced defensively – 'Anybody may blame me who likes' – it is a passage about need, demand and desire that exceed social possibility and challenge social prejudice. In Jane's soliloquy, inspired by a view reached through raising the 'trap-door of the attic', the Romantic aesthetic is reasserted for women, together with a passionate refusal of the terms of feminine difference. Moved by a 'restlessness' in her 'nature' that 'agitated me to pain sometimes', Jane paces the top floor of Thornfield and allows her 'mind's eye to dwell on whatever bright visions rose before it':

> to let my heart be heaved by the exultant movement which, while it swelled it in trouble, expanded it with life; and, best of all, to open my inward ear to a tale that was never ended – a tale my imagination created, and narrated continuously; quickened with all of incident, life, fire, feeling, that I desired and had not in my actual existence.
>
> (Brontë 1976, p. 110)

This reverie is only partly quoted by Woolf, who omits the 'visionary' section, moving straight from 'pain . . .' to the paragraph most familiar to us through her citation of it:

> It is in vain to say that human beings ought to be satisfied with tranquillity; they must have action; and they will make it if they cannot find it. Millions are condemned to a stiller doom than mine, and millions are in silent revolt against their lot. Nobody knows how many rebellions besides political rebellions ferment in the masses of life which people earth. Women are supposed to be very calm generally: but women feel just as men feel; they need exercise for their faculties, and a field for their efforts as much as their brothers do; they suffer from too rigid a restraint, too absolute a stagnation, precisely as men would suffer; and it is narrow-minded in their more privileged fellow-creatures to say that they ought to confine themselves to making puddings and knitting stockings, to playing on the piano and embroidering bags. It is thoughtless to condemn them, or laugh at them, if they seek to do more or learn more than custom has pronounced necessary for their sex.
>
> When thus alone I not unfrequently heard Grace Poole's laugh . . .

This shift from feminist polemic to the laugh of Grace Poole is the 'jerk', the 'awkward break' of 'continuity' that Woolf criticizes. The writer of such a flawed passage

will never get her genius expressed whole and entire. Her
books will be deformed and twisted. She will write in a rage
where she should write calmly. She will write foolishly where
she should write wisely. She will write of herself when she
should write of her characters. She is at war with her lot. How
could she help but die young, cramped and thwarted?

(Woolf 1973, p. 70)

It is a devastating, controlled, yet somehow uncontrolled
indictment. What elements in this digression, hardly a formal
innovation in nineteenth-century fiction, can have prompted
Woolf to such excess? Elaine Showalter analyses this passage
and others as part of Woolf's 'flight into androgyny', that
aesthetic chamber where masculine and feminine minds meet
and marry. Showalter's analysis focuses on Woolf's aesthetic as
an effect of her inability to come to terms with her sexuality,
with sexual difference itself. Showalter's analysis is persuasive
in individual terms, but it does not deal with all of the questions
thrown up by Brontë's challenge and Woolf's violent response
to it. In the sentences that Woolf omits in her own citation,
Brontë insists that even the confined and restless state could
produce 'many and glowing' visions. Art, the passage
maintains, can be produced through the endless narration of the
self, through the mixed incoherence of subjectivity spoken from
subordinate and rebellious positions within culture. It was this
aesthetic that Woolf as critic explicitly rejected.

However, the passage deals with more than sexual difference.
In the references to 'human beings' and to unspecified 'millions', Brontë deliberately and defiantly associates political and
sexual rebellion even as she distinguishes between them. In the
passage the generic status of 'men' is made truly trans-class and
transcultural when linked to 'masses', 'millions' and 'human
beings', those larger inclusive terms. In 1847, on the eve of the
second great wave of modern revolution, it was a dangerous
rhetoric to use.

Its meaningful associations were quickly recognized by contemporary reviewers, who deplored the contiguous relationship between revolution and feminism. Lady Eastlake's
comments in the *Quarterly Review* of 1849 are those most often
quoted:

> We do not hesitate to say, that the tone of mind and thought
> which has overthrown authority and violated every code
> human and divine abroad, and fostered chartism and rebel-
> lion at home is the same which has also written *Jane Eyre*.

Yet Charlotte Brontë was no political radical. She is pulled
towards the positive linking of class rebellion and women's
revolt in this passage through her anger at the misrepresen-
tation and suppression of women's identity, not via an already
held sympathy with the other masses and millions. It is a
tentative, partial movement in spite of its defiant rhetoric, and it
is checked in a moment by the mad, mocking female laughter,
and turned from its course a few pages later by the introduction
of Rochester into the narrative. For Woolf, Jane's soliloquy
spoils the continuity of the narrative with its 'anger and rebellion'. Woolf turns away, refuses to comprehend the logical
sequence of the narration at the symbolic level of the novel.

Jane's revolutionary manifesto of the subject, which has its
own slightly manic register, invokes that sliding negative signification of women that we have described. At this point in the
story the 'low, slow ha'ha!' and the 'eccentric murmurs' which
'thrilled' Jane are ascribed to Grace Poole, the hard-featured
servant. But Grace is only the laugh's minder, and the laugh
later becomes 'correctly' ascribed to Rochester's insane wife,
Bertha Mason. The uncertain source of the laughter, the narrator's inability to predict its recurrence – 'There were days
when she was quite silent; but there were others when I could
not account for the sounds she made' – both mark out the
'sounds' as the dark side of Romantic female subjectivity.

Retroactively, in the narratives the laughter becomes a threat
to all that Jane had desired and demanded in her roof-top
reverie. Mad servant, mad mistress, foreigner, nymphomaniac,
syphilitic, half-breed, aristocrat, Bertha turns violently on
keeper, brother, husband and, finally, rival. She and her noises
become the condensed and displaced site of unreason and
anarchy as it is metonymically figured through dangerous
femininity in all its class, race and cultural projections. Bertha
must be killed off, narratively speaking, so that a moral, Protestant femininity, licensed sexuality and a qualified, socialized
feminism may survive. Yet the text cannot close off or recuper-

ate that moment of radical association between political rebellion and gender rebellion, cannot shut down the possibility of a positive alliance between reason, passion and feminism. Nor can it disperse the terror that speaking those connections immediately stirs up – for Woolf in any case.

Woolf was at her most vehement and most contradictory about these issues, which brought together for her, as for many other feminists before and after, a number of deeply connected anxieties about subjectivity, class, sexuality and culture. Over and over again in her critical writing, Woolf tries to find ways of placing the questions inside an aesthetic that disallows anger, unreason and passion as productive emotions. Like Wollstonecraft before her, she cannot quite shake off the moral and libidinal economies of the Enlightenment. In 'Women and Fiction' (1929) she frames the question another way:

> In *Middlemarch* and in *Jane Eyre* we are conscious not merely of the writer's character, as we are conscious of the character of Charles Dickens, but we are conscious of a woman's presence – of someone resenting the treatment of her sex and pleading for its rights. This brings into women's writing an element which is entirely absent from a man's, unless, indeed, he happens to be a working man, a Negro, or one who for some other reason is conscious of disability. It introduces a distortion and is frequently the cause of weakness. The desire to plead some personal cause or to make a character the mouthpiece of personal discontent or grievance always has a distressing effect, as if the spot at which the reader's attention is directed were suddenly two-fold instead of single.
>
> (Woolf 1979, p. 47)

Note how the plea for a sex, a class, a race becomes reduced to individual, personal grievance, how subordinate position in a group becomes immediately pathologized as private disability, weakness. Note too how 'man' in this passage loses its universal connotation, so that it only refers normatively to men of the ruling class. In this passage, as in *Jane Eyre*, the metonymic evocation of degraded subjectivities is expressed as an effect of subordination, not its rationale nor its cause. But the result is still a negative one. For the power to resist through fictional language, the language of sociality and self; the power to move and enlighten, rather than blur and distress through the double focus, is denied. Instead, Woolf announces the death of the feminist text, by proclaiming, somewhat prematurely, the triumph of feminism.

> The women writer is no longer bitter. She is no longer angry. She is no longer pleading and protesting as she writes. . . . She will be able to concentrate upon her vision without distraction from outside.
>
> (Woolf 1979, p. 48)

This too is a cry from the roof-tops of a desire still unmet by social and psychic experience.

Although the meanings attached to race, class and sexuality have undergone fundamental shifts from Wollstonecraft's (and Woolf's) time to our own, we do not live in a post-class society any more than a post-feminist one. Our identities are still constructed through social hierarchy and cultural differentiation, as well as through those processes of division and fragmentation described in psychoanalytic theory. The identities arrived at through these structures will always be precarious and unstable, though *how* they will be so in the future we do not know. For the moment, women still have a problematic place in both social and psychic representation. The problem for women of woman-as-sign has made the self-definition of women a resonant issue within feminism. It has also determined the restless inability of feminism to settle for humanist definitions of the subject, or for materialism's relegation of the problem to determinations of class only. I have emphasized in this chapter some of the more negative ways in which the Enlightenment and Romantic paradigms of subjectivity gave hostage to the making of subordinate identities, of which femininity is the structuring instance. Although psychoanalytic theories of the construction of gendered subjectivity stress difficulty, antagonism and contradiction as necessary parts of the production of identity, the concept of the unconscious and the psychoanalytic view of sexuality dissolve in great part the binary divide between reason and passion that dominates earlier concepts of subjectivity. They break down as well the moralism attached to those libidinal and psychic economies. Seen from this perspective, 'individualism' has a different and more contentious history within feminism than it does in androcentric debates.

It is that history which we must uncover and consider, in both its positive and its negative effects, so that we can argue convincingly for a feminist rehabilitation of the female psyche in non-moralized terms. Perhaps we can come to see it as neither sexual outlaw, social bigot nor dark hiding-place for treasonable regressive femininity waiting to stab progressive feminism in the back. We must redefine the psyche as a structure, not as a content. To do so is not to move away from a feminist politics which takes race and class into account, but to move towards a fuller understanding of how these social divisions and the inscription of gender are mutually secured and given meaning. Through that analysis we can work towards change.

References

Alexander, Sally (1984) 'Women, Class and Sexual Difference', *History Workshop*, 17, pp. 125–49.

Bakhtin, M. M. (1981) *The Dialogic Imagination: Four Essays*, ed. Michael Holquist. Austin, Texas: University of Texas Press.

Brontë, Charlotte (1976) *Jane Eyre* (1847) ed. Margaret Smith. London: Oxford University Press.

Cott, Nancy F. (1978) 'Passionlessness: An Interpretation of Victorian Sexual Ideology, 1790–1850', *Signs*, 2, 2, pp. 219–33.

Hartmann, Heidi (1981) 'The Unhappy Marriage of Marxism and Feminism: Towards a More Progressive Union'. In Lydia Sargent (ed.), *The Unhappy Marriage of Marxism and Feminism: A Debate on Class and Patriarchy*, pp. 1–42. London: Pluto Press.

Jacobus, Mary (1979) 'The Buried Letter: Feminism and Romanticism in *Villette*'. In Mary Jacobus (ed.), *Women Writing and Writing about Women*, pp. 42–60. London: Croom Helm.

Marxist-Feminist Literature Collective (1978) 'Women's Writing: *Jane Eyre, Shirley, Villette, Aurora Leigh*'. In *1848: The Sociology of Literature*, proceedings of the Essex conference on the Sociology of Literature (July 1977), pp. 185–206.

Newton, Judith Lowder (1981) *Women, Power, and Subversion: Social Strategies in British Fiction 1778–1860*. Athens, Ga.: University of Georgia Press.

Radcliffe, Ann (1966) *The Mysteries of Udolpho* (1794). London: Oxford University Press.

Robinson, Lillian S. (1978) 'Dwelling in Decencies: Radical Criticism and the Feminist Perspective'. In *Sex, Class and Culture*, pp. 3–21. Bloomington, Ind.: Indiana University Press.

Rousseau, Jean-Jacques (1974) *Emile* (1762). London: Dent.

Said, Edward W. (1978) *Orientalism*. London: Routledge & Kegan Paul.

Stedman Jones, Gareth (1983) *Languages of Class: Studies in English Working Class History 1832–1982*. Cambridge: Cambridge University Press.

Wollstonecraft, Mary (1975a) *A Vindication of the Rights of Woman* (1792). New York: Norton.

Wollstonecraft, Mary (1975b) *Maria, or The Wrongs of Woman* (1798). New York: Norton.

Woolf, Virginia (1973) *A Room of One's Own* (1929). Harmondsworth: Penguin.

Woolf, Virginia (1979) 'Women and Fiction'. In Michèle Barrett (ed.), *Women and Writing*, pp. 44–52. London: Women's Press.

Wordsworth, William, and Coleridge, Samuel Taylor (1971) *Lyrical Ballads* (1798, 1800), ed. R. L. Brett and A. R. Jones. London: Methuen.

7
What has never been:
an overview of
lesbian feminist criticism
BONNIE ZIMMERMAN

Bonnie Zimmerman outlines the historical development of lesbian scholarship in literature, investigating the achievements, problems and future needs of a developing lesbian feminist criticism. She begins by describing heterosexism in feminist criticism, identifying the sources of emergent lesbian criticism, discussing competing definitions of 'lesbian writer' and 'lesbian text', and mapping a lesbian tradition or canon. The critical approaches she considers include the analysis of myths, images and stereotypes of lesbians in literature; attempts to define a lesbian aesthetic, and 're-visions' of traditional literature through a lesbian perspective. Noting the problems still to be addressed by lesbian critics, she calls upon all feminist scholars to develop a 'double vision' by using the insights of lesbian criticism to 'read lesbian' whenever possible.

*

In the 1970s a generation of lesbian feminist literary critics came of age. Some, like the lesbian professor in Lynn Strongin's poem, 'Sayre', had been closeted in the profession; many had 'come out' as lesbians in the women's liberation movement. As academics and as lesbians, we cautiously began to plait together the strands of our existence by teaching lesbian literature, establishing networks and support groups, and exploring assumptions about a lesbian-focused literary criticism. Beginning with nothing, as we thought, this generation quickly began to expand the limitations of literary scholarship by pointing to what had been for decades 'unspeakable' – lesbian existence – thus phrasing, in the novelist June Arnold's words, 'what has never been' (Arnold 1976, p. 28). Our process has paralleled the development of feminist literary criticism – and, indeed, pioneering feminist critics and lesbian critics are often one and the same. As women in a male-dominated academy, we explored the way we write and read from a different or 'other' perspective. As lesbians in a heterosexist academy, we have continued to explore the impact of 'otherness', suggesting dimensions previously ignored and yet necessary to understand fully the female condition and the creative work born from it.

Lesbian critics, in the 1980s, may have more questions than answers, but the questions are important not only to lesbians but to all feminists teaching and criticizing literature. Does a woman's sexual and affectional preference influence the way she writes, reads and thinks? Does lesbianism belong in the classroom and in scholarship? Is there a lesbian aesthetic distinct from a feminist aesthetic? What should be the role of the lesbian critic? Can we establish a lesbian 'canon' in the way in which feminist critics have established a female canon? Can lesbian feminists develop insights into female creativity that might enrich all literary criticism? Different women, of course, answer these questions in different ways, but one set of assumptions underlies virtually all lesbian criticism: that a woman's identity is not defined only by her relation to a male world and male literary tradition (a relationship brilliantly dissected by feminist critics), that powerful bonds between women are a crucial factor in women's lives, and that the sexual and emotional orientation of a woman profoundly affects her consciousness and thus her creativity. Those critics who have consciously chosen to read as lesbians argue that this perspective can be uniquely liberating and provide new insights into life and literature because it assigns the lesbian a specific vantage-point from which to criticize and analyse the politics, language and culture of patriarchy:

> We have the whole range of women's experience and the other dimension too, which is the unique viewpoint of the dyke. This extra dimension puts us a step outside of so-called normal life and lets us see how gruesomely abnormal it is. . . .

[This perspective] can issue in a world-view that is distinct in history and uniquely liberating.

(Boucher 1977, p. 43)

The purpose of this essay is to analyse the current state of lesbian scholarship, to suggest how lesbians are exercising this unique world-view, and to investigate some of the problems, strengths and future needs of a developing lesbian feminist literary criticism.[1]

I

One way in which this unique world-view takes shape is as a 'critical consciousness about heterosexist assumptions' (Bulkin 1978, p. 8). Heterosexism is the set of values and structures that assumes heterosexuality to be the only natural form of sexual and emotional expression, '*the* perceptual screen provided by our [patriarchal] cultural conditioning' (Stanley 1979, pp. 4–5). Heterosexist assumptions abound in literary texts, such as feminist literary anthologies, that purport to be open-minded about lesbianism. When authors' biographies make special note of husbands, male mentors, and male companions, even when that author was primarily female-identified, but fail to mention the female companions of prominent lesbian writers – that is heterosexism. When anthologists ignore historically significant lesbian writers such as Renée Vivien and Radclyffe Hall – that is heterosexism. When anthologies include only the heterosexual or non-sexual works of a writer like Katherine Philips or Adrienne Rich who is celebrated for her lesbian or homo-emotional poetry – that is heterosexism. When a topically organized anthology includes sections on wives, mothers, sex objects, young girls, ageing women and liberated women, but not lesbians – that is heterosexism. Heterosexism in feminist anthologies, like the sexism of androcentric collections, serves to obliterate lesbian existence and maintain the lie that women have searched for emotional and sexual fulfilment only through men – or not at all.

Lesbians have also expressed their concern that the absence for many years of lesbian material in women's studies journals such as *Feminist Studies*, *Women's Studies* and *Women and Literature* indicates heterosexism either by omission or by design. Only in

1979 did lesbian-focused articles appear in *Signs* and *Frontiers*. Most lesbian criticism first appeared in alternative, non-establishment lesbian journals, particularly *Sinister Wisdom* and *Conditions*, which are unfamiliar to many feminist scholars. For example, in *Signs*' first review article on literary criticism (1975), Elaine Showalter makes no mention of lesbianism as a theme or potential critical perspective, not even to point out its absence. Annette Kolodny, in *Signs*' second review article (1976), does call Jane Rule's *Lesbian Images* (1975) 'a novelist's challenge to the academy and its accompanying critical community', and further criticizes the homophobia in then current biographies, calling for 'candor and sensitivity' in future work (Kolodny 1976, pp. 416, 419). However, neither this nor subsequent review articles, even as late as 1980, familiarize the reader with 'underground' sources of lesbian criticism, some of which had appeared by this time, nor do they explicate lesbianism as a literary theme or critical perspective. Ironically, during the 1970s more articles on lesbian literature had appeared in traditional literary journals than in the women's studies press, just as in preceding years only male critics felt free to mention lesbianism. Possibly, feminist critics have felt that they will be identified as 'dykes', and that this would invalidate their work.

The perceptual screen of heterosexism is also evident in most of the pioneering works of feminist literary criticism. Ellen Moers's *Literary Women*, germinal work as it is, is both homophobic and heterosexist. Lesbians, she points out, appear as monsters, grotesques and freaks in works of Carson McCullers, Djuna Barnes (her reading of *Nightwood* is at least questionable) and Diane Arbus, but she seems to concur in this identification rather than calling it into question or explaining its historical context. Although her so-called defence of unmarried women writers against the 'charge' of lesbianism does criticize the way in which this word has been used as a slur, she neither condemns such anti-lesbianism nor entertains the possibility that some women writers were, in fact, lesbians. Her chapter on 'Loving Heroinism' is virtually textbook heterosexism, assuming as it does that women writers only articulate love for men (Moers 1977, pp. 108–9, 145). Perceptual blinders also mar Spacks's *The Female Imagination*, which never uses the word 'lesbian' (except in the index) or 'lover' to describe either the 'sexual ambiguity' of the bond between Jane and Helen in *Jane Eyre*, nor Margaret Anderson's relationship with a 'beloved older woman'. Furthermore, Spacks claims that Gertrude Stein, 'whose life lack[ed] real attachments' (a surprise to Alice B. Toklas), also 'denied whatever is special to women' (which lesbianism is not?) (Spacks 1976, pp. 89, 214, 363). The latter judgement is particularly ominous because heterosexuals often have difficulty accepting that a lesbian, even a role-playing 'butch', is in fact a woman. More care is demonstrated by Elaine Showalter, who in *A Literature of their Own* uncovers the attitudes toward lesbianism held by the nineteenth-century writers Eliza Lynn Linton and Mrs Humphrey Ward. However, she does not integrate lesbian issues into her discussion of the crucial genera-tion of early twentieth-century writers (Woolf, Sackville-West, Richardson and Lehmann, among others; Radclyffe Hall is mentioned but not *The Well of Loneliness*), all of whom wrote about sexual love between women. Her well-taken point that modern British novelists avoid lesbianism might have been balanced, however, by a mention of Maureen Duffy, Sybille Bedford or Fay Weldon (Showalter 1977, pp. 178, 229, 316). Finally, the word 'lesbian' does not appear in the index of Sandra Gilbert's and Susan Gubar's *The Madwoman in the Attic*; the lone reference made in the text is to the possibility that 'Goblin Market' describes 'a covertly (if ambiguously) lesbian world' (Gilbert and Gubar 1979a, p. 567). The authors' tenden-cy to interpret all pairs of female characters as aspects of the self sometimes serves to mask a relationship that a lesbian reader might interpret as bonding or love between women.

Lesbian critics, who as feminists owe much to these critical texts, have had to turn to other resources, first to develop a lesbian canon, and then to establish a lesbian critical perspec-tive. Barbara Grier, who as Gene Damon reviewed books for the pioneering lesbian journal *The Ladder*, laid the groundwork for this canon with her incomparable but largely unknown *The Lesbian in Literature: A Bibliography* (Damon *et al.* 1975). Equally obscure was Jeannette Foster's *Sex Variant Women in Literature*, self-published in 1956 after having been rejected by a university press because of its subject matter. An exhaustive chronological account of every reference to love between women from Sappho and Ruth to the fiction of the 1950s, *Sex Variant Women* has proven to be an invaluable starting-point for lesbian readers and scholars. Out of print almost immediately after its publication and lost to all but a few intrepid souls, it was finally reprinted by Diana Press in 1975 (Foster 1975). A further resource and gathering-point for lesbian critics was the special lesbian issue of *Margins*, a review of small press publications which appeared in 1975, the first issue of a literary journal devoted entirely to lesbian writing. In 1976 its editor, Beth Hodges, produced a second special issue, this time in *Sinister Wisdom* (1975, 1976). Along with the growing visibility and solidarity of lesbians within the academic profession, and the increased availability of lesbian literature from feminist and mass-market presses, these two journal issues provided a starting-point for the development of lesbian feminist literary criticism.

The literary resources available to lesbian critics form only part of the story, for lesbian criticism is equally rooted in political ideology. Although not all lesbian critics are activists, most have been strongly influenced by the politics of lesbian feminism. These politics travel the continuum from civil rights advocacy to separatism; however, most, if not all, lesbian feminists assume that lesbianism is a healthy lifestyle chosen by women in virtually all eras and all cultures, and thus strive to eliminate the stigma historically attached to lesbianism. One way to remove this stigma is to associate lesbianism with positive and desirable attributes, to divert women's attention away from male values and towards an exclusively female *communitas*. Thus the influential Radicalesbians essay, 'The Woman-Identified Woman', argues that lesbian feminism assumes 'the primacy of women relating to women, of women creating a new consciousness of and with each other. . . . We see ourselves as prime, find our centers inside of ourselves' (Radicalesbians 1973, p. 245). Many lesbian writers and critics have also been profoundly influenced by the politics of separatism, which provides a critique of heterosexuality as a political institution rather than a personal choice – 'because relationships between men and women are essentially political . . . [they involve] power and dominance' (Bunch 1975, p. 30). As we shall see, the notion of 'woman-identification', that is, the primacy of women bonding with women emotionally and politically, as well as the premisses of separatism, that lesbians have a unique and critical place at the margins of patriarchal society, are central to much current lesbian literary criticism.

II

Unmasking heterosexist assumptions in feminist literary criticism has been an important but hardly the primary task for lesbian critics. We are more concerned about developing a unique lesbian feminist perspective or, at the very least, determining whether or not such a perspective is possible. In order to do this, lesbian critics have had to begin with a special question: 'When is a text a "lesbian text" or its writer a "lesbian writer"?' (Lanser 1979, p. 39). Lesbians are faced with this special problem of definition: we presumably know when a writer is a 'Victorian writer' or a 'Canadian writer'. To answer this question, we have to determine how inclusively or exclusively we define 'lesbian'. Should we limit this appellation to those women for whom sexual experience with other women can be proven? This is an almost impossible historical task, as many have noted, for what constitutes proof? Women have not left obvious markers in their private writings. Furthermore, such a narrow definition 'names' lesbianism as an exclusively sexual phenomenon – which, many argue, may be an inadequate construction of lesbian experience, both today and in less sexually explicit eras. This sexual definition of lesbianism also leads to the identification of literature with life, and thus can be an over-defensive and suspect strategy.

Nevertheless, lesbian criticism continues to be plagued with the problem of definition. One perspective insists that 'desire must be there and at least somewhat embodied. . . . That carnality distinguishes it from gestures of political sympathy for homosexuals and from affectionate friendships in which women enjoy each other, support each other, and commingle their sense of identity and well-being' (Stimpson 1981, p. 364). A second perspective, which might be called a school, claims, on the contrary, that 'the very meaning of lesbianism is being expanded in literature just as it is being redefined through politics' (Smith 1977, p. 39). An articulate spokeswoman for this 'expanded meaning' school of criticism is Adrienne Rich, who offers a compelling inclusive definition of lesbianism:

> I mean the term *lesbian continuum* to include a range – through each woman's life and throughout history – of woman-identified experience; not simply the fact that a woman has had or consciously desired genital sexual experience with another woman. If we expand it to embrace many more forms of primary intensity between and among women, including the sharing of a rich inner life, the bonding against male tyranny, the giving and receiving of practical and political support . . . we begin to grasp breadths of female history and psychology which have lain out of reach as a consequence of limited, mostly clinical, definitions of 'lesbianism'.
>
> (Rich 1980, pp. 648–9)

This definition has the virtue of de-emphasizing lesbianism as a static entity and of suggesting interconnections among the various ways in which women bond together. However, all inclusive definitions of lesbianism risk blurring the distinctions between lesbian relationships and non-lesbian female friendships, or between lesbian identity and female-centred identity. Some lesbian writers would deny that there are such distinctions, but this position is reductive and of mixed value to those who are developing lesbian criticism and theory and who may need limited and precise definitions. In fact, reductionism is a serious problem in lesbian ideology. Too often, we identify 'lesbian' with 'woman', or 'feminist'; we equate lesbianism with any close bonds between women or with political commitment to women. These identifications can be fuzzy and historically questionable – as, for example, in the claim that lesbians have a unique relationship with nature or (as Rich also has claimed) that all female creativity is lesbian. By so reducing the meaning of 'lesbian', we have in effect eliminated lesbianism as a meaningful category.

A similar problem arises when lesbian theorists redefine lesbianism politically, equating it with strength, independence and resistance to patriarchy. This new political definition then influences the interpretation of literature: 'If in a woman wri-ter's work a sentence refuses to do what it is supposed to do, if there are strong images of women, and if there is a refusal to be linear, the result is innately lesbian literature' (Smith 1977, p. 33). The concept of an 'innately' lesbian perspective or aesthetic allows the critic to separate lesbianism from bio-graphical content – which is an essential development in lesbian critical theory. Literary interpretation will, of course, be sup-ported by historical and biographical evidence, but perhaps lesbian critics should borrow a few insights from textual criti-cism. If a text lends itself to a lesbian reading, then no amount of biographical 'proof' ought to be necessary to establish it as a lesbian text. Barbara Smith, for example, interprets Toni Morri-son's *Sula* as a lesbian novel, regardless of the author's affection-al preference. But we need to be cautious about what we call 'innately' lesbian. Why is circularity or strength limited to lesbians, or why is love of nature or creativity? It is certainly not evident that women, are 'innately' anything. And while it might require a lesbian perspective to stress the dominant relationship between Nel and Sula ('All that time, all that time, I thought I was missing Jude'), the critic cannot ignore the heterosexuality that pervades this novel.

Almost midway between the inclusive and exclusive approaches to a definition of lesbianism lies that of Lillian Faderman in her extraordinary overview, *Surpassing the Love of Men: Romantic Friendship and Love Between Women*. Faderman's precise definition of lesbianism provides a conceptual framework for the 400 years of literary history explored by the text:

> 'Lesbian' describes a relationship in which two women's strongest emotions and affections are directed toward each other. Sexual contact may be a part of the relationship to a greater or lesser degree, or it may be entirely absent. By preference the two women spend most of their time together and share most aspects of their lives with each other.
>
> (Faderman 1981, pp. 17–18)

Broader than the exclusive definition of lesbianism – for Fader-man argues that not all lesbian relationships may be fully embodied – but narrower than Rich's 'lesbian continuum', this definition is both specific and discriminating. The book is slightly marred by a defensive, over-explanatory tone, caused, no doubt, by her attempt to neutralize the 'intense charge of the word *lesbian*' (Rich 1979, p. 202); note, for example, that this charged word is omitted from the title. Furthermore, certain problems remain with her framework, as with any that a lesbian critic or historian might establish. The historical relationship between genital sexuality and lesbianism remains unclear; nor can we easily identify lesbianism outside a monogamous relationship. Nevertheless, despite problems in definition that may be inherent in lesbian studies, the strength of *Surpassing the Love of Men* derives partly from the precision with which Faderman defines her topic and chooses her texts and subjects.

This problem of definition is exacerbated by the problem of silence. One of the most pervasive themes in lesbian criticism is that woman-identified writers, silenced by a homophobic and misogynistic society, have been forced to adopt coded and obscure language and internal censorship. Emily Dickinson counselled us to 'tell all the truth / but tell it slant', and critics are now calculating what price we have paid for slanted truth. The silences of heterosexual women writers may become lies for lesbian writers, as Adrienne Rich warns: 'a life "in the closet" . . . [may] spread into private life, so that lying (described as *discretion*) becomes an easy way to avoid conflict or complication' (Rich 1979, p. 190). Gloria T. Hull recounts the moving story of just such a victim of society, the black lesbian poet Angelina Weld Grimké, whose 'convoluted life and thwarted sexuality' marked her slim output of poetry with images of self-abnegation, diminution, sadness and the wish for death. The lesbian writer who is working class or a woman of colour may be particularly isolated, shackled by conventions and, ultimately, silenced 'with [her] real gifts stifled within' (Hull 1979, pp. 23, 20).

What does a lesbian writer do when the words cannot be silenced? Critics are pointing to the codes and strategies for literary survival adopted by many women. For example, Willa Cather may have adopted her characteristic male persona in order to express safely emotional and erotic feelings for other women (Russ 1979; Lambert 1982). Thus a writer some call anti-feminist or at least disappointing may be better appreciated when her lesbianism is taken into account. Similarly, many ask whether Gertrude Stein cultivated obscurity, encoding her

lesbianism in order to express hidden feelings and evade potential enemies. Or, on the other hand, Stein may have been always
a declared lesbian, but a victim of readers' (and scholars')
unwillingness or inability to pay her the close and sympathetic
attention she requires (Secor 1979).

The silence of 'Shakespeare's [lesbian] sister' has meant that
modern writers have had little or no tradition with which to
nurture themselves. Feminist critics such as Moers, Showalter,
Gilbert and Gubar have demonstrated the extent and significance of a female literary tradition, but the lesbian writer
developed her craft alone (and perhaps this is the significance of
the title of *the* lesbian novel about novel-writing, *The Well of
Loneliness*). Elly Bulkin's much-reprinted article on lesbian
poetry points out that lesbian poets 'have had their work
shaped by the simple fact of their having begun to write without
knowledge of such history and with little or no hope of support
from a woman's and/or lesbian writing community' (Bulkin
1978, p. 8). If white women can at least imagine a lesbian
literature, the black lesbian writer, as Barbara Smith demonstrates, is even more hampered by the lack of tradition: 'Black
women are still in the position of having to "imagine", discover
and verify Black lesbian literature because so little has been
written from an avowedly lesbian perspective' (Smith 1977, p.
39). Blanche Cook points out further that all lesbians are
affected by this absence of tradition and role models, or the
limiting of role models to Hall's Stephen Gordon. She also
reminds us that our lesbian foremothers and networks were not
simply lost and forgotten; rather, our past has been 'erased',
obliterated by the actions of a hostile society (Cook 1979).

It would appear, then, that lesbian critics are faced with a set
of problems that make our work particularly delicate and
problematic, requiring caution, sensitivity and flexibility as
well as imagination and risk. Lesbian criticism begins with the
establishment of the lesbian text: the creation of language out of
silence. The critic must first define the term 'lesbian' and then
determine its applicability to both writer and text, sorting out
the relation of literature to life. Her definition of lesbianism will
influence the texts she identifies as lesbian, and, except for the
growing body of literature written from an explicit lesbian
perspective since the development of a lesbian political

movement, it is likely that many will disagree with various identifications of lesbian texts. It is not only *Sula* that may provoke controversy, but even the 'coded' works of lesbian writers like Gertrude Stein. The critic will need to consider whether a lesbian text is one written by a lesbian (and, if so, how do we determine who is a lesbian?), one written about lesbians (which might be by a heterosexual woman or by a man) or one that expresses a lesbian 'vision' (which has yet to be satisfactorily described). But, despite the problems raised by definition, silence and coding, and absence of tradition, lesbian critics have begun to develop a critical stance. Often this stance involves peering into shadows, into the spaces between words, into what has been unspoken and barely imagined. It is a perilous critical adventure, with results that may violate accepted norms of traditional criticism, but it may also transform our notions of literary possibility.

III

One of the first tasks of this emerging lesbian criticism has been to provide lesbians with a tradition, even if a retrospective one. Jane Rule, whose *Lesbian Images* appeared about the same time as Moers's *Literary Women*, first attempted to establish this tradition (Rule 1975). Although her text is flawed, relying too much on biographical evidence and derivative interpretations and including some questionable writers (such as Dorothy Baker) while omitting others, *Lesbian Images* was a milestone in lesbian criticism. Its importance is partially suggested by the fact that it took five years for another complete book – Faderman's – to appear on lesbian literature. In a 1976 review of *Lesbian Images*, I questioned the existence of a lesbian 'great tradition' in literature, but I now think I was wrong (Zimmerman 1976). Along with Rule, Dolores Klaich in *Woman + Woman* (1974) and Louise Bernikow in the introduction to *The World Split Open* (1974) have explored the possibility of a lesbian tradition, and recent critics such as Faderman and Blanche Cook, in particular, have begun to define that tradition, who belongs to it, and what links the writers who can be identified as lesbians. Blanche Cook's review of lesbian literature and culture in the early twentieth century proposes 'to analyze the literature and attitudes out of which the present lesbian feminist works have emerged, and to examine the continued denials and invalidation of the lesbian experience' (Cook 1979, p. 720). Focusing on the recognized lesbian networks in France and England that included Virginia Woolf, Vita Sackville-West, Ethel Smyth, Gertrude Stein, Radclyffe Hall, Natalie Barney and Romaine Brooks, Cook provides an important outline of a lesbian cultural tradition and an insightful analysis of the distortions and denials of homophobic scholars, critics and biographers.

Lillian Faderman's *Surpassing the Love of Men*, like her earlier critical articles, ranges more widely through a literary tradition of romantic love between women (whether or not one calls that 'lesbian') from the sixteenth to the twentieth century. Her thesis is that passionate love between women was labelled neither abnormal not undesirable – probably because women were perceived to be asexual – until the sexologists led by Krafft-Ebing and Havelock Ellis 'morbidified' female friendship around 1900. Although she does not always clarify the dialectic between idealization and condemnation that is suggested in her text, Faderman's basic theory is quite convincing. Most readers, like myself, will be amazed at the wealth of information about women's same-sex love that Faderman has uncovered. She rescues from heterosexual obscurity Mary Wollstonecraft, Mary Wortley Montagu, Anna Seward, Sarah Orne Jewett, Edith Somerville, 'Michael Field', and many others, including the Scottish schoolmistresses whose lesbian libel suit inspired Lillian Hellman's *The Children's Hour*. Faderman has also written on the theme of same-sex love and romantic friendship in the poems and letters of Emily Dickinson; in novels by James, Holmes and Longfellow; and in popular magazine fiction of the early twentieth century (Faderman 1978a, 1978b, 1978c, 1978d).

Faderman is pre-eminent among those critics who are attempting to establish a lesbian tradition by rereading writers of the past previously assumed to be heterosexual or 'spinsters'. As the songwriter Holly Near expresses it: 'Lady poet of great acclaim / I have been misreading you / I never knew your poems were meant for me' (Near 1976). It is in this area of lesbian scholarship that the most controversy – and some of the most exciting work – has occurred. Was Mary Wollstonecraft's passionate love for Fanny Blood, recorded in *Mary, A Fiction*, lesbian? Does Henry James dissect a lesbian relationship in *The Bostonians*? Did Emily Dickinson address many of her love poems to a woman, not a man? How did Virginia Woolf's relationships with Vita Sackville-West and Ethyl Smyth affect her literary vision? What was the nature of Alice Dunbar–Nelson's affection for other women? Not only are some lesbian critics increasingly naming such women and relationships 'lesbian', but they are also suggesting that criticism cannot fail to take into account the influence of sexual and emotional orientation on literary expression.

In the establishment of a self-conscious literary tradition, certain writers have become focal points both for critics and for lesbians in general, who affirm and celebrate their identity by 'naming names', establishing a sense of historical continuity and community through the knowledge that incontrovertibly great women were also lesbians. Foremost among these heroes (or 'heras') are the women who created the first self-identified lesbian feminist community in Paris during the early years of the twentieth century. With Natalie Barney at its hub, this circle included such notable writers as Colette, Djuna Barnes, Radclyffe Hall, Renée Vivien and, peripherally, Gertrude Stein. Contemporary lesbians – literary critics, historians and lay readers – have been drawn to their mythic and myth-making presence, seeing in them a vision of lesbian society and culture that may have existed only once before on the original island of Lesbos (Klaich 1974; Harris 1973; Rubin 1976). More interest, however, has been paid to their lives so far than to their art. Barnes's portraits of decadent, tormented lesbians and homosexuals in *Nightwood* and silly, salacious ones in *The Ladies' Almanack* often prove troublesome to lesbian readers and critics (Lanser 1979). However, Elaine Marks's perceptive study of French lesbian writers (1979) traces a tradition and how it has changed, modified by circumstance and by feminism, from the Sappho of Renée Vivien to the Amazons of Monique Wittig.

The problem inherent in reading lesbian literature primarily for role-modelling is most evident with Radclyffe Hall – the most notorious of literary lesbians – whose archetypal 'butch', Stephen Gordon, has troubled readers since the publication of

The Well of Loneliness. Although one critic praises the novel as 'the standard by which all subsequent similar works are measured', most contemporary lesbian feminists would, I believe, agree with Faderman's harsh condemnation of it for 'helping to wreak confusion in young women' (Vincent n.d.; Faderman 1978b). Such an extraliterary debate is not limited to lesbian novels and lesbian characters; I am reminded of the intense disappointment expressed by many feminists over George Eliot's disposal of Dorothea Brooke in *Middlemarch*. In both cases, the cry is the same: why haven't these writers provided us with appropriate role models? Blanche Cook may be justified in criticizing Hall for creating a narrow and debilitating image for lesbians who follow; however, Catharine Stimpson's analysis of the ironic levels of the text and Claudia Stillman Franks's demonstration that Stephen Gordon is a portrait of an artist deepen our understanding of this classic, suggesting that its hero and message are highly complex (Stimpson 1981; Franks 1982; see also Newton 1984). In looking to writers for a tradition, we need to recognize that that tradition may not always be a happy one. It encompasses Stephen Gordons alongside characters like Molly Bolt in Rita Mae Brown's *Rubyfruit Jungle*. Lesbians may also question whether or not the incarnation of a 'politically correct' but elusive and utopian mythology provides our only appropriate role model.

As with Radclyffe Hall, some readers and critics have been strongly antipathetic to Gertrude Stein, citing her reactionary and anti-feminist politics and her role-playing relationship with Alice B. Toklas. However, other critics, by carefully analysing Stein's actual words, establish that she did have a lesbian and feminist perspective, calling into question assumptions about coding and masculine role-playing. Cynthia Secor, who has developed an exciting lesbian feminist interpretation of Stein, argues that her novel *Ida* attempts to discover what it means to be a female person, and that the author profited from her position on the boundaries of patriarchal society: 'Stein's own experience as a lesbian gives her a critical distance that shapes her understanding of the struggle to be one's self. Her own identity is not shaped as she moves into relation with a man' (Secor 1978, p. 99; also 1982a and 1982b). Similarly, Elizabeth Fifer points out that Stein's situation encouraged her to experiment with parody, theatricality, role-playing and 'the diversity of ways possible to look at homosexual love and at her love object' (Fifer 1979, p. 478). Recently Fifer suggests that Stein pursued the two contradictory goals of concealment and exposure of her personal life (Fifer 1982). Deirdre Vanderlinde finds in *Three Lives* 'one of the earliest attempts to find a new language in which to say, "I, woman-loving woman, exist"' (Vanderlinde 1979, p. 10). Catharine Stimpson places more critical emphasis on Stein's use of masculine pronouns and conventional language, but, despite what may have been her compromise, Stimpson feels that female bonding provides Stein with a private solution to a woman's mind–body split (Stimpson 1977; also Burke 1982; O'Brien 1984).

Along with Stein, Emily Dickinson's woman-identification has drawn the most attention from recent critics, and has generated considerable controversy between lesbian and other feminist critics. Faderman insists that Dickinson's love for women must be considered homosexual, and that critics must take into account her sexuality (or affectionality). Like most critics who accept this lesbian identification of Dickinson, she points to Susan Gilbert Dickinson as Emily's primary romantic and sexual passion. Both Faderman and Louise Bernikow thus argue that Dickinson's 'muse' was sometimes a female figure as well as a male (Faderman 1978a; also Morris 1981). Some of this work can be justifiably criticized for too closely identifying literature with life; however, by altering our awareness of what is *possible* – namely, that Dickinson's poetry was inspired by her love for a woman – we also can transform our response to the poetry. Thus Paula Bennett daringly suggests that Dickinson's use of crumbs, jewels, pebbles and similar objects was an attempt to create 'clitoral imagery' (Bennett 1977). In a controversial paper on the subject, Nadean Bishop argues forcefully that the poet's marriage poems must be reread in light of what she considers to have been a consummated sexual relationship with her sister-in-law (Bishop 1980; see also Patterson 1951; Morris 1983).

Feminist critics working on other major literary figures, particularly the early twentieth-century modernists, increasingly uncover evidence of the impact lesbian love had on their literary production. For example, Louise DeSalvo analyses how the love shared by Virginia Woolf and Vita Sackville-West enabled them 'to look inward and backward together, to reexamine a past that was difficult for each of them to deal with alone': a process of interspection that 'is preserved in the score of literary works that they wrote while they were lovers and loving friends' (DeSalvo 1982, p. 214). Similarly, the work of Susan Friedman and Rachel Blau Duplessis explores the 'sexualities' – both lesbian and heterosexual – of H.D. (Friedman and Duplessis 1981; Friedman 1983). It is becoming evident that many women writers, especially in the twentieth century, can be understood only if the critic is willing and able to adopt a lesbian point of view.

IV

The establishment of a lesbian literary tradition, a 'canon', as my discussion suggests, has been the primary task of critics writing from a lesbian feminist perspective. But it is not the only task to emerge. For example, lesbian critics, like feminist critics in the early 1970s, have begun to analyse the images, stereotypes and mythic presence of lesbians in fiction by or about lesbians. Bertha Harris, a major novelist as well as a provocative and trail-blazing critic, considers the lesbian to be the prototype of the monster and 'the quintessence of all that is female; and Female enraged. . . . a lesbian is . . . that which has been unspeakable about women' (Harris 1977, p. 7). She offers this monstrous lesbian as a female archetype who subverts traditional notions of female submissiveness, passivity and virtue. Her 'tooth-and-claw' image of the lesbian is ironically similar to that of Ellen Moers, although from a lesbian rather than heterosexual point of view. But the very fact that Moers presents the lesbian-as-monster in a derogatory context and that Harris presents it in a celebratory one suggests that there is an important dialectic between how the lesbian articulates herself and how she is articulated and objectified by others. Popular culture, in particular, exposes the objectifying purpose of the lesbian-as-monster image, such as the lesbian vampire first created by LeFanu's 1871 ghost story, 'Carmilla', and revived in early 1970s 'B' films, as a symbolic attack on women's struggle for self-identity (Zimmerman 1980).

Other critics too have analysed the negative symbolic appearance of the lesbian in literature. Ann Allen Shockley, reviewing black lesbian characters in American fiction, notes that 'within these works exists an undercurrent of hostility, trepidation, subtlety, shadiness, and in some instances, ignorance culling forth homophobic stereotypes' (Shockley 1979, p.136). Homophobic stereotypes are also what Maureen Brady and Judith McDaniel find in abundance in recent commercial fiction (such as *Kinflicks*, *A Sea Change*, *Some Do* and *How to Save Your Own Life*) by avowedly feminist novelists. Although individuals might disagree with Brady and McDaniel's severe criticism of specific novels, their overall argument is unimpeachable: contemporary feminist fiction, by perpetuating stereotyped characters and themes (such as the punishment theme so dear to pre-feminist lesbian literature), serves to 'disempower the lesbian' (Brady and McDaniel 1980, p. 83). Lesbian, as well as heterosexual, writers present the lesbian as Other, as Julia Penelope Stanley discovered in pre-feminist fiction: 'the lesbian character creates for herself a mythology of darkness, a world in which she moves through dreams and shadows' (Stanley 1975, p. 8). Lesbian critics may wish to avoid this analysis of the lesbian as Other because we no longer wish to dwell upon the cultural violence done against us. Yet this area must be explored until we strip these stereotypes of their inhibiting and dehumanizing presence in our popular culture and social mythology.

Lesbian critics have also delved into the area of stylistics and literary theory. If we have been silenced for centuries and speak an oppressor's tongue, then liberation for the lesbian must begin with language. Some writers may have reconciled their internal censor with their speech by writing in code, but many critics maintain that modern lesbian writers, because they are uniquely alienated from patriarchy, experiment with its literary style and form. Julia Penelope Stanley and Susan Wolfe, considering such diverse writers as Virginia Woolf, Gertrude Stein, Kate Millett and Elena Dykewoman, claim that 'a feminist aesthetic, as it emerges out of women's evolution, grounds itself in female consciousness and in the unrelenting language of process and change' (Stanley and Wolfe 1978, p. 66). In this article the authors do not call their feminist aesthetic a lesbian feminist aesthetic, although all the writers they discuss are, in fact, lesbians. Susan Wolfe later confronted this face: 'Few women who continue to identify with men can risk the male censure of "women's style", and few escape the male perspective long enough to attempt it' (Wolfe 1978, p. 3). Through examples from Kate Millett, Jill Johnston and Monique Wittig, she illustrates her contention that lesbian literature is characterized by the use of the continuous present, unconventional grammar and neologism; and that it breaks boundaries between art and the world, between events and our perceptions of them, and between past, present and the dream world. It is, as even the proponents of this theory admit, highly debatable that all lesbian writers are modernists, or that all modernists are lesbians. If Virginia Woolf wrote in non-linear, stream-of-consciousness style because she was a lesbian (or 'woman-identified'), how does one explain Dorothy Richardson, whose *Pilgrimage*, despite one lesbian interlude, is primarily heterosexual? If both Woolf and Richardson can be called 'feminist' stylists, then how does one explain the non-linear experimentation of Joyce or Robbe-Grillet, for example?

Nevertheless, the suggestive overlap that exists between experimental writing and lesbian writing is leading to a rethinking of the literary meaning of lesbianism. If it is difficult to define authoritatively a lesbian writer or a lesbian style, it may be more fruitful to ask how lesbianism functions as a sign within the text. Bertha Harris and Barbara Smith, as discussed above, attempted to locate an inherent lesbianism in texts not intended to be read as lesbian. Many other critics are turning to the self-defined lesbian literature produced since the late 1960s, using it as a laboratory in which to explore the notions of a lesbian aesthetic, a lesbian imagery and symbolism, a lesbian ethics and epistemology.

Among the most interesting work is that being done on the French novelist and theorist Monique Wittig. Her literary project has been to shape a 'lesbian writing' that locates the lesbian subject outside the male linguistic universe. Using the language and concepts of contemporary French feminism, critics have shown how Wittig attacks phallogocentrism by 'overwriting' metaphors, 'translating' cultural myths and 'restructuring' genres. As a writer and theorist, argues Diane Griffin Crowder, Wittig unites the realms of language and politics: '"Lesbian writing" is a tool for transforming the female subject's relation to all cultural systems which are, by definition, political' (Crowder 1983, p. 131). In the neat conclusion to her study of *Le Corps lesbien*, Namascar Shaktini defines '*Ecriture lesbienne* [as] a *coup d'écriture*' (Shaktini 1982, p. 44; also Rosenfeld 1978; Wenzel 1981).

Other critics also demonstrate how lesbian writing transforms the traditional elements of fiction and poetry, creating new paradigms in the process. Marilyn Schuster carefully analyses the way in which Jane Rule, a stylistically conservative novelist, subverts traditional symbols of western culture in order to tell a true story about lesbian lovers (Schuster 1981). Catherine Stimpson's historical and thematic study of the lesbian novel from the 1920s to the 1970s explores two patterns, the 'dying fall' and the 'enabling escape', used by lesbian novelists to respond to the stigmatization of homosexuality (Stimpson 1981, p. 364). My own work on the lesbian novel of development illustrates a similar pattern of repression and liberation, as well as demonstrating the similarities and differences between lesbian and traditional *Bildungsroman* (Zimmerman 1983; also Gurko 1980).

Studies of lesbian poetry, in particular, suggest the emergence of a lesbian poetics. Elly Bulkin first traced the various sources of contemporary poetry and analysed the 'range of lesbian voices' (Bulkin 1978, p. 10). Mary Carruthers, in asking why so much contemporary feminist poetry is also lesbian, observed that the 'lesbian love celebrated in contemporary women's poetry requires an affirmation of the value of femaleness, women's bodies, women's sexuality – in women's language' (Carruthers 1979, p. 301). In a more recent article, Carruthers deepens her concept of a lesbian poetics. She identifies a 'distinctive movement in contemporary American poetry' that she names 'Lesbian poetry' because

> the 'naming and defining' of this phrase is its central poetic preoccupation. These poets [Adrienne Rich, Audre Lorde, Judy Grahn and Olga Broumas] choose to deal with life at the level of metaethics – its social, psychic, and aesthetic underpinnings, which are articulable only in myth; their

metaethics takes its structure from a complex poetic image of lesbian relationship.

(Carruthers 1983, p. 293)

For these poets, love for and between women forms the basis of a 'common language' replacing patriarchal discourse (see also McDaniel 1978; Diehl 1980; Clausen 1982; Libertin 1982).

Curruthers is a notable example of a critic searching out the ethical imperative of contemporary lesbian writing. Such also is the intention of Sally Gearhart and Jane Gurko, in an essay that compares the success of lesbian and gay male writers in transforming heterosexual ideology. The authors claim that, in contrast to gay male literature, lesbian literature 'does express a revolutionary model of sexuality which in its structure, its content, and its practice defies the fundamental violent assumptions of patriarchal culture' (Gurko and Gearhart 1979, p. 3). This article, admirable in many ways, also illustrates one danger inherent in the attempt to establish a lesbian vision, paradigm or value-system. In the attempt to say *this* is what defines a lesbian literature, the critic may be tempted to read selectively, omitting what is foreign to her theory. Most contemporary lesbian literature does embrace a rhetoric of nonviolence, but this is not universally true; for example M. F. Beal's *Angel Dance* and Camarae Grey's *The Winged Dancer* are hardboiled detective novels, and *Le Corps lesbien* is infused with a violent eroticism that is, nevertheless, intensely antipatriarchal. Violence, role-playing, disaffection, unhappiness, suicide and self-hatred, to name a few 'taboo' subjects, all exist within lesbian culture, and a useful criticism will have to effectively analyse these as *lesbian* themes and metaphors, regardless of the dictates of ideological purity.

V

As lesbian feminist criticism has developed over a decade, it has changed, and it has changed the criticism of others. Lesbian criticism was originally influenced primarily by the politics of lesbian separatism. This position is exemplified by a statement from *Sinister Wisdom*, a journal that developed a consistent and articulate separatist politics:

'lesbian consciousness' is really a point of view, a view from the boundary. And in a sense everytime a woman draws a circle around her psyche, saying 'this is a room of *my own*', and then writes from within that 'room', she's inhabiting lesbian consciousness.

(Desmoines 1976, p. 29)

The value of separatism, which has always provided the most exciting theoretical developments in lesbian ideology, is precisely this marginality: the notion that lesbians exist 'on the periphery of patriarchy' (Wolfe 1978, p. 16). Separatism has provided criticism, as it has lesbian politics, with a cutting edge and radical energy that impels us forward rather than allowing us to slip backward from fear or complacency. Those critics who maintain a consciously chosen position on the boundaries (and not one imposed by a hostile society) help keep lesbian and feminist criticism radical and provocative. Understandably, those critics and scholars willing to identify themselves publicly as lesbians have also tended to hold radical politics of marginality. Exposing oneself to public scrutiny as a lesbian may in fact entail marginality through denial of tenure or loss of job, and those lesbians willing to risk those consequences often have a political position that justifies their risk.[2] But, increasingly, lesbian criticism has developed diversity in theory and approach, encorporating the insights of Marxist, structuralist, semiotic and even psychoanalytic criticism. Although lesbians, perhaps more than heterosexual feminists, may mistrust systems of thought developed by and associated with men and male values, our work is in fact richer and subtler for this incorporation.

At this time, lesbian criticism and cultural theory in general must continue to grow by developing a greater specificity, historically and culturally. We have written and acted as if lesbian experience – which is perceived as that of a contemporary white middle-class feminist – is universal and unchanging. Although most lesbians know that it is not, we too often forget to apply rigorous historical and cross-cultural tools to our scholarship. Much of this ahistoricity occurs around the shifting definitions of lesbianism from one era and one culture to another. To state simply that Mary Wollstonecraft 'was' a lesbian because she passionately loved Fanny Blood, or Susan

B. Anthony because she wrote amorous letters to Anna Dickinson, without accounting for historical circumstances, may serve to distort or dislocate the actual meaning of these women's lives (just as it is distorting to *deny* their love for women). There are also notable differences among the institution of the *berdache* (the adoption by one sex of the opposite gender role) in Native American tribes; *faute de mieux* lesbian activity tolerated in France (as in Colette's *Claudine* novels); idyllic romantic friendships (such as that of the famous Ladies of Llangollen); and contemporary self-conscious lesbianism. It may be that there is a common structure – a lesbian 'essence' – that may be located in all these specific historical existences, just as we may speak of a widespread, perhaps universal, structure of marriage or the family. However, in each of these cases – lesbianism, marriage, the family – careful attention to history teaches us that differences are as significant as similarities, and vital information about female survival may be found in the different ways in which women have responded to their historical situation. This tendency towards simplistic universalism is accompanied by what seems to me to be a dangerous development of biological determinism and a curious revival of the nineteenth-century feminist notion of female (now lesbian) moral superiority – that women are uniquely caring and superior to inherently violent males. Although only an undertone in some criticism and literature, any such sociobiological impulse should be questioned at every appearance.

The denial of meaningful differences among women is being challenged, particularly around the issue of racism. Elly Bulkin has raised criticisms about the racism of white lesbian feminist theory:

> if I can put together – or think someone else can put together – a viable piece of feminist criticism or theory whose base is the thought and writing of white women/lesbians and expect that an analysis of racism can be tacked on or dealt with later as a useful addition, it is a measure of the extent to which I partake of that white privilege.

> (Bulkin 1980, p. 16)

Implicit in the criticism of Bulkin and other anti-racist writers is the belief that lesbians, because of our experience of stigma and exclusion from the feminist mainstream, ought to be particularly sensitive to the dynamic between oppression and oppressing. White lesbians who are concerned about eradicating racism in criticism and theory have been greatly influenced as well by the work of such black lesbian feminist literary critics as Gloria Hull, Barbara Smith and Lorraine Bethel (see Bethel 1982; Hull 1982; Clarke *et al.* 1983). A similar concern is not yet present over the issue of class, although the historical association of lesbianism with upper-class values has often been used by left-wing political groups and governments to deny legitimacy to homosexual rights and needs (see Kaye 1980). Lesbian critics studying the Natalie Barney circle, for example, might analyse the historical connections between lesbianism and class status. Lesbian critics might also develop comparisons among the literatures of various nationalities, since the lesbian canon is of necessity cross-national. We have barely explored the differences between American, English, French and German lesbian literature (although *Surpassing the Love of Men* draws some distinctions), let alone non-western literature. Recent articles on the lesbian coding in Colette's *The Pure and the Impure*, as well as those on Wittig, suggest, however, that we may soon see a truly international lesbian literary canon (Dranch 1983; Cothran 1981).

VI

As lesbian criticism continues to mature, we may anticipate the development of ongoing and compelling political and practical concerns. At this time, for example, lesbians are still defining and discovering texts. We are certainly not as badly off as we were in the early seventies, when the only lesbian novels in print were *The Well of Loneliness*, Isabel Miller's *Patience and Sarah* and Rita Mae Brown's *Rubyfruit Jungle*. However, texts published prior to 1970 are still difficult to find, and even *The Well of Loneliness* is intermittently available at the whim of publishers. Furthermore, the demise of Diana Press, Daughters Inc. and Persephone Press (which were among the most active lesbian publishing houses) leaves many major works unavailable, possibly for ever. As the boom in gay literature subsides, teachers of literature will find it very difficult to unearth teachable texts.

Scholars have the excellent Arno Press series, *Homosexuality: Lesbians and Gay Men in Society, History, and Literature*, but, as Faderman's monumental scholarship reveals, far more lesbian literature exists than anyone has suspected. This literature needs to be unearthed, analysed, explicated, perhaps translated, and made available to readers.

As lesbian critics, we also need to address the exclusion of lesbian literature from not merely the traditional but also the feminist canon. Lesbian literature has not yet been integrated into the mainstream of feminist texts, as evidenced by what is criticized, collected and taught. It is a matter of serious concern that lesbian literature is omitted from anthologies or included in mere token amounts, or that critical works and MLA panels still exclude lesbianism.[3] Lesbianism is still perceived as an unimportant and somewhat discomforting variation within the female life cycle, when it is perceived at all. It may as yet be possible for heterosexual feminists to claim ignorance about lesbian literature, but lesbian critics should make it impossible for that claim to stand much longer. And, just as we need to integrate lesbian material and perspectives into the traditional and feminist canons, we might also apply lesbian theory to traditional literature. Feminists have not only pointed out the sexism in many canonical works, but have also provided creative and influential rereadings of these works; lesbians might similarly contribute to rereadings. For example, *The Bostonians*, an obvious text, has been reread often from a lesbian perspective, and we could reinterpret D. H. Lawrence's anti-feminism or Doris Lessing's compromised feminism (particularly in *The Golden Notebook*) by relating these to their fear of, or discomfort with, lesbianism. Other texts or selections of texts – such as Rossetti's 'Goblin Market' or the relationship between Lucy Snowe and Ginevra Fanshawe in *Villette* – might reveal a subtext that could be called lesbian. Just as few texts escape a feminist re-vision, few might evade a lesbian transformation.

This last point – that there is a way in which we might 'review' literature as lesbians – brings me to my conclusion: that in a brief period of a few years critics have begun to demonstrate the existence of a distinct lesbian aesthetic, just as feminists have outlined elements of a female aesthetic. Certain components of this aesthetic or critical perspective have been suggested by Judith McDaniel:

> lesbian feminist criticism [or literature, I would add] is a political or thematic perspective, a kind of imagination that can see beyond the barriers of heterosexuality, role stereotypes, patterns of language and culture that may be repressive to female sexuality and expression.
>
> (McDaniel 1976, p. 2)

A lesbian artist very likely would express herself differently about sexuality, the body and relationships. But are there other, less obvious, unifying themes, ideas and imagery that might define a lesbian text or subtext? How, for example, does the lesbian's sense of outlaw status affect her literary vision? Might lesbian writing, because of the lesbian's position on the boundaries, be characterized by a particular sense of freedom and flexibility or, rather, by images of violently imposed barriers, the closet? Or, in fact, is there a dialectic between freedom and imprisonment that is unique to lesbian writing? Do lesbians have a special perception of suffering and stigma, as so much pre-feminist literature seems to suggest? What about the 'muse', the female symbol of literary creativity: do women writers create a lesbian relationship with their muse as May Sarton asserts? If so, do those writers who choose a female muse experience a freedom from inhibition because of that fact, or might there be a lack of creative tension in such a figurative same-sex relationship?

Lesbian literature may present a unified tradition of thematic concerns, such as that of unrequited longing, a longing of almost cosmic totality because the love object is denied not by circumstance or chance but by necessity. The tension between romantic love and genital sexuality takes a particular form in woman-to-woman relationships, often articulated through musings on the difference between purity and impurity (culminating in Colette's study of variant sexuality, *The Pure and the Impure*). Lesbian literature approaches the theme of development or the quest in a manner different from that of men or heterosexual women. Lesbian literature, like lesbian culture in general, is particularly flexible on issues of gender and role identification; even *The Well of Loneliness* hints at the tragedy of rigid gender roles. Because of this flexibility, lesbian artists and writers have always been fascinated with costuming, since dress is an external manifestation of gender roles that lesbians often reject (see Gubar 1981). As we read and reread literature from a lesbian perspective, I am confident we shall continue to expand our understanding of a lesbian aesthetic and literary tradition.

This chapter has suggested the vigour of lesbian criticism and its value to all feminists in raising awareness of entrenched heterosexism in existing texts, clarifying the lesbian traditions in literature through scholarship and reinterpretation, pointing out barriers that have stood in the way of free lesbian expression, explicating the recurring themes and values of lesbian literature, and exposing the dehumanizing stereotypes of lesbians in our culture. Many of the issues that face lesbian critics – expanding the canon, creating a non-racist and non-classist critical vision, transforming our readings of traditional texts and exploring new methodologies – are the interests of all feminist critics. Since feminism concerns itself with the removal of limitations and impediments in the way of female imagination, and lesbian criticism helps to expand our notions of what is *possible* for women, then all women would grow by adopting for themselves a lesbian vision. Disfranchised groups have had to adopt a double vision for survival; one of the political transformations of recent decades has been the realization that enfranchised groups – men, whites, heterosexuals, the middle class – would do well to adopt that double vision for the survival of us all. Lesbian literary criticism simply restates what feminists already know, that one group cannot name itself 'humanity' or even 'woman'. As Adrienne Rich suggests, 'We're not trying to become part of the old order misnamed "universal" which has tabooed us; we are transforming the meaning of "universality"' (Bulkin 1977, p. 58).

Whether lesbian criticism will survive depends as much upon the external social climate as it does upon the creativity and skill of its practitioners. If political attacks on gay rights and freedom grow; if the so-called 'moral majority' wins its fight to eliminate gay teachers and texts from the schools (as it apparently has done at Long Beach State); and if the academy, including feminist teachers and scholars, fails to support lesbian scholars, eradicate heterosexist values and assumptions, and incorporate the insights of lesbian scholarship into the mainstream: then current lesbian criticism will probably suffer the same fate as did Jeanette Foster's *Sex Variant Women* in the fifties. Lesbian or heterosexual, we should all suffer from that loss.

Notes

1 This survey is limited to published and unpublished essays in literary criticism that present a perspective either sympathetic to lesbianism or explicitly lesbian in orientation. It is limited to *literature* and to theoretical and scholarly articles and books (not book reviews). The sexual preference of the authors is irrelevant; this is an analysis of lesbian feminist *ideas*.

2 The National Women's Studies Association in the USA now has a 'fired lesbians' caucus, not all of whom would identify themselves as separatist. The most dramatic attack on lesbians in academia occurred at California State University, Long Beach, in 1981–2, resulting in the decimation of that institution's women's studies programme.

3 For example, recent anthologies such as *Shakespeare's Sisters* (Gilbert and Gubar 1979b) and *Gender and Literary Voice* (Todd 1980) include no articles on lesbian ideas or authors. *Women's Autobiographies* (Jelinek 1980) includes four articles on writers for whom lesbianism was clearly a significant aspect of the self, but the subject is addressed only in Annette Kolodny's article on Kate Millett (1980). At many points in *The Female Hero* (Pearson and Pope 1981), lesbian texts and concepts could have deepened and extended the authors' analyses. Many important essays of the past few years (Abel 1981; Homans 1983) develop theories about such subjects as female bonding and linguistic representation that beg for some attention to lesbian texts. It is encouraging to note that lesbian criticism seems to have influenced other critics. Two notable examples are *Archetypal Patterns in Women's Fiction* (Pratt 1981) and 'Soldier's Heart: Literary Men, Literary Women, and the Great War' (Gilbert 1983).

References

Abel, Elizabeth (1981) '(E)Merging Identities: The Dynamics of Female Friendship in Contemporary Fiction by Women', *Signs*, 6, 3, pp. 413–35.

Arnold, June (1976) 'Lesbian Fiction', *Sinister Wisdom*, 2, p. 28.

Bennett, Paula (1977) 'The Language of Love: Emily Dickinson's Homoerotic Poetry', *Gai Saber* (Spring).

Bernikow, Louise (1974) *The World Split Open.* New York: Vintage Books.

Bethel, Lorraine (1982) '"This Infinity of Conscious Pain": Zora Neale Hurston and the Black Female Literary Tradition'. In Gloria T. Hull, Patricia Bell Scott and Barbara Smith (eds), *All the Women are White, All the Blacks are Men, But Some of us are Brave: Black Women's Studies*, pp. 176–88. Old Westbury, NY: Feminist Press.

Bishop, Nadean (1980) 'Renunciation in the Bridal Poems of Emily Dickinson', unpublished paper presented at the National Women's Studies Association Conference.

Boucher, Sandy (1977) 'Lesbian Artists', *Heresies*, 3, p. 43.

Brady, Maureen, and McDaniel, Judith (1980) 'Lesbians in the Mainstream: Images of Lesbians in Recent Commercial Fiction', *Conditions: Six*, p. 83.

Bulkin, Elly (1977) 'An Interview with Adrienne Rich: Part II', *Conditions: Two*, p. 58.

Bulkin, Elly (1978) '"Kissing/Against the Light": A Look at Lesbian Poetry', *Radical Teacher*, 10, p. 8.

Bulkin, Elly (1980) 'Racism and Writing', *Sinister Wisdom*, 13, p. 16.

Bunch, Charlotte (1975) 'Lesbians in Revolt'. In Nancy Myron and Charlotte Bunch (eds), *Lesbianism and the Women's Movement.* Baltimore, Md: Diana Press.

Burke, Carolyn (1982) 'Gertrude Stein, the Cone Sisters, and the Puzzle of Female Friendship', *Critical Inquiry*, 8, 3, pp. 543–64.

Carruthers, Mary (1979) 'Imagining Women: Notes Toward a Feminist Poetic', *Massachusetts Review*, 10, 2, p. 301.

Carruthers, Mary (1983) 'The Re-Vision of the Muse: Adrienne Rich, Audre Lorde, Judy Grahn, Olga Broumas', *The Hudson Review*, 36, 2, pp. 293–322.

Clarke, Cheryl, *et al.* (1983) 'Conversations and Questions: Black Women on Black Women Writers', *Conditions: Nine*, 3, 3, pp. 88–137.

Clausen, Jan (1982) *A Movement of Poets: Thoughts on Poetry and Feminism.* Brooklyn, NY: Long Haul Press.

Cook, Blanche Wiesen (1979) '"Women Alone Stir my Imagination": Lesbianism and the Cultural Tradition', *Signs*, 4, 4, pp. 718–39.

Cothran, Ann (1981) '*The Pure and the Impure*: Codes and Constructs', *Women's Studies*, 8, 4, pp. 335–57.

Crowder, Diane (1983) 'Amazons and Mothers? Monique Wittig, Hélène Cixous and Theories of Women's Writing', *Contemporary Literature*, 24, 2, pp. 114–43.

Damon, Gene, Watson, Jan, and Jordan, Robin (1975) *The Lesbian in Literature: A Bibliography.* Weatherby Lake, MO: Naiad Press.

DeSalvo, Louise (1982) 'Lighting the Cave: The Relationship between Vita Sackville-West and Virginia Woolf', *Signs*, 8, 2, p. 214.

Desmoines, Harriet (1976) 'Notes for a Magazine II', *Sinister Wisdom*, 1, 1, p. 29.

Diehl, Joanne Feit (1980) ' "Cartographies of Silence": Rich's *Common Language* and the Woman Poet", *Fem. ust Studies*, 6, 3, pp. 530–46.

Dranch, Sherry A. (1983) 'Reading through the Veiled Text: Colette's *The Pure and the Impure*', *Contemporary Literature*, 24, 2, pp. 176–89.

Faderman, Lillian (1978a) 'Emily Dickinson's Homoerotic Poetry', *Higginson Journal*, 18.

Faderman, Lillian (1978b) 'Emily Dickinson's Letters to Sue Gilbert', *Massachusetts Review* (Summer).

Faderman, Lillian (1978c) 'Female Same-Sex Relationships in Novels by Longfellow, Holmes and James', *New England Quarterly*, 2, 3, pp. 309–32.

Faderman, Lillian (1978d) 'Lesbian Magazine Fiction in the Early Twentieth Century', *Journal of Popular Culture*, 11, 4, pp. 800–17.

Faderman, Lillian (1978e) 'The Morbidification of Love Between Women by 19th-Century Sexologists', *Journal of Homosexuality*, 4, 1, pp. 73–90.

Faderman, Lillian (1981) *Surpassing the Love of Men: Romantic Friendship and Love between Women from the Renaissance to the Present*. New York: William Morrow.

Faderman, Lillian, and Bernikow, Louise (1978) 'Comment on Joanne Feit Diehl's "Come Slowly, Eden" ', *Signs*, 4, 1, pp. 188–95.

Faderman, Lillian, and Williams, Ann (1977) 'Radclyffe Hall and the Lesbian Image', *Conditions: One*, p. 40.

Fifer, Elizabeth (1979) 'Is Flesh Advisable: The Interior Theater of Gertrude Stein', *Signs*, 4, 3, p. 478.

Fifer, Elizabeth (1982) 'Rescued Readings: Characteristic Deformations in the Language of Gertrude Stein's Plays', *Texas Studies in Literature and Language*, 24, 4, pp. 394–428.

Foster, Jeannette (1975) *Sex Variant Women in Literature*. Baltimore, Md: Diana Press.

Franks, Claudia Stillman (1982) 'Stephen Gordon, Novelist: A Reevaluation of Radclyffe Hall's *The Well of Loneliness*', *Tulsa Studies in Women's Literature*, 1, 2, pp. 125–39.

Friedman, Susan (1983) ' "I Go Where I Love": An Intertextual Study of H.D. and Adrienne Rich', *Signs*, 9, 2, pp. 228–45.

Friedman, Susan, and Duplessis, Rachel Blau (1981) 'The Sexualities of H.D.'s *Her*', *Montemora*, 8, pp. 7–30.

Gilbert, Sandra M. (1983) 'Soldier's Heart: Literary Men, Literary Women, and the Great War', *Signs*, 8, 3, pp. 422–50.

Gilbert, Sandra M., and Gubar, Susan (1979a) *The Madwoman in the Attic: The Woman Writer and the Nineteenth-Century Literary Imagination*. New Haven, Conn.: Yale University Press.

Gilbert, Sandra M., and Gubar, Susan (eds) (1979b) *Shakespeare's Sisters: Feminist Essays on Women Poets*. Bloomington, Ind.: Indiana University Press.

Gubar, Susan (1981) 'Blessings in Disguise: Cross-Dressing as Re-Dressing for Female Modernists', *Massachusetts Review*, 22, 3, pp. 477–508.

Gurko, Jane (1980) 'The Shape of Sameness: Contemporary Lesbian Autobiographical Narratives', unpublished paper presented to the Gay Rhetoric Panel at MLA, December.

Gurko, Jane, and Gearhart, Sally (1979) 'The Sword and the Vessel versus the Lake on the Lake: A Lesbian Model of Non-Violent Rhetoric', unpublished paper presented at MLA.

Harris, Bertha (1973) 'The More Profound Nationality of their Lesbianism: Lesbian Society in Paris in the 1920s'. In *Amazon Expedition*. New York: Changing Times Press.

Harris, Bertha (1977) 'What We Mean to Say: Notes toward Defining the Nature of Lesbian Literature', *Heresies*, 3, p. 7.

Hodges, Beth (ed.) (1975) *Lesbian Writing and Publishing, Margins* (special issue), 23.

Hodges, Beth (ed.) (1976) *Lesbian Literature and Publishing, Sinister Wisdom* (special issue), 2.

Homans, Margaret (1983) ' "Her Very Own Howl": The Ambiguities of Representation in Recent Women's Fiction', *Signs*, 9, 2, pp. 186–205.

Hull, Gloria T. (1979) ' "Under the Days": The Buried Life and Poetry of Angelina Weld Grimké', *Conditions: Five*, pp. 20–3.

Hull, Gloria T. (1982) 'Researching Alice Dunbar-Nelson: A Personal and Literary Perspective'. In Gloria T. Hull, Patricia Bell Scott and Barbara Smith (eds), *All the Women are White, All the Blacks are Men, But Some of us are Brave: Black Women's Studies*, pp. 189–95. Old Westbury, NY: Feminist Press.

Jelinek, Estelle C. (ed.) (1980) *Women's Autobiography*. Bloomington, Ind.: Indiana University Press.

Kaye, Melanie (1980) 'Culture-Making: Lesbian Classics', *Sinister Wisdom*, 13, pp. 23–4.

Klaich, Dolores (1974) *Woman + Woman: Attitudes toward Lesbianism*. New York: William Morrow.

Kolodny, Annette (1976) 'Review Essay: Literary Criticism', *Signs*, 2, 2, pp. 404–21.

Kolodny, Annette (1980) 'The Lady's Not for Spurning: Kate Millett and the Critics'. In Jelinek (1980), pp. 238–59.

Lambert, Deborah G. (1982) 'The Defeat of a Hero: Autonomy and Sexuality in *My Ántonia*', *American Literature* 53, 4, pp. 676–90.

Lanser, Susan Sniader (1979) 'Speaking in Tongues: *Ladies' Almanack* and the Language of Celebration', *Frontiers*, 4, 3, p. 39.

Libertin, Mary (1982) 'Female Friendship in Women's Verse: Toward a New Theory of Female Poetics', *Women's Studies*, 9, 3, pp. 291–308.

McDaniel, Judith (1976) 'Lesbians and Literature', *Sinister Wisdom*, 2.

McDaniel, Judith (1978) *Reconstituting the World: The Poetry and Vision of Adrienne Rich*. Argyle, NY: Spinsters, Ink.

Marks, Elaine (1979) 'Lesbian Intertextuality', In George Stambolian and Elaine Marks (eds), *Homosexualities and French Literature*, pp. 353–77. Ithaca, NY: Cornell University Press.

Moers, Ellen (1977) *Literary Women: The Great Writers*. Garden City, NY: Anchor Press/Doubleday.

Morris, Adalaide (1981) 'Two Sisters Have I: Emily Dickinson's Vinnie and Susan', *Massachusetts Review*, 22, 2, pp. 323–32.

Morris, Adalaide (1983) ' "The Love of Thee – A Prism Be": Men and Women in the Bridal Poems of Emily Dickinson'. In Susan Juhasz (ed.), *Feminist Critics Read Emily Dickinson*, pp. 98–113. Bloomington, Ind.: Indiana University Press.

Near, Holly (1976) 'Imagine My Surprise', *Imagine My Surprise!* Redwood Records.

Newton, Esther (1984) 'The Mythic Mannish Lesbian: Radclyffe Hall and the New Woman', *Signs*, 9, 4, pp. 557–75.

O'Brien, Sharon (1984) ' "The Thing Not Named": Willa Cather as a Lesbian Writer', *Signs*, 9, 4, pp. 576–99.

Patterson, Rebecca (1951) *The Riddle of Emily Dickinson*. Boston, Mass.: Houghton Mifflin.

Pearson, Carol, and Pope, Katherine (1981) *The Female Hero*. New York: R. R. Bowker.

Pratt, Annis (1981) *Archetypal Patterns in Women's Fiction*, with Barbara White, Andrea Loewenstein and Mary Wyer. Bloomington, Ind.: Indiana University Press.

Radicalesbians (1973) 'The Woman-Identified Woman'. In *Radical Feminism*. New York: Quadrangle/New York Times Book Co.

Rich, Adrienne (1979) 'It Is the Lesbian in Us . . .' In *On Lies, Secrets, and Silence: Selected Prose 1966–1978*, p. 202. New York: Norton.

Rich, Adrienne (1980) 'Compulsory Heterosexuality and Lesbian Existence', *Signs*, 5, 4, pp. 648–9.

Rosenfield, Marthe (1978) 'Linguistic Experimentation in Monique Wittig's *Le Corps lesbien*', unpublished paper presented at MLA.

Rubin, Gayle (1976) Introduction to *A Woman Appeared to Me* by Renée Vivien, pp. iii–xli. Reno, NV: Naiad Press.

Rule, Jane (1975) *Lesbian Images*. Garden City, NY: Doubleday.

Russ, Joanna (1979) 'To Write "Like a Woman": Transformations of Identity in Willa Cather', unpublished paper presented at MLA.

Schuster, Marilyn (1981) 'Strategies for Survival: The Subtle Subversion of Jane Rule', *Feminist Studies*, 7, 3, pp. 431–50.

Secor, Cynthia (1978) '*Ida*, A Great American Novel', *Twentieth Century Literature*, 24, 1, p. 99.

Secor, Cynthia (1979) 'Can We Call Gertrude Stein a Non-Declared Lesbian Writer?' unpublished paper presented at MLA.

Secor, Cynthia (1982a) 'Gertrude Stein: The Complex Force of Her Femininity'. In Kenneth W. Wheeler and Virginia Lee Lussier (eds), *Women, the Arts, and the 1920s in Paris and New York*. New Brunswick, NJ: Transaction Books.

Secor, Cynthia (1982b) 'The Question of Gertrude Stein'. In Fritz Fleischmann (ed.), *American Novelists Revisited: Essays in Feminist Criticism*, pp. 299–310. New York: G. K. Hall.

Shaktini, Namascar (1982) 'Displacing the Phallic Subject: Wittig's Lesbian Writing', *Signs*, 8, 1, p. 44.

Shockley, Ann Allen (1979) 'The Black Lesbian in American Literature: An Overview', *Conditions: Five*, p. 136.

Showalter, Elaine (1975) 'Review Essay: Literary Criticism', *Signs*, 1, 2, pp. 435–60.

Showalter, Elaine (1977) *A Literature of Their Own: British Women Novelists from Brontë to Lessing*. Princeton, NJ: Princeton University Press.

Smith, Barbara (1977) 'Towards a Black Feminist Criticism', *Conditions: Two*, p. 39.

Spacks, Patricia Meyer (1976) *The Female Imagination*. New York: Avon Books.

Stanley, Julia Penelope (1975) 'Uninhabited Angels: Metaphors for Love', *Margins*, 23, p. 8.

Stanley, Julia Penelope (1979) 'The Articulation of Bias: Hoof in Mouth Disease', unpublished paper presented at National Council of Teachers of English Convention.

Stanley, Julia Penelope, and Wolfe, Susan J. (1978) 'Toward a Feminist Aesthetic', *Chrysalis*, 6, p. 66.

Stimpson, Catherine (1977) 'The Mind, the Body and Gertrude Stein', *Critical Inquiry*, 3, 3, pp. 489–506.

Stimpson, Catherine (1981) 'Zero Degree Deviancy: The Lesbian Novel in English', *Critical Inquiry*, 8, 2, p. 364.

Todd, Janet M. (ed.) (1980) *Gender and Literary Voice*. New York: Holmes & Meier.

Vanderlinde, Deirdre (1979) 'Gertrude Stein: Three Lives', unpublished paper presented at MLA.

Vincent, Sybil Korff (n.d.) 'Nothing Fails Like Success: Radclyffe Hall's *The Well of Loneliness*', unpublished paper.

Wenzel, Helene (1981) 'The Text as Body/Politics: An Appreciation of Monique Wittig's Writings in Context', *Feminist Studies*, 7, 2, pp. 264–87.

Wolfe, Susan J. (1978) 'Stylistic Experimentation in Millett, Johnston and Wittig', unpublished paper presented at MLA.

Zimmerman, Bonnie (1976) 'The New Tradition', *Sinister Wisdom*, 2, pp. 34–41.

Zimmerman, Bonnie (1980) '"Daughters of Darkness": Lesbian Vampires', *Jump Cut*, 24–5, pp. 23–4.

Zimmerman, Bonnie (1983) 'Exiting from Patriarchy: The Lesbian Novel of Development'. In Elizabeth Abel, Marianne Hirsch and Elizabeth Langland (eds), *The Voyage In: Fictions of Female Development*. Hanover, NH: University Press of New England, pp. 244–57.

8

Black women writers: taking
a critical perspective
SUSAN WILLIS

Susan Willis singles out three central concerns in writing by black women – community, journey and sexuality – through which they articulate a perspective on black experience in America. Illustrating this perspective by reference to the work of Toni Morrison, Alice Walker, Paule Marshall and Zora Neale Hurston, Willis shows how each writer comes to terms with the past and constructs a critique of the present. She finds that they problematize community, by contrasting the vital bonds uniting their mothers' generation to the erosion of black cultural identity and surrender to commodification which occurred under capitalism. Similarly, they treat journey as a means of self-knowledge through re-entry into collective historical experience, itself defined by the journeys from Africa into slavery, and from the rural south to the urban north. Finally, they see black women's sexual experience as distorted by a male-dominated heterosexuality, burdened by contradiction and ambivalence, but rich in the capacity for joyous sensuality, especially in communities of women.

*

> working
> and recognizing beauty
>   (Alice Walker)

In one of her poems, Alice Walker remarks, 'it is hard for me to write / what everybody already knows' (Walker 1980, p. 48). I think this simple statement defines exactly what black women writers do. And, although we may already know about racial oppression, sexual oppression, class oppression, we may not know how extensive oppression is, how it works and how these modes are interrelated. Black women's writing confronts oppression, in an astute and critical way, on the basis of deeply felt human needs and desires.

The following discussion will offer three ways into black women's writing: community, journey, and sensuality versus sexuality. These are not thematic motifs, but central concerns which focus and modulate the critical perspective black women bring to their work. The discussion will draw upon the more familiar texts by contemporary American black women writers simply because these are the most available. In choosing the familiar, my aim is to avoid having to summarize texts that many readers have not had the opportunity to read, and to develop a theoretical perspective. My hope is that, on the basis of this discussion, readers will want to seek out the newer novels, the in-and-out-of-print novels, so that future critical discussion will draw upon a greater critical awareness and a more comprehensive body of literature.

The community

'In that place, where they tore the nightshade and blackberry patches from their roots to make room for the Medallion City Golf Course, there was once a neighborhood' (Morrison 1980, p. 3). This is how Toni Morrison begins to tell about Sula, her most contradictory and perhaps her most prophetic woman character. Sula, who when confronted by a gang of white boys lopped off the tip of her own finger and scared them all away; Sula, who accidentally killed a child, flung him in the river and watched him sink; Sula, whose lover once gave her the present of a room full of yellow butterflies; Sula, who grew up in the Bottom, went to college, was hated by most and never really fitted in anywhere. Why, with so marvellous a tale to tell, and a character so strong yet enigmatic, does Morrison begin with a place – and a seemingly inconsequential one at that? Why, before we ever meet Sula, must we first read about Shadrack, the First World War casualty who invented National Suicide Day? Why too, before we read about Sula's interesting three-woman household, must we travel all the way to New Orleans, there to discover Nel's grandmother, the Creole prostitute? Why not simply begin with Sula? We might imagine Morrison drawing upon the oldest form of black writing in this country, the slave narrative, and writing along the lines of its formulaic opening, 'Sula was born . . .'

But times have changed the mode of articulation, just as history has changed the mode of black women's struggle for selfhood. If the slave narratives begin by positing the 'I', they do so dramatically to wrest the individual black subject out of anonymity, inferiority and brutal disdain. The 'I' stands against and negates the perception of the black person as indistinguishable from the mass, as slave, as animal. The 'I' proclaims voice, subject, and the right to history and place.

The definition of the subject has undergone significant change with the transition from slavery (which according to dependency economic theory[1] is a capitalist mode of labour control) to more modern forms of capitalism (which include the transition from monopoly capitalism to multinational or commodity capitalism). While traditional society defined the subject in terms of community, advanced capitalism has generated a society in which subjects are isolated individuals. If the struggle against oppression (which involves the struggle for selfhood) is waged for the sake of the individual, it will necessarily end in the isolation of the subject and the fragmentation of social relationships. Morrison's *Sula* – and, to varying degrees, all contemporary novels by black women – resists the tendency in bourgeois fiction to isolate the individual. Sula may be prophetically singular, but it is absolutely impossible to see her as an individual in the bourgeois sense of the term. Neither is she so intimately shaped and bound by her community as to be inseparable from it. She is not the Bottom nor the black middle west in general, but she is their contradiction. She is not the embodiment of black womanhood, but she does articulate many black women's unrealizable possibilities. Sula is a prophet of change[2] on the imaginative and metaphoric plane in the same way that Alice Walker's Meridian embodies change on a political level.

So Morrison begins with the Bottom, which, in the opening line, she refers to as a 'neighborhood' but will later simply call a 'place'. She eschews the word 'community', a term that was central to the civil rights movement for its ability to evoke the many separate neighbourhoods and towns, north and south, but that has now been perhaps too loosely used, too often on the lips of media politicians, black and white.

> These young ones kept talking about the community, but they left the hills to the poor, the old, the stubborn – and the rich white folks. Maybe it hadn't been a community, but it had been a place. Now there weren't any places left, just separate houses with separate televisions and separate telephones and less and less dropping by.
>
> (Morrison 1980, p. 143)

These lines come shortly before the novel's conclusion and reiterate the notion of change depicted in the book's opening line. The Bottom, the place, the community (in the sense of a small organic neighbourhood, daily defined by people's interaction) no longer exists. Rather than the 'dropping by', the visits that meant women would have to share in each other's work and childrearing, now there are 'separate houses' linked by technology to each other and to the larger world. The telephone may facilitate gossip, but it denies women the possibility of sharing domestic toil.

In their writing, black women problematize the notion of community. Rather than paying it lip service, they scrutinize the community as it existed in the past in order to question whether or not and in what form it might exist in the future. Contemporary black women writers tend to associate the existence of community with their mothers' generation, while they see themselves struggling and writing against the devastating influence of late capitalist society, particularly as it erodes the cultural identity of black people, replacing cultural production with commodity consumption. Toni Morrison's Hagar from *Song of Solomon*, although an extreme case, offers the heart-rending example of the impossibility of defining black womanhood according to a mode of consumption evolved in relation to capitalism and white domination. Finding her lover no longer interested in her and believing that there must be something wrong with her personally (a typical response in a society whose basis is individualism), Hagar decides that she must make herself right for him (since, in this society, a heterosexual woman can't find affirmation except in the eyes of a male lover). Of course, 'right', in a racist capitalist society, means 'white'; and capitalism offers a way to whiteness (which, in economic terms, means an approximation of the bourgeois class) through the consumption of commodities and the style these evoke. The great illusion of commodity capitalism is that, while we may not all be white and middle class, we might (if we have a little cash) trade in its signs; and Hagar buys into two pages' worth of brand names:

> She bought a Playtex garter belt, I. Miller No Color hose, Fruit of the Loom panties, and two nylon slips – one white, one pink – one pair of Joyce Fancy Free and one of Con Brio ('Thank heaven for little Joyce heels').
>
> (Morrison 1978, p. 314)

– and on, and on and on.

Paule Marshall is equally condemning in her view of how bourgeois society penetrates and supplants black cultural practice. Her recent novel, *Praise Song for the Widow*, portrays a black woman in her sixties who, after years of secretarial work and as a consequence of her husband's upward mobility, finds herself fulfilling white bourgeois society's dream of leisure: a Caribbean cruise. Her body softened by years of desk work, her stomach stuffed with the rich food prepared for tourists, Avey Johnson begins to reflect upon her past. The novel gradually reveals how the climb up the wage ladder and the move to the suburbs lifted Avey out of culture and community and divorced her from an active sense of self. Avey would never have confronted the hollowness of her life had it not been for the intrusion of black Caribbean culture, which interrupts her cruise.

The Caribbean, for Morrison as well as for Marshall, is often posited as the New World home and culture source for black Americans. Its utopian realization is the maroon encampment which lurks in the impenetrable swamplands and dream visions of Morrison's *Tar Baby*. More often, the antecedent community is defined by an island – Carriacou in Marshall's *Praise Song* – where ritual practice and Creole and African dance are kept alive.

For Alice Walker, the notion of community is related to the rural south, as it also was for the great precursor of contemporary black women writers, Zora Neale Hurston, who in the late 1920s left New York and the Harlem Renaissance, with her college degree (largely in anthropology) in hand, to return to the black southern town of her birth, Eatonville, Florida. From there, she travelled the back roads to towns and mill camps, seeking out and recording the music, the stories, the conversation and the rituals of root workers and hoodoo conjurers – the lifeblood of the traditional black community, which Hurston sensed was already passing out of existence in the late 1920s. In contrast, Alice Walker's notion of community is less defined as a cultural practice. Rather, it tends to embrace the whole of the black south, but is hardly cohesive, having been rent and mutilated by the history of racist domination first through slavery, then sharecropping, and now wage labour. In Walker's opinion, if there is to be a community supportive of people's needs and capable of satisfying their desires, then it will only be realized by understanding the past (this is the lesson of *The Third Life of Grange Copeland*) and grappling with the future (these are the lessons taught by Meridian, who struggles for political transformation; and Celie in *The Color Purple*, who realizes both sexual and economic transformation). As always, Walker's female characters stand in contradictory and prophetic relationships (she might say 'saintly'[3]) to black southern society as it has been formed and deformed under white domination.

Writers of the urban northern black experience tend to define the community in terms of more narrowly focused social units, and it is here that we begin to see what community means once it no longer has a rich infusion of traditional culture. Many contemporary black women writers of the city often see the community in a single city street. This is the case in Gloria Naylor's *The Women of Brewster Place*, whose self-contained neighbourhood is composed of two rows of inward-facing apartment buildings, open at one end and closed at the other by a dead-end street. Similarly, the neighbourhood in Paule Marshall's *Brown Girl, Brownstones* is defined by the intersection of Chauncey Street, where families live; and Fulton Street, the avenue of commerce and night life. But community requires something more than geographic space. As Morrison would see it, the definition of 'place' is necessarily a definition of a group's social practice, their mode of 'dropping in'.

However, not all communal social practices are truly progressive in nature. This is the problematic of Marshall's *Brown Girl, Brownstones*, whose Barbadian Association represents the definition of black community according to a capitalist model, based upon patriotism, college education, exclusionary local business, and individual property ownership. In contrast to this image of black capitalism, the book offers an alternative sense of community in its depiction of domestic space. Although Selina's mother is caught up, like the rest of the immigrant Barbadians, in the obsession to 'buy house', her kitchen provides a very different social model from the one suggested by the Association. Here, neighbour women come to chat and help in the preparation of food, children listen, taking in the Bajan accent in equal doses with the tales. This is community defined by culture and practice. It brings together the generations and spans the distance between Caribbean peasant society and the immigrants' urban environment.

But there is yet another notion of community in the novel, more comprehensive and more contradictory than the mother's kitchen community. This is the household rather than the family, since the latter is torn by the father's desire to return to an idyllic island setting and the mother's headlong drive towards integration with bourgeois society – but the household as it is defined by Selina, who listens to and brings together all the lives of the people living in her mother's house. This notion of community is not only black, but includes Miss Mary, the aged white servant, and her tales of life in the house under its former white owners. It also includes Suggie, a Barbadian maid, who spends her weekends drinking, loving and telling Selina about Barbados. Miss Mary is as different from Suggie as Selina's mother is from her father. What's important about Selina's household community has to do both with its individual components (their histories and class desires), and with the way Selina, out of great curiosity and compassion, brings them all together in the course of her 'dropping in'. The community lives in the telling and the listening. However, in this household only Selina is listening and only she perceives the community. The other inhabitants remain isolated in their rooms, never talking to one another – the mother in the kitchen, Suggie in her room, Miss Mary in the attic and the father in the sun porch. Selina is the rudimentary structural articulation of the sort of communication which, if fully realized, would define a community on a scale larger than the household.

Most often in black women's writing the notion of community is defined by what it is not, rather than what it is. Pilate's household in Song of Solomon, based on non-accumulation and the delights of cottage-style industry, is known throughout Detroit by its address on Not-Doctor Street. The negation of bourgeois social models is the substance of the black community. In Meridian, community is not the university, which, not withstanding its all-woman student body, is still a bastion of élitist tradition, but rather the southern town where Meridian leads the community in facing down a Second World War army tank. In Praise Song for the Widow community is not the comfortable North White Plains suburb, nor the elegant cruise ship, nor even Grenada, whose possibility for community (in this pre-Jewel-Movement version) had been co-opted by tourist high-rise hotels; rather, community is the tiny offshore island whose native-born population yearly return from their mainland jobs to replenish themselves and their culture. And in Sula community is not the real town, Medallion, the white town; but its annex, the Bottom, a not-town.

What the Bottom is tells us something more about the social practices that define black community. Aside from the 'dropping in', it is clear that the Bottom's commercial establishments have little to do with the economics of exchange and a lot to do with the exchange of social life. The Time and a Half Pool Hall, Reba's Grill, Edna Finch's Mellow House and Irene's Palace of Cosmetology – these are not the sites of production, but zones for social reproduction. The Bottom itself is not a workplace but a daily-life place. This is not to say that people in the Bottom do not work. Most work in the real town, and the few whose business is in the Bottom are involved in the production of a social space. The tremendous difference between Medallion and the Bottom, which we perceive racially as the segregation between white and black, and financially as the separation between rich and poor, is in social economics the difference between production and accumulation on the one hand, and reproduction and social exchange on the other. While the white people of Medallion may remember their small-town heritage with fondness, theirs was probably not the experience of community in the fullest sense, simply because the economics of accumulation defines the white small town – no matter how slight its economic importance – as part of a larger network based on inter-regional trade. For the Bottom, the impossibility of being a part of production and trade (except as the supplier of a labour pool) creates a space for the generation of community.

It is striking that nowhere in black women's writing is the workplace ever seen as the basis for community as it might be in proletarian fiction. Factory work, like domestic service before it, and like slavery before that, is shown to be yet another alienating mode of labour. Nowhere is this more evident than in *Brown Girl, Brownstones*, where a factory job means just as many hours away from home as domestic service, and quicker integration into property ownership and bourgeois alienation. When, at the end of *The Color Purple*, Celie finds a way of bringing her workplace and living space together, she defines an alternative economic basis for community. We may find the production of customized pants a fanciful, updated version of cottage industry, hardly a viable prescription for the great number of black people who, whether employed or unemployed, have suffered the alienation associated with wage labour under capitalism. Rather than a universal solution, Walker's portrayal of Celie might be seen as emblematic of the sort of social imagination that all people must begin to practise if community is to be reinvented under late capitalist economics.

The journey

Ever since Zora Neale Hurston hit the back roads in her chevvy, gathering up the folk tradition and defining herself in relation to that tradition and her project as a writer, journey has been central to black women writers. Even before Zora Neale, journey had given structure and pattern to the slave narratives, as escaped slaves recounted the transformation in both condition and consciousness that the journey produced in their lives and then came to signify in their narrations. And, long before that, journey meant Middle Passage, the cataclysmic mediation between African tribal society and plantation slavery. Yet even here, even as journey led to the horrors of slavery, it also stirred the consciousness, propelling newly arrived Africans to ponder the radical discontinuity between their lives in Africa and their enslavement. This too can be seen in the few extant slave narratives produced by Africans. The journey into slavery, the journey into freedom, and finally the journey made by many contemporary black women writers – the journey back into history, reversing the migration of Afro-Americans from south to north – each of these journeys, no matter how arduous, has generated a growth in consciousness. Each of these journeys, no matter how perilous to the self, has provided a means for defining the self. This most recent form of journey – whether it is real and accompanied by the dust or the salt spray of Hurston's and Marshall's journeys to the south and to the Caribbean, or whether it is in the spirit of the writer's imagination as in Morrison's *Song of Solomon* – enacts the retrieval of the collective past.

Many critics commenting upon writing by black women have remarked upon the frequency of the journey in their work.[4] Calling it motif, theme or literary strategy, the criticism groups this along with other common and recurrent themes in the attempt to define a black women's aesthetic. What's wrong with such a formula is its shortsightedness. Black women's writing is not a mere collection of motifs and strategies, but a mode of discourse which enables a critical perspective upon the past, the present and sometimes into an emerging future. Journey in the novels by black women is not just a structuring device upon which the author might conveniently string the incidents of plot. Rather, the notion of travelling through space is integral to the unfolding of history and the development of the individual's consciousness with regard to the past. The voyage over geographic space is an expanded metaphor for the process of one person's coming to know who she is – not as an individual, but as a subject who gathers up the collective experience of black Americans; and who then, in writing about that experience, gives shape and substance to the self in history.

In writing *The Third Life of Grange Copeland*, Alice Walker achieves a vision of history equal to Diego Rivera's great National Palace mural. Both record the dialectic of history in the Americas through the representation of the economic modes that have defined production and culture in this hemisphere. While Diego's visual narrative extends back to the moment of Conquest, Walker's literary text allows us to imagine plantation slavery by extrapolation out of Grange Copeland's experience as a sharecropper. While Diego's vision culminates in a Marx-inspired revolution, Walker's final vision is more modest but perhaps just as radical. Her conclusion projects a feminist revision of the past which sets the book upon the brink of a not yet knowable future. The novel scrutinizes three economic modes: sharecropping, wage labour (as Grange journeys to the north) and something like the rural homestead, which Grange brings into being upon his return to the south when he buys a small farm and experiences, with the help of his granddaughter, the pleasures of rural self-sufficiency. In many ways, this is a rural precursor of the cottage-industry solution Walker finds at the end of *The Color Purple*.

Sharecropping, wage labour and rural self-sufficiency – these are the broad stages of history's dialectic, whose lived experience has been marked by exploitation, violence and brutality. Walker's portrayal of history, defined by Grange's movement through geographical space, examines male domination as it has been influenced by racism and by the various economic modes. The possibility of Grange's liberation from the ruthlessness of sharecropping and the false promises of wage labour is shown to be based upon the rape of women – their money, their labour and their sex; and upon the murder of women – the mutilation of their spirit and imagination, and the assassination of their potential and bodies. If Grange achieves a transformation in his economic situation, he does so because women created the necessary material conditions for his liberation. If he finally reaches a deep and comprehensive understanding of himself, his consciousness-raising is equal to his realization of the toll paid by women. Although Grange Copeland makes the journey and, in so doing, defines himself in relation to Afro-American history, he who has accumulated the dead possibilities of women cannot bring the future into being. Rather, he bequeathes the journey and the lessons he learned to his granddaughter, Ruth, who at the end of the novel, with the civil rights movement growing around her, becomes the new defining figure of history. In shifting to a female protagonist, Walker gathers up the generations of brutalized women, demanding that the reader reconstruct history – not upon Grange's journey through time, space and consciousness which has constituted the novel up to this point, but upon the non-journeys of Ruth's mother, grandmother and all the other women who gave Grange the possibility for progress. Ruth's story will be the affirmation of all the futures these women never realized – never even hoped to dream.

The matrilineal re-evaluation of history is the substance of Paule Marshall's *Praise Song for the Widow*. Here, too, the vision of history and the individual's process of coming to consciousness is accomplished through journey. Again the movement into and out of different space/time frames, whether in dream or in the novel's real world, offers a means for conceptualizing different modes of production. The novel's present is defined by wage labour, the coming into being of the black bourgeoisie. Its protagonist, Avey Johnson, is lifted out of the present and made to confront the southern plantation and accept it as part of her heritage when, during a Caribbean cruise, she dreams of her great aunt Cuney, a Sea Islander whose stories summon up images of slavery. The end-point of Avey's voyage is, however, not the plantation, but the island of Carriacou, where she discovers the New World source of her black culture.

Previous to her voyage, Avey's life had been narrowly defined by her husband's upward mobility and their move to the suburbs, which resulted in the erosion of their black cultural heritage. Avey's journey is a process both of self-discovery and cultural retrieval. Contrasted with the vital collective experience of dance and the songs of the African nations, Avey's North White Plans home – its wood panelling, her silver and china – offers little more than décor and display for a museum of bourgeois culture. But, for Avey, the process of discovery is neither instantaneous nor painless. Journey, as Marshall portrays it, is a soul-purging, body-rending and highly physical means to understanding. Only thus can the self emerge as an active subject prepared to redefine the future. While we might take Avey's decision to transform her great-aunt's home into a summer camp for wayward city kids as far less radical than Meridian's civil disobedience and acts of confrontation, none the less both characters and their creators suggest that commitment to the future and the ability to conceive of future visions can only be achieved through struggle – and struggle is a violent and draining experience.

Avey's ability to apprehend critically the way her life had been dominated by her husband's demands and desires, to step outside the sphere of his influence (which continued to shape her life long after his death), and then to acquire a feminist perspective on history, is the ground and goal of her first struggle. Rather than thrashing out the past with her husband (which, while confronting male domination, would have been conditioned by their shared history of appeasement and compromise), Marshall gives Avey's struggle a specifically feminist orientation when she portrays her in a tooth-and-nail struggle with the ghost of her great-aunt. Confronted by the old woman in a dream, Avey lashes out at Cuney, beats at her breasts, begs for release – begs to put aside her memory of her great-aunt and her responsibility to the past. Waking the next morning to bruises and aching muscles, Avey has taken the first arduous step upon her journey into consciousness.

The rest of her trip is no less painful. Overfed on commodities, her body and her sensuality trapped in the elastic confines of a girdle, Avey's journey to Carriacou involves both a stripping away of the accoutrements of commodity culture – her watch, her purse and stylish clothes – and an internal purge as well. A victim of the most violent seasickness, Avey retches until she can retch no more; undergoes violent spasms of diarrhoea; and, half fainting, comes to see her individual suffering in terms of the collective suffering of black people in Middle Passage:

> she had the impression as her mind flickered on briefly of other bodies lying crowded in with her in the hot, airless dark. A multitude it felt like lay packed around her in the filth and stench of themselves, just as she was. Their moans, rising and falling with each rise and plunge of the schooner, enlarged upon the one filling her head. Their suffering – the depth of it, the weight of it in the cramped space – made hers of no consequence.
>
> (Marshall 1983, p. 209)

Marshall occasionally uses metaphoric images such as

Avey's glimpse into the hold of a slave ship to enact the recovery of the collective past. But her project involves more than rendering history tangible, and is aimed precisely at retrieving the cultural heritage. As Avey ponders her life with her husband, she summons up the times they listened and danced to blues recordings in their New York tenement. She comes to see their progress up and out of poverty in direct proportion to the waning importance of black poetry and music in their lives. Later her dream encounter with her great-aunt calls to mind the Sea Island ring-shouts she witnessed as a child during her summertime visits with her aunt. Both the blues music she knew as an adult and the ring-shouts of her childhood are finally seen as partialities, parts of a larger cultural tapestry, whose centre – which gives meaning to all its separate and partial realizations – is in the Caribbean, where ritual practice and the body of African tribal songs are kept alive.

If it appears that many of the characters in black women's fiction can't do or think anything without embarking upon a journey, then this is certainly the case for Toni Morrison's Milkman in *Song of Solomon*. Frozen in the dead weight of his privileged and self-satisfying existence (which, like Alice Walker's Grange Copeland, has been accomplished upon the death of many women's aspirations), Milkman is a young black man going nowhere and incapable of making himself or anyone else happy. The journey he undertakes, defined nominally as a quest for gold, is in reality a search for self. Leaving Detroit, which represents the present defined by class society and race hatred, Milkman journeys south and into the past. Finally arriving in Shalimar, West Virginia, where he will eventually solve the riddle of the song of Solomon and, in so doing, put together his own genealogy, Milkman is first of all struck by the fact that women there had nothing in their hands. 'No pocketbook, no change purse, no wallet, no keys, no small paper bag, no comb, no handkerchief. They carried nothing' (Morrison 1978, p. 262). We, like Milkman, are made to see what strange appendages handbags are – and by extension how alienating commodity culture is. Milkman's journey enables the demystification of the late capitalist society he previously saw as 'normal'. During the course of the journey, Milkman comes to experience more traditional modes of social behaviour, based on reciprocity, barter and self-sufficiency. These prepare him for his final integration with his African heritage and his metaphoric leap to freedom.

While Milkman's 'flight' unites the novel's themes and metaphors and leaves the reader with a strong and lasting impression, this is not his most profound accomplishment during the course of the journey. Rather, his ability to have a reciprocal, non-sexist love relationship with a woman suggests the basis for radical social transformation:

> She put salve on his face. He washed her hair. She sprinkled talcum on his feet. He straddled her behind and massaged her back. She put witch hazel on his swollen neck. He made up the bed. She gave him gumbo to eat. He washed the dishes. She washed his clothes and hung them out to dry. He scoured her tub. She ironed his shirt and pants. He gave her fifty dollars. She kissed his mouth. He touched her face. She said please come back. He said I'll see you tonight.
>
> (Morrison 1978, pp. 288–9)

The fact that Sweet is a prostitute and Milkman gives her fifty dollars is secondary to the fact that he responds to each of her caring gestures in equal and reciprocal fashion. This is not the Milkman who so disdained Hagar's love that she became obsessively possessive, or who occasioned his sister's angry rebuke:

> You are a sad, pitiful, stupid, selfish, hateful man. I hope your little hog's gut stands you in good stead, and that you take good care of it, because you don't have anything else . . . you have pissed your last in this house.
>
> (Morrison 1978, p. 218)

While the journey has enabled Milkman to put aside the practice of male sexual domination, it has also given him the means for appreciating the uniqueness of his aunt Pilate's house. As a child he knew the pleasures of her household and way of life, but he had no way to articulate what these signified. Only by experiencing traditional small-town society has he gained a means by which to evaluate Pilate's house, not that it represents the simple transplantation of the small town into the big city, but that it includes certain of the small town's defining characteristics:

She had no electricity because she would not pay for the service. Nor for gas. At night she and her daughter lit the house with candles and kerosene lamps; they warmed themselves and cooked with wood and coal, pumped kitchen water into a dry sink through a pipeline from a well and lived pretty much as though progress was a word that meant walking a little farther on down the road.

(Morrison 1978, p. 27)

No meal was ever planned or balanced or served. Nor was there any gathering at the table. Pilate might bake hot bread and each one of them would eat it with butter whenever she felt like it. Or there might be grapes, left over from the winemaking, or peaches for days on end. . . . They ate what they had or came across or had a craving for. Profits from their wine-selling evaporated like sea water in a hot wind – going for junk jewelry for Hagar, Reba's gifts to men, and he didn't know what all.

(Morrison 1978, p. 29)

Pilate's household, based upon spontaneity, shared activity and non-accumulation, represents a utopian reworking of the small-town principle with none of the latter's narrowminded attitudes or the poverty generated by the town's unequal and dependent relationship to the city. None of this would have been apparent had we – or Milkman – been permitted only the rigidly dichotomized opposition between Pilate's utopia and her brother's bourgeois capitalism which structures the novel's opening. But, because the terrain of the journey is history, both social formations are recast in relation to their historical evolution.

Sensuality and sexuality

Black women write against the erosion and the repression of female sexuality as it is channelled by male desire and stifled by domestic life. Recall Milkman's mother, Ruth, in *Song of Solomon*, as she has been defined by her father's overprotection and her husband's rejection. Experience with her the dead air of her entombing domestic space and the empty longing of her passion, which, finding no response in her husband, caused her to nurse her child for six years, substituting the sensual pleasure of his mouth at her breast for the sexual gratification of penetration and orgasm.

Toni Morrison's depiction of Ruth is but one example in a body of literature profoundly moved and angered by the sexual deformation and repression of women. Remember the widow Avey Johnson in Paule Marshall's *Praise Song*. Feel the numbness in her thighs. How long has her flesh felt the airless pinch of a girdle? When was the last time she felt her husband's warm caress? Certainly long before he died he was already treating sex and her body as something mechanical. Feel, then, with Avey, the warm and wonderous delight when, awaking on Carriacou, she is bathed and massaged by her hostess. Recognize, with her, her initial timidity and gradual yielding up to pleasure. Realize, along with Avey, the newly discovered zones of delight, and how simple, how natural sensual pleasure is; and then be appalled along with Avey at the years of fastidious denial – the decades of entombment.

Toni Morrison, in *The Bluest Eye*, refers to sensual pleasure as 'funk'. Marvelling at the 'thin brown girls who have looked long at hollyhocks in the backyards of Meridian, Mobile, Aiken and Baton Rouge' (Morrison 1972, p. 67), she traces their development through 'land grant colleges and normal schools' in preparation for 'white man's work' (p. 68) and a black man's domestic needs. Theirs is a cautious and careful process of growing up and out of adolescent sensuality and into womanly repression: their project is 'to get rid of the funkiness. The dreadful funkiness of passion, the funkiness of nature, the funkiness of the wide range of human emotions' (p. 68).

Sex, finally, is something that such a woman's body does 'sparingly and partially' (p. 69). Alienated from her own body and more closely attuned to her hair curlers, she hopes 'that she will remain dry between her legs – she hates the glucking sound they make when she is moist' (p. 69). And, while she only vaguely participates in intercourse, such a woman is still defined by the dictates of her husband's desire. Rather than denying him, 'when she senses some spasm about to grip him, she will make rapid movements with her hips, press her fingernails into his back, suck in her breath, and pretend she is having an orgasm' (p. 69).

For these black women, as for Ruth Dead and Avey Johnson,

the repression of sexuality is related to their assimilation into the bourgeois class, a phenomenon both Morrison and Marshall portray as the commodification of experience. What takes the place of spontaneity and caresses, and what fills in the dreadful gap created between women and men in non-reciprocal heterosexual relationships, are the commodities – the 'orange-colored Lifebuoy soap', 'the Cashmere Bouquet talc', 'The little Joyce heels'; and the more traditional class-defined objects – 'the special crystal', the 'silverplate – all eighty pieces – in its felt-lined case' and the 'great oval-shaped table' (Marshall 1983, p. 26).

But entrée into the bourgeois class only partially explains the deformation of black women's sexuality. Sexual repression is also related to race hatred in a class society. Polly Breedlove in *The Bluest Eye* is a battered woman, beaten down in body and soul, crippled in spirit, her emotional and physical death summarized in the word 'ugly'. But she was not always like that:

> Pauline was leaning idly on the fence, her arms resting on the crossrail between the pickets. She had just put down some biscuit dough and was cleaning the flour from under her nails. Behind her at some distance she heard whistling. One of these rapid, high-tone riffs that black boys make up as they go while sweeping, shoveling, or just walking along. A kind of city-street music where laughter belies anxiety, and joy is as short and straight as the blade of a pocketknife. She listened carefully to the music and let it pull her lips into a smile. The whistling got louder, and still she did not turn around, for she wanted it to last. While smiling to herself and holding fast to the break in somber thoughts, she felt something tickling her foot. She laughed aloud and turned to see. The whistler was bending down tickling her broken foot and kissing her leg. She could not stop her laughter – not until he looked up at her and she saw the Kentucky sun drenching the yellow, heavy-lidded eyes of Cholly Breedlove.
>
> (Morrison 1972, p. 91)

Her stance, 'leaning idly on the fence', her lips pulled into a smile by the music, suggest a languorous sensuality. This is the Polly Breedlove who once knew how to delight in colour – in the june-bug green and the trickle-down-your-legs-deep-berry-purple colour and sensuality she would later recall and experience only as fragments when the pleasure of orgasm briefly restores her to the plenitude of childhood sensuality:

> I begin to feel those little bits of color floating up into me – deep in me. That streak of green from the june-bug light, the purple from the berries trickling along my thighs, Mama's lemonade yellow runs sweet in me. Then I feel like I'm laughing between my legs, and the laughing gets all mixed up with the colors, and I'm afraid I'll come, and afraid I won't. But I know I will. And I do. And it be rainbow all inside.
>
> (Morrison 1972, pp. 103–4)

As in *Song of Solomon*, where Pilate's only remembrance of her mother is the colour of her ribbons, so, too, for Polly Breedlove, colour is the medium for gathering up all significant past experience, including activities associated with her specific childhood and the rural south in general. Colour is here not just a visual perception, but a deeply physical experience. In a number of novels by black women writers, colour is the code for describing a woman's capability of achieving sensual gratification. This is the case in *The Color Purple* for Celie, whose growing awareness of her own body as a source of pleasure coincides with her ability to remark upon colours and how they affect her.

When Polly first meets her future husband, it is her passivity that betrays the basis for the deformation of her sensuality that we come to associate with her life as wife and mother. For Polly, pleasure is something bestowed by someone else, and therefore determined in its time, place and duration by the man. This puts Polly in a position of dependency, wanting the delight of *his* whistling, *his* tickling and finally *his* intercourse 'to last'. It is not heterosexuality *per se* that eventually narrows Polly's experience of gratification, but heterosexuality as it has been defined by male control.

The way Polly later experiences sex is determined by the terms under which she first met Cholly, when she is defined as the receiver of his provocation to pleasure rather than an initiator in her own right. This is how she describes her desire:

> I know he wants me to come first. But I can't. Not until he does. Not until I feel him loving me. Just me. Sinking into me. Not until I know that my flesh is all that be on his mind. That

he couldn't stop if he had to. That he would rather die than
take his thing out of me. Of me. Not until he has let go of all he
has, and give it to me. To me. To me. When he does, I feel a
power. I be strong, I be pretty, I be young.

(Morrison 1972, p. 103)

Polly's possessiveness ('loving me. Just me') is her response to
seeing her pleasure as something under Cholly's control. She
attributes to Cholly the power of defining her possibilities: he
has the 'power' to make her 'strong', 'pretty' and 'young'. In a
sense, and in accordance with what the book is all about, the
unspoken connection is that to be strong, pretty and young is to
be white – not in a specifically racial sense, but in the sense that
in this society achievements and aspirations are class privileges
that coincide with whiteness.

It becomes clear in the novel that Polly's desire and her
sexuality are not hers alone to define, but are grounded in a
traumatic incident which, while it did not include her personally, would shape her husband's entire relationship to her. The
incident I am referring to – the interruption of his first act of
intercourse by a flashlight's probing beam – marked Cholly's
initiation into sex and is the basis for the novel's definition of
sexuality in terms of racial oppression. The ray of white light
cast into Cholly's backside is a metonym for the white hunters
who hold the flashlight and who, as voyeurs, symbolize the
plantation overseer, who 'screw' Cholly, inferiorizing his heterosexual manhood and 'screwing him up' for life. Cholly's
response is hatred, aimed not at the white men, but at the black
face and kinky hair of the girl under his body. This incident
suggests the foundation of black male misogyny, whose historical basis is white male domination and the lynch mob. In
capitalist society, where race is the means by which the white
bourgeoisie defines its domination, the hatred of the oppressed
class is deflected away from the source of domination and
channelled upon those in the most inferior position: black
women.

The connection of desire and hatred is a contradiction generated by the male domination of heterosexual relationships.
Black women's fiction grapples with this contradiction not only
as it shapes adult heterosexual relationships, but also as it
pertains to women's feelings towards their children and mother-

ing. Recall the fate of Wile Chile in Alice Walker's *Meridian*, herself scarcely an adolescent and grossly pregnant, struck down by a truck, child-mother and unborn babe killed. Recall in the same book the brutal murder of the young child Camara and Meridian's own elective abortion, not to mention the child she gave away in order to attend college. We cannot help but be struck by the deep ambivalence attached to childbearing and children in the fiction written by black women.

There is a single, brief but complex incident in Toni Morrison's *Sula*, which articulates the love–hate contradiction and how it bears upon the definition of a black woman's sexuality. Sula who is 12 at the time, is just on her way out of the house to spend the day at the river with her bosom buddy, Nel. Passing by the kitchen, she overhears her mother discussing children with some neighbour women. Her mother's words are fatal: 'You love her, like I love Sula. I just don't like her. That's the difference' (Morrison 1980, p. 49).

Ambivalence is the possibility of separating liking from loving. It is the way women experience contradiction in heterosexual relationships – precisely because these are male-determined in a society which valorizes maleness. And, as children are for the most part born of heterosexual relationships, they are the living embodiments of the contradictions that have shaped their mother's life possibilities and sexuality. Nowhere is this more clear than when Meridian, caressing and marvelling upon her dear black baby, fantasizes scratching and tearing his flesh with her fingernails. The love and hate are one, just as her desire for his future is one with the recognition that in this society he is but one more black body for the labour pool.

This is the contradiction Nel and Sula confront when, out of the house and away from the mother's words and influence, they experience the deep sensuality of their companionship. 'They ran in the sunlight, creating their own breeze, which pressed their dresses into their damp skin' (Morrison 1980, p. 49). They lie in the grass, feeling the points of contact between the ground and their adolescent bodies, 'their small breasts just now beginning to create some pleasant discomfort when they were lying on their stomachs' (p. 49). The scene is very like the one described in *Brown Girl, Brownstones*, when Selina and her girlhood friend cut themselves free of mothers and domestic enclosure to spend the day in the park, similarly passing the time poking at the grass and talking about sex. I have been making a distinction between sensuality and sexuality which these two literary examples will help clarify. The heightened sensual perception and the range of sensual gratification experienced by Nel and Sula, Selina and her friend, depicted in the intimate relationship between their bodies and nature and between themselves, will soon be lost as adult sexuality channels their desire towards purely sexual gratification. In her much-debated essay on *Sula*, Barbara Smith sees in the childhood relationship between Nel and Sula a primary expression of Sula's lesbianism, which as an adult she is not able to fully realize.[5] Although Smith's essay is aimed at unfolding the radical nature of Morrison's novel, I think she errs in couching her argument solely in terms of sexuality and in assimilating all of Sula's radical behaviour to an innate but thwarted lesbianism. Sula is an extremely political figure whose passionate articulation of contradiction casts a critical perspective upon all forms of domination.

I want to continue with Sula's day at the river, to show how Morrison brings contradiction to light. While Nel and Sula lie in the grass, a little boy comes along, about 3 or 4 years old; his name is Chicken Little. After helping him up and down a tree, Sula beings to twirl him around and around, high in the air, until her hands give way, propelling Chicken Little into the river, where he sinks from sight. The drowning of Chicken Little enacts the same ambivalence Sula is made to feel about herself as the result of her mother's fatal words – the same ambivalence Meridian feels towards her babe-in-arms. Sula is 12 years old; and, in that precarious zone called adolescence, she is able to identify with both the child and the mother. Morrison's portrayal of Sula's accidental murder of Chicken Little ought to be read in the light of Alice Walker's depiction of Meridian's decision to terminate a pregnancy. Both the accidental and the purposeful are acts fraught with the contradictions that heterosexuality and childrearing bestow on women. Recall that Sula's day at the river is bracketed on one side by her mother's cutting definition of the contradiction between loving and liking, and on the other by Shadrack's equally fatal word, 'Always', which he whispers to Sula soon after she kills Chicken

Little. If we put aside for a moment the fact that Shadrack is a lunatic and that he meant his word to be of solace, and instead see him in his structural relationship to Sula as an adult male, then his single word voices the imprisonment that adult female heterosexuality means for women in this society, and for black women in particular.

Sula's life is a challenge to male-dominated heterosexual roles for women. Only if we see her struggling within and against heterosexuality can we realize the full impact of her critical perspective and the potential of her challenge. Sula is an affront to the way men have traditionally defined heterosexual women as either mothers or whores. The mother in the novel is Helen, Nel's mother, whose sexuality was determined by her husband's long absences and sublimated into her care for her daughter. The prostitute in the novel is Nel's Creole grandmother, whose clothes, perfume and patois were equally determined by and responsive to male desire. Nel, in her adult life, lives out her mother's model. Abandoned by her husband, she recognizes that a life devoted to rearing her children will be as devoid of pleasure as her relationship to her husband probably was, except that his presence and demands made it impossible for her to question the lack of gratification. Sula's challenge to Nel is not that she specifically adopt the lesbian alternative, but that she bring the terms of their childhood relationship into the adult world – reinvent their girlhood exuberance, fearlessness, supportiveness and delight. Otherwise – and this is what finally happens to Nel and Sula – the development of adult female sexuality, because it develops under male domination, drives a wedge between women, which in their sensual but pre-sexual girlhood did not exist.

Sula's challenge couldn't be more explicit or more direct. In having sex with Nel's husband, she strikes at the way male domination controls women's freedom and mobility, condemning them to the anguish of possessive love. First, when as an adolescent Sula chases off a gang of white boys by cutting off the tip of her own finger to dramatize her refusal of racially motivated male domination; and then, as an adult, when she steals Nel's husband to reveal how heterosexual, nuclear family life stifles women's aspirations, Sula's challenge has been to suggest the possibility of creating a female equivalent to male bonding.

Sula's challenge is, finally, directed to the reader – to imagine Sula and Nel's adolescent twosome evolved into adulthood. The real challenge, of course, would be for them to bond as adult heterosexual women. Such a relationship would avoid the exclusionary and inferiorizing tendencies associated with male bonding. Nor would it fall prey to separatism, whose power to undermine and destroy male sexual domination is checked by the very nature of separatism. The embryo of such a feminist union exists in Nel and Sula's childhood companionship. And, while they never bring it to fruition as adults, Nel, at the end of the novel, does finally come to recognize the terms of Sula's challenge when she remarks:

> 'All that time, all that time, I thought I was missing Jude.'
> And the loss pressed down on her chest and came up into her throat. 'We was girls together,' she said as though explaining something. 'O Lord, Sula,' she cried, 'girl, girl, girlgirlgirl.'
> (Morrison 1980, p. 149)

Nel's reiterating cry captures the grief of an opportunity missed. Its profound effect is to cause the reader to reflect back upon the novel, questioning: will I in my lifetime lose such a chance, or will I, as a heterosexual woman, accept Sula's challenge?

Utopian visions

While Sula is the halcyon figure of challenge, there is, at the heart of the novel, an alternative vision which Sula does not perpetuate, but which nevertheless nurtured her and made it possible for her to articulate a radical perspective on heterosexuality. I am referring to the three-woman household, comprised of Sula's grandmother, Eva Peace; her mother, Hannah; and Sula herself. The three-woman household is a living arrangement that crops up throughout Morrison's writing to suggest an alternative and utopian possibility for redefining the space and the relationships associated with social reproduction. In *The Bluest Eye* the three-woman household is the upstairs apartment belonging to three prostitutes, where Pecola often goes for refuge and companionship. Here, in sharp contrast to the grim hostility and oppression of her mother's house, Pecola finds three heterosexual women who do not live with men or in families, who share chores, food and conversation, who do not work as domestics, but who make money off men. The point is not whether Morrison suggests prostitution as a viable alternative for women, but how the living arrangements defined by prostitution give rise to a non-nuclear, non-sexist community.

In *Song of Solomon* the three-woman household finds its utopian realization in Pilate's house, and its dystopian cancellation in the house Ruth shares with Macon Dead. Aside from the fact that both houses are comprised of women and defined upon different economic models (accumulation versus non-accumulation), Ruth's house fails to bring the feminist principle into being. It represents, instead, male domination in the form of Macon's ruthless authority and his son's petulant egotism. In contrast, Pilate's household, again composed of three heterosexual women (although Pilate has transcended the need for sex), negates male domination simply because, while the women may have relationships with men, men do not live in or define the space and economy of the household.

Eva Peace's three-woman household offers perhaps the most fully evolved vision of utopian social relationships in that the basic three-woman core is expanded by the inclusion of numerous unofficially adopted children and boarders – both singles and couples. Eva's house itself is a *bricolage* of stairways, rooms and porches, as befits its ever-changing social make-up. It stands in sharp contrast to the boxed-in atmosphere and shape of the nuclear family, which is defined by male domination, whether it be based upon a heterosexual couple or a single abandoned mother (as was Eva's lot at the beginning of the book). In the nuclear family, male domination is enacted either by the actual presence of a man (husband or father) or, in a large sense, by the notion of male sexual and economic domination which defines all women as ultimately dependent.

In all its versions, whether its composition is familial or non-familial, the three-woman household represents a challenge to bourgeois living arrangements and the economics of capitalism. This is particularly the case for Eva Peace, who, abandoned by her husband, with three children, and no job or food, allows her leg to be severed by a locomotive in order to collect damages from the railroad company. Eva's bold act of self-mutilation, although done out of desperation, is neither self-destructive nor despairing. Rather it represents her manipulation of corporate capitalism.

Finally, the most important aspect of the three-women household is that it allows women a space outside male domination to exercise heterosexuality. None of the households represents separatist politics (either sexual or economic). But, like the challenging figure of Sula, they are in dynamic involvement with and critical opposition to the larger system in which they occur. These are the characters and the visions that define black women's writing as a critical perspective upon the forms of oppression generated by capitalism.

Notes

1 Dependency economic theory originates with the work of André Gunder Frank (see *Capitalism and Underdevelopment in Latin America* (New York: Monthly Review Press, 1969)), and has been greatly elaborated by Immanuel Wallerstein, whose definition of the global capitalist system is based upon the distinction between core, semi-periphery and periphery. To date, little has been done towards the application of dependency theory to literary and cultural criticism. My article on Faulkner's 'The Bear' represents a step in this direction (see 'Aesthetics of the Rural Slum', *Social Text*, 2 (1979)).

2 I see Pecola in *The Bluest Eye* as a prophet denied. Like Sula, she is the focal point of deep contradiction; but, unlike Sula, she (her spirit and her body) is beaten down. The end of the novel finds Pecola chanting the prophecy of despair – locked in a perpetual conversation with herself, unable to reach out to another or to be touched by anyone.

3 In speaking of her mother's and grandmother's eras, Alice Walker describes black women as 'creatures so abused and mutilated in body, so dimmed and confused by pain, that they considered themselves unworthy even of hope'. In the selfless abstractions their bodies became to the men who used them, they became more than 'sexual objects', more even than mere women: they became 'Saints'.

Walker goes on to say: 'these grandmothers and mothers of ours were not Saints, but Artists; driven to a numb and bleeding madness by the springs of creativity in them for which there was no release' (Walker 1983, pp. 232–3).

4 Deborah E. McDowell, 'New Directions for Black Feminist Criticism', *Black American Literature Forum* (Winter 1980), pp. 153–9.

5 Barbara Smith, 'Towards a Black Feminist Criticism', *Conditions: Two*, 1 (October 1977), p. 27.

References

Bell, Roseann P., Parker, Bettye J., and Guy-Sheftall, Beverly (eds) (1979) *Sturdy Black Bridges*. New York: Doubleday.

Davis, Angela (1981) *Women, Race and Class*. New York: Random House.

Evans, Mari (ed.) (1984) *Black Women Writers*. New York: Doubleday.

Gates, Henry Louis, Jr (ed.) (1984) *Black Literature and Literary Theory*. London: Methuen.

Hooks, Bell (1982) *Aint I a Woman*. Boston, Mass.: South End Press.

Hull, Gloria T., Scott, Patricia Bell, and Smith, Barbara (eds) (1982) *All the Women are White, All the Blacks are Men, But Some of us are Brave: Black Women's Studies*. Old Westbury, NY: Feminist Press.

Lerner, Gerda (1972) *Black Women in White America*. New York: Random House.

Lorde, Audre (1984) *Sister Outsider*. New York: Crossing Press.

Marshall, Paule (1983) *Praise Song for the Widow*. New York: Putnam's.

Moraga, Cherríe, and Anzaldúa, Gloria (eds) (1981) *This Bridge Called My Back: Writings by Radical Women of Color*. Watertown, Mass.: Persephone Press.

Morrison, Toni (1972) *The Bluest Eye*. New York: Simon & Schuster.

Morrison, Toni (1978) *Song of Solomon*. New York: New American Library.

Morrison, Toni (1980) *Sula*. New York: Bantam.

Smith, Barbara (ed.) (1983) *Home Girls*. New York: Kitchen Table, Women of Color Press.

Snitow, Ann, Stansell, Christine, and Thompson, Sharon (eds) (1983) *Powers of Desire*. New York: Monthly Review Press.

Walker, Alice (1980) *Good Night Willie Lee, I'll See You in the Morning*. New York: Dial Press.

Walker, Alice (1983) *In Search of our Mothers' Gardens*. New York: Harcourt Brace Jovanovich.

9
Notorious signs, feminist criticism and literary tradition
ADRIENNE MUNICH

Adrienne Munich argues that the male-authored works of the literary canon are properly as much the object of feminist criticism as is women's writing. Turning to the traditional reading of Genesis as a myth of male dominance – in particular, dominance by means of language – she shows how tropes of male authority serve to deny the presence and power of women. In a feminist reading of an episode from *Don Quixote*, she deconstructs the ways in which literature mythologizes woman and man's desire for woman. Finally, she suggests that critical discourse, in defending against texts which don't wholly substantiate patriarchal definitions of gender, is often more misogynistic than the texts themselves.

*

According to Scripture's second (but earlier) account of creation, Adam was the first philologist, interpretative as well as onomastic: 'the Lord God formed every beast of the field and every fowl of the air, and brought them unto the man to see what he would call them; and whatsoever the man called every living creature, that was the name thereof' (Genesis 2:19). By naming creation, he possessed for himself language's power. To validate further his authority and to avoid possible controversy, he performed these acts before Eve was created.

Many critics, including feminist ones, find in this fable a paradigm for male dominance over language. For some, such as

Mary Daly, woman has apparently allowed man to steal from her the power to shape language:

> women have had the power of *naming* stolen from us. We have not been free to use our own power to name ourselves, the world, or God. The old naming was not the product of dialogue – a fact inadvertently admitted in the Genesis story of Adam's naming the animals and the woman. Women are now realizing that the universal imposing of names by men has been false because partial. That is, inadequate words have been taken as adequate.   (Daly 1973, p. 8)

Daly believes that the text 'inadvertently' admits the truth about gender and names, as if Scripture's claim were a Freudian slip rather than being a masculinist assertion, a canny political statement, and a myth used to impose male ownership upon a complex realm of human experience. On the basis of the strong scriptural assertion, Daly hands over language to the patriarchy. Then, because she believes the Bible's claim, she imagines a universal male monopoly over names; she believes that words themselves and not this biblical text are inadequate.

Particularly for the French feminists, 'men's' language is not simply inadequate because incomplete; rather, they claim that a patriarchal monopoly upon naming has left no voice whatever for women. Hélène Cixous, Luce Irigaray and Marguerite Duras (Marks and Courtivron 1980), among others, ascribe a male gender to language and find the feminine at the level of the silent, the unconscious. Discourse – linear, logical and theoretical – is masculine. When women speak, therefore, they cannot help but enter male-dominated discourse; speaking women are silent as women.

In its recognition of the power of the word over creation, certainly, the Genesis passage can suggest this 'truth' about the culturally ascribed characteristics of gender. The text gives the man privileged access to language. Adam's acts of naming dramatize a male will to power and a willing of female absence. The text thus provides an instance of sexual polarizing that requires feminist literary criticism. By ascribing a gender role to naming, Genesis asserts a polemical position that cannot be an origin of feminist analysis but rather must itself be the object of that analysis. Daly's position escalates without changing the essentially dualistic terms of a sex war in which language, having been stolen, becomes part of the patriarchal loot to be reclaimed. Either to wish with Daly to steal language back or to discover with Duras a uniquely female speech is to leave the text's authority intact – as an instance of male dominion. To allow Genesis – or any other text – such power without a more thorough consideration of its tropes of authority grimly cedes the culture's language to males and in ladylike fashion allows to literature itself a male gender.

I begin with a primal example of gender politics from the Bible, to emphasize that feminist literary criticism cannot ignore the intriguing instances of gender politics inscribed in the patriarchal tradition. If its myth of naming has influenced our thinking, its gender politics and the politics of its interpretations need to remain open to critical enquiry. This chapter will argue the essential importance of questions raised for feminist criticism by male-authored works. Although the traditional literary canon has justifiably been labelled misogynist, I question the sufficiency of that label. Literary texts linked by common inheritance and cultural recognition have been shaped by both men and women. Revisionary interpretations which explore female influence in male-authored works are a vital enterprise for feminist criticism. Before attributing a gender to language and, by extension, to all literature, feminist critics need first to examine canonical ideology to find out if the absence of Eve in fact screens women's significant role.

But for one notable exception, we do not know Adam's reasons for his names. When God brings him a female the man bursts into formal verse and gives a lyric explanation of her name:

> This one at last
> bone of my bones
> and flesh of my flesh.
> This one shall be called woman
> For from man was this one taken.
>
> (Genesis 2:23, trans. Robert Alter)

Robert Alter explains the inset of formal verse as 'a common convention in biblical narrative for direct speech that has some significantly summarizing or ceremonial function' (Alter 1981,

p. 28). It is particularly notable here that the first instance of biblical verse subjects woman to man by means of a politically useful but a false etymology. The lonely man appropriates by misinterpretation the one who will complete his paradise. If woman and man become 'one flesh', because she was taken from him, the man's naming conquers his loneliness. It is only after God's judgement upon the couple that Adam names the woman Eve, meaning, he says, the 'mother of all living'. He allows woman her function as life-bearer only after the Fall, when this female power bears the taint of sin, pain and death. Monique Wittig's *Les Guérillères* restates the idea: 'What belongs to you on this earth? Only death' (Wittig 1973, p. 116).

The trope of reversal (metalepsis or *transumptio*) that governs these biblical chapters is reversal. Time sequences are reversed and/or collapsed: man not woman gives birth not to an infant but to a contemporary. One can infer from the trope that the one who gives birth was considered superior. By turning the normal sequence around and having her arrive second, Eve becomes second-best, subordinate – as child to parent.

In addition, the birthing trope reinforces the gender politics of the myth of naming. In inventing names for animals, Scripture claims for Adam absolute priority over names in defiance of what the experience of language acquisition has been for most people. Usually the first namer is female. Mothers convey names to children; the metalepsis suggests that their nearly absolute pedagogic control over the years of infancy, when people learn words, threatens male dominance (Dinnerstein 1976; Chodorow 1978). As an extreme effort to obliterate any female role in shaping language, the fable's reversal detaches woman from her function. How could she be a namer if she had not yet been created? Not satisfied to silence her by oppression, the trope suppresses her entirely. The violence of the wish to obliterate women's role in language-making is masked by denial. Denying her existence absolves the text of its violence. The woman can be disregarded by all – by women who object to her absence, and even by those who interpret her absence as a metaphor for the woman's silence in patriarchal discourse.

Yet the female presence shines through the text's negation of it. By recognizing in the myth an angry defensive reach for authority, a feminist reading robs the text of its ontological claim. We can view the text as a complex tale of gender relations. Once we name the trope, we can reverse its reversal and claim its opposite: female authority occasions the myth.

This feminist assertion requires a feminist qualification, however, because the myth we have considered here is a received version which, by its conventions of naming, translating and interpreting, has created a gender-polarized story. The researches of Phillis Trible (1973) show that patriarchal interpretation has made a generic word – *'adham*, meaning 'humanity' – into a male proper name. As Casey Miller and Kate Swift report, *adamah* (soil or earth) is a feminine noun, suggesting a derivation from a Hebrew concept of mother earth (1976, pp. 150–1). Interpretation, then, has taken an idea, possibly more female than male, polarized the genders, and then erased the female.

In pondering this female absence, feminist criticism has taken various stances. One of the first feminist projects was to examine portrayals of female characters in male-authored texts (de Beauvoir 1952; Ellmann 1968; Millett 1969). Finding abundant evidence of misogyny in these characters and in gender characterizations in general, many feminist critics were persuaded that male authors could not speak truly about women. Consequently, they proposed that whatever one could consider as a female presence in a male-authored text would necessarily be filtered through the complex workings of male desire. To read male-authored texts, therefore, would be merely to encounter those stereotypes and those attitudes towards women that constitute a dreary record of women's oppression.

As a second strategy, feminist criticism concentrated upon recovering works written by women, to set the record straight, to correct the imbalance, and to restore to critical attention authentic female voices. As a result of this work, discredited and disregarded women authors, such as Jean Rhys, Kate Chopin, Christine de Pizan and Zora Neale Hurston, have been accorded, if not full literary honours, at least a serious consideration and a small corner of the literary canon. Such writers as Mary Shelley, Dorothy Wordsworth, Charlotte Brontë, George Eliot and Elizabeth Barrett Browning are receiving feminist reinterpretation (Spacks 1975; Moers 1976; Showalter 1977). Some – Eliot and Brontë – who had always been in the literary canon are newly considered from a feminist point of view, and others – Wordsworth, Shelley, Barrett Browning – whose recent fame resided in their famous male family members are newly considered on their own merit.

Some recent American feminist literary theory focuses upon what Elaine Showalter (1981) calls 'gynocentric criticism'. This criticism, opposed to 'androcentric criticism', follows from earlier feminist re-evaluations of women's writing. Privileging women's writing and women's language, Showalter counsels 'feminist criticism . . . to concentrate on women's access to language, on the available lexical range from which words can be selected, on the ideological and cultural determinants of expression'. By polarizing literary criticism into gynocentric and androcentric criticism, however, Showalter replicates the social categories of gender. The paradox engendered by her eloquent argument is contained in her title, 'Feminist Criticism in the Wilderness', which echoes dialectically Geoffrey Hartman's *Criticism in the Wilderness* (1980), a work that Showalter herself describes as discussing no women critics. So, whereas she opposes her position to Hartman's androcentric view, she incorporates his paradigm. Annette Kolodny's intelligent and important 'A Map for Rereading' (1980) which addresses Harold Bloom's exclusively male-oriented *A Map of Misreading* (1975), also reveals in its title dependence and alliance (even homage) rather than separation.

The relation of women to literary culture can be discovered not only in women's fiction and poetry but in 'gynocriticism' of the literary canon. Although Showalter defines the 'essential subject of feminist criticism, the close and extensive knowledge of women's texts', she appears to exclude women's critical writing. She seems to assume that women's writing about male-authored texts is not quite women's writing, since she devalues or even prohibits women's writing about literary tradition. This particular limitation reinforces, however unwittingly, a primitive patriarchal taboo forbidding women to approach sacred objects. Unless gender definitions – sexual differences as enforced by culture – are explicated by feminist critics, traditional texts will remain encrusted with patriarchal interpretation, and civilization will continue to be enthralled by them.

We should neither limit the scope of feminist interpretation nor cling to a narrow idea of authorship. Instead of viewing the criticism of male-authored texts as a mere act of interpreting works by the 'other', feminist criticism can consider the active role of women in their production – how this two-sexed culture has produced gendered polarities which inform all its writings. Suppression, distancing, alteration or any other defences against woman's role in a text's creation are compelling examples of women's history, and are therefore a vital subject for feminist criticism. No matter what critical methodology or political programme the varieties of feminist criticism employ, in order to imagine a different future we cannot exclude any portion of our past.

In a literary tradition in which there are few recognized women writers, feminist critics assert their power rather than their victimhood by revising traditional wisdom and altering the meaning of the canon. The concept of authorship enlarges to include forces that shape texts. One cannot neatly equate a work with the sex of its author; the identity of an individual writer may not necessarily be coterminous with her or his sexual organs. Variable physiology and varieties of nurturing bear upon an individual author's imagination in ways more unpredictable than logical categories (which tend to be dualistic) or anatomy (which looks at external structures). The exclusive categories of masculine and feminine are dominated by a hierarchical mentality which inevitably regards one category as more favoured than the other. Rigid dualism of sexual stereotyping causes great human suffering; how destructive of the rich ambiguities of variety, then, to subject literary texts to the absolute polarities of sex. To do so identifies with dominant (patriarchal) thinking. Whether the text is male- or female-authored, the literary canon contains, not a uniform example of male as subject and female as object, but a valuable record of a conflict between sex, gender and common humanity. These texts convey the working myths of the culture. We are to blame if we read them as gospel instead of as myth.

To varying degrees, texts convey a subversive knowledge of the gendered arena of their production. An exceptionally clear use of that knowledge can be found in a passage from one of the 'great' books, *Don Quixote*, a work in which the complexity of gender roles is further complicated by its gloss on the way ideas of the feminine become traditional. As Eve was the last to be created, so Don Quixote fashions his lady Dulcinea as the final item in his chivalric equipment:

> Now that his armour was scoured, his morion made into a helmet, his horse and himself newly named, he felt nothing was wanting but a lady of whom to be enamoured, for a knight-errant who was loveless was a tree without leaves and fruit, a body without soul.

> (Cervantes 1964)

His need for a motivating emotion (rather than for a 'real' woman) was engendered by books. Because she is refined (or sublimed) from the country lass Aldonza, Dulcinea requires constant idealization. The complex energies required to satisfy a male need for a feminine character – a heroine as opposed to a woman – is one major theme of the book. But, since Dulcinea's role is often commented on by means of the interpolated tales, we can discover how she mediates between male desire and female reality not only by examining the knightly adventures but also by considering an early and particularly crucial 'digression'. The story of Marcela (part I, chs 12–14) is about the objectifying strategies that create a female character in a male-authored work. Told by a goatherd to Don Quixote, it replicates one paradigm of literary tradition: stories (about women) conveyed from one man to another.

Marcela, a beautiful heiress, has become a shepherdess as an escape from the horde of swains who pursue her against her will and contrary to her interests. The heroine embodies the essence of conventional, even archetypal, virtues. First, Marcela encompasses all beauty, both of the day and of the night. Her looks surpass those of her dead mother, whose face had the 'sun on one side and the moon on the other'. Second, although rich, she is none the less legally dependent. As an orphan, her marriage and great wealth are controlled by an uncle whose interest in her fate is compromised by her commodity value.

Faced with importunate and powerful males, Marcela, asserting her youth and incapacity to bear the 'burden of matrimony', retreats to the woods to become a shepherdess. She escapes, in other words, into a literary genre, the pastoral. But literature, as part of patriarchal tradition, provides no true refuge. No longer invisible behind the walls of her 'guardian's' house, as shepherdess she becomes more visible, and therefore more vulnerable. The pastoral female role traps her as the conventional object of shepherds' laments. The shepherd Chrysostom fatally succumbs to Marcela's beauty and to the protestations of his own poetry.

By means of the parodic filters through which most literary conventions in *Don Quixote* pass, the tale of Marcela presents the convention of women in the pastoral specifically as a convention, making possible a critique of its own methods and allowing an interpretation of gender dynamics. That is to say, the text itself juxtaposes a 'real' woman whose independence from men allows her to stand apart from the gender behaviour of her culture with the conventional woman of the western literary tradition. The tantalizing Marcela of male fantasies is distinct from her demure and neutral behaviour. The distinction between the two is asserted not only by Marcela but also by male spectators:

> Don't, however, think for a moment that because Marcela adopted that free and unfettered life with its lack of privacy, she has given any occasion, or even the hint of one, that might imperil her modesty or virtue. On the contrary, she is so watchful of her own honor that not one of her many suitors has boasted, nor has the right to boast, that she has ever given him the slightest hope of obtaining his desire. Although she does not ignore or avoid the company of shepherds but treats them in a friendly and courteous manner, if one of them starts showing his intentions, even though it be with a proper and holy proposal of matrimony, like a flash, she flings him off as with a catapult.
>
> (Cervantes 1964 ch. 12)

The teller of this tale interprets Marcela's behaviour in a traditionally male way. Although he recognizes his distortion, he attempts to deny it by describing her as 'cruel', 'unkind' and 'sinister'; he makes her into a literary type, a *femme fatale*, whose nature ensures literary tradition – laments, *chansons d'amour*, romances. At this point in the narrative, Marcela joins the procession of Stellas, Sylvias and Diaphenias – pastoral ladies who are ciphers for male desire. As feminist critics point out, she is now merely an object, found in paeans where, as in the following example by Sidney, the closing of her eyes is as the eclipse of the sun:

> *Strephon.* For she, whose parts maintained a perfect music,
>   Whose beauties shined more than the blushing morning,
>   Who much did pass in state the stately mountains,
>   In straightness passed the cedars of the forests,
>   Hath cast me, wretch, into eternal evening,
>   By taking her two suns from these dark valleys.
>
> *Klaius.* For she, with whom compared, the Alps are valleys,
>   She, whose least word brings from the spheres their
>   music,
>   At whose approach the sun rose in the evening,
>   Who, where she went, bore in her forehead morning,
>   Is gone, is gone from these our spoiled forests,
>   Turning to deserts our best pastured mountains.

('Ye goat-herd Gods that love the grassy mountains')

As one of these 'shes' whose force transforms the landscape, Marcela represents that type the tale criticizes or deconstructs.

At the moment that mourners at Chrysostom's funeral revile her as 'that mortal enemy of the human race', Marcela herself leaps from a thicket and, standing above them on a high rock, pleads her own case. Her deductive argument rationally asserts her identity apart from the imago of her admirers' and detractors' fantasies. Why, she argues, should she love a man simply because he loves her? She chose neither to be beautiful nor to be loved. If Chrysostom persisted in spite of her clear words, his stubbornness and not her beauty killed him: 'Those whom my looks have captivated, my words have undeceived.' No one has accused Marcela of false speaking, but her eloquent words cannot compete with the language of her flesh; women's words have no force to speak the truth or 'undeceive'. Her female body as counter-text to her words does not speak her language. The tale presents woman's words estranged from woman's body, allowing interpretation to distinguish between discourses, between woman as object and woman as subject, between male desire and female consciousness.

No common goatherd, the teller of Marcela's story is a

version of Pan, a singer of male lust; Cervantes allows the reader
to see Pan's discourse imposing its own desires upon male–
female interaction and, by the force of its authority, making up
the canonical text. But the text is situated so that we can see his
story as it floats in a larger reality, or, to change the metaphor,
the story allows a different discourse in the fissures of its telling;
it presents a feminist critique of male love and comments about
its commentary on the female as subject.

Chrysostom is buried with his love poetry, some of which is
quoted in the narrative. By parodying such poems as the Sidney
poem quoted above, this lament clearly labels the object as
desire itself and not as Marcela:

> At last I die, and since I lost all hope
> Of more luck in death than in life I have,
> I shall keep loyal to my fantasy . . .

But, in spite of the poem's avowal of loyalty to the fantasy of
possessing Marcela, the poet blames the woman:

> Thou whose unreasoning scorn was the cause
> That spurred me on to violence against
> My youth, and to quit this life I now loathe,
> Since by notorious signs thou art aware
> How deep the wound that now consumes my heart,
> And how cheerfully I have faced thy scorn.
>
> (Cervantes 1964, ch. 14)

As opposed to Marcela, whose body contradicts (speaks
against) her words, Chrysostom claims that his body speaks for
him. The 'notorious signs' (*notorias muestras*) are obvious for
anyone to read; they tell of a profound and true inner condition–
a deep wound (*profunda llaga*). The poem claims congruence in
men of body sign, language and inner state. From the male point
of view, women's words and their bodies are incongruous,
disjuncted; their own words, however, are clear, even notorious
– that is, giving information. Everyone knows and recognizes
them for what they are: conventional, traditional.

But the convention and the tradition (another meaning of
notorious signs) of which the words are a part tell a partial truth.
Chrysostom's poem goes on for pages in the same fashion, as if
Cervantes were showing by its tediousness how long was this
tradition and how easy to continue it, line upon line. But,

immediately after it is read, one man points out that, although the poem pleases everyone, it lies about Marcela. To complicate further the commentary upon modes of literature and their means of encoding females, another man reveals that the shepherd composed his canonical work while he was far from Marcela:

> I must tell you that when the unfortunate man wrote this song, he was absent from Marcela, from whom he had voluntarily withdrawn to see if absence would have its usual effect upon him. And as there is nothing that does not vex the absent lover and no fear that does not haunt him, so Chrysostom was tormented by imaginary jealousies and suspicions as frightening as if they were real. So Marcela's goodness, therefore, is as genuine as fame proclaims it, and but for cruelty, a little haughtiness, and much scorn, envy itself cannot justly find fault with her.
>
> (Cervantes 1964, ch. 14)

Thus the swain's poem deliberately distances even the conventionalized Marcela from its real subject, which is masochistic, celibate desire. Because the solipsistic fantasy is conventional, men describe it without understanding it. Yet the same men believe in the poem's fiction while they revile Marcela. Unusually candid male critics, they resemble 'those lost adventurers my peers', as Browning's quixotic Childe Roland calls them, whose stake in the solidarity which bonded them to tradition's fables takes priority over the more complex truths of gender.

The subtext of Marcela's tale concerns the shared male authorship (another meaning of tradition) of female characters by the process of masculine critical enquiry. To reinforce this subtext, the interpolated tale itself is interrupted by a long discussion of the role of the lady in the adventures of Amadis of Gaul, Felixmarte of Hyrcania, Tirante the White and Sir Belianis of Greece – declining eventually to the lineage of Dulcinea del Toboso, the archetype of dream ladies, the sovereign of the heart. So the interrupted text, itself an interruption, is enclosed by and comments upon the main lady. As its discourse on female character-making unfolds, it subverts its own claims, shifting the grounds of its fiction-making. At the end, the subtext is ironically distanced by the masculinist comment upon Marcela: 'She should be honored and esteemed by all good men in the world, for she has demonstrated that she is the only woman living with such pure intentions.'

After we view from various perspectives the dynamics of her creation, Cervantes then turns Marcela, alone of all her sex – like the Virgin Mary – into the exception that proves the rule. In other words, the text finally closes off the radical possibilities it had admitted, but without erasing them entirely. Feminist interpretation can reopen Marcela's case by addressing the conflict encoded in its competing voices.

To deconstruct the discourses on femininity and male desire that this text thematizes is not, however, to deny that it is written by a male. Nor do I claim that the male signature is irrelevant. However, what its relevancy means – what the relationship is between a male author and the work he produces – cannot be resolved by dismissing the canon because of its misogyny. Like the whole of *Don Quixote*, the Marcela episode calls into question any ultimate formulation about reality. Lying about women is one of tradition's fictions. That such lies lead to disaster is one compelling reason for feminists to decode them. Furthermore, misogynist aspects of literature are an essential part of our cultural heritage. One might imagine a female-authored work, contemporary with Cervantes, in which Marcela's speech did not undo itself. But the story we have suggests why female-authored works are rare, fragmentary or non-existent. Woman, mythologized, fragmented, interpreted, exists as a colonized element of patriarchy. None the less, the Marcela story imagines the problems of female subjectivity in a way that few Renaissance Spanish women could express, a way that startles many in the twentieth century. That Cervantes was a male writer is a fact of *women's* history.

To argue that literature preserves a two-sexed world is not the same as agreeing with Virginia Woolf that the great male writers' imaginations are 'androgynous' and 'incandescent'. Cervantes' text shows that the second sex has exerted a disproportionate impact upon sexual mythology. Marcela's tale exhibits profound disjunctions and throws barriers around its 'feminist consciousness' that betray profound discomfort about what is being expressed. I would argue that all western literature will exhibit some defensiveness about this subject. Female-

authored work cannot escape varieties of sexual malaise; identification with dominance has colonized most imaginations.

Although inevitably reflecting in some way the gender politics of the patriarchy, the canon may not be as masculinist as
some feminist criticism has assumed. The interpretation of
texts, however, has created a narrowly patriarchal discourse
that limits reading. Shoshana Felman has shown how the
critical exegesis of Balzac's story 'Adieu' has situated the
importance of the story in its 'male' themes by ignoring those
elements (a third of the text) that deal with the woman.
'Madness and women', she states, 'turn out to be the two
outcasts of the establishment of readability' (Felman 1975,
p. 6). For this reason alone, it would be mistaken for feminists to
polarize criticism according to the genitals of the author, or to
attend only to 'women's writing'. This reification of gender will
retard the changes in reading that is one of feminist criticism's
goals.

Critical discourse has tended to be more misogynist than the
texts it examines. Tagged with a patriarchal interpretation,
canonical texts pass into the culture validated by what the
Institution of Reading has understood. How many of us, for
example, were taught that the *Oresteia* is about the establishment of justice for western civilization, rather than that it is a
great act of mythopoeia in which politics are sexualized and
where the idea of justice becomes defined as 'masculine'? Froma
I. Zeitlin's feminist enquiry (1978) into the 'dynamics of misogyny' in that monumental trilogy has made ignorance of its
sexual politics an irresponsible act both of scholarship and of
pedagogy.

Ideally, a feminist critique would question not only the
inadequate representation of other voices in the western literary
canon but the inadequate explication of received tradition. The
blindness of patriarchal criticism to female-authored works
does not mean that its acuity to subjects it has called its own is
thereby sharpened. On the contrary, the defensive strategies
that males use to avoid what has become a main subject for
feminist critics – the 'invisible' sexual politics of literature –
have lamed their interpretation of the canon as well. To privilege certain forms as great, certain themes as important and
certain genres as major has required traditional criticism to

disregard or elide those very aspects in the 'great' texts that are incongruent with patriarchal gender definitions.

Feminist critics can question received interpretation, refusing to regard the text as an icon, isolated from the world in which it was produced, refusing to accept texts as unaffected by women. We can read signs of real female power, untapped because unexplicated. Rather than invent female language, we can appropriate what is at least half ours anyway. Feminist critics of the literary canon can expose women's presence in writing by men as well as in writing by women (Johnson 1980; Jehlen 1981–2; Auerbach 1982; Froula 1983). Canon revision requires cultural change; one strategy for such change is feminist critique of the canon.

The blindness of traditional criticism to subjects of interest to feminist criticism suggests a rationale for the claim voiced in Charlotte Brontë's *Shirley*: 'women read men more truly than men read women.' The observation is limited; it says nothing, for example, about men reading men or women reading women. It may seem to raise the spectre of 'feminine intuition', spooky extra-rational knowledge, compensation for inferior ratiocinative power. Nevertheless, Brontë's proposition is useful. Marginality empowers the feminist reader to prise open mythologies that govern patriarchal texts. A feminist critic may not write or even seek a woman's language, but she can exile herself from language's patrimony. Hence her own writing can establish a different bond with traditional texts. Feminist critics should not claim a privileged relationship to female-authored works and complain about the inadequate reading of male-authored ones. A more fruitful enterprise would not limit scrutiny but would instead frame feminist questions appropriate to any cultural production.

Marginality, however, cannot be considered an uncomplicated blessing. Interpretation from the margins may distort while it illuminates. A passage in Toni Morrison's remarkable novel *Sula* suggests a strategy and some limitations of reading male-authored texts from the margins. I cite Morrison's passage, then, as an elaboration, though still limited, upon Brontë's claim.

Sula is about a black female friendship that flourishes in the desperate and intimate conditions of a black neighbourhood.

Sula, who tries to reject gender socialization in favour of autonomy, and Nel, who accepts a conventional gender role as a complaisant wife and mother, are confronted with a canonical male text. Nel's husband Jude finds being a waiter emasculating compared to his dream of turning his tray and platter into more manly tools – a pick, a shovel, a sledge-hammer. Returning home fresh from a 'personal insult', he begins to complain in front of the two women about his black man's life in a white man's world, 'a whiney tale that peaked somewhere between anger and a lapping desire for comfort'. Jude interprets his own tale, then depends upon the two women to reflect back an enhanced view of his interpretative strategy:

> He ended it with the observation that a Negro man had a hard row to hoe in this world. He expected his story to dovetail into milkwarm commiseration, but before Nel could excrete it, Sula said she didn't know about that – it looked like a pretty good life to her.
>
> (Morrison 1975, p. 88–9)

Jude's interpretation excludes women entirely. By focusing upon black men, he avoids confronting his allegiance with all men. His idea of 'the world' is as patriarchal as the white man's. Second, he looks to the women for nurturance. He wants a woman to suffer his misery, but he does not want to suffer hers. And Nel, rather than voicing her less canonical tales of woe (she is ironing when Jude enters), is ready to respond maternally rather than as his equal. That is, both Jude and Nel regard Nel's role as one of nurturer – the one whose milkwarm commiseration cannot be depleted. Because its supply is endless, it requires no reciprocity.

It is important to recognize, however, that Jude's interpretation is not completely false but that it is a cliché, reinforcing whatever he wants to know about his powerlessness. He is oppressed by the system: 'white man running it – nothing good.' Racial politics masks sexual politics. Jude's real difficulties allow him to maintain his male identity, to exploit women, and not to examine himself. Sula's extended reading of Jude's text rejects its overt, even platitudinous, message by reframing it. She redefines attraction, calling it 'love', and attention, which she calls 'envy'. Thereby, she avoids the conventional role of woman readers of male texts which presupposes empathetic homage. Audacious if not perverse, Sula decodes a subversive message in Jude's story by changing its perspective:

> I mean, I don't know what the fuss is about. I mean, everything in the world loves you. White men love you. They spend so much time worrying about your penis they forget their own. The only thing they want to do is cut off a nigger's privates. And if that ain't love and respect I don't know what is. And white women? They chase you all to every corner of the earth, feel for you under every bed. I know a white woman wouldn't leave the house after 6 o'clock for fear one of you would snatch her. Now ain't that love? They think rape soon's they see you, and if they don't get the rape they looking for, they scream it anyway just so the search won't be in vain. Colored women worry themselves into bad health just trying to hang on to your cuffs. Even little children – white and black, boys and girls – spend all their childhood eating their hearts out 'cause they think you don't love them. And if that ain't enough, you love yourselves. Nothing in this world loves a black man more than another black man. You hear of solitary white men, but niggers? Can't stay away from one another a whole day. So. It looks to me like you the envy of the world.

> (Morrison 1975, p. 89)

In order to turn Jude's story of powerlessness into a tale of power, Sula draws upon its context. She reads its setting – the wife washing, ironing and cooking, the children hanging around, the white world in which Jude is an oppressed, because feared, victim. Hers is an inspired unreading, freeing Jude to imagine a different future. Jude's characterization of the black man, on the other hand, like the goatherd's characterization of Marcela, calls upon a typology that reproduces itself.

Of course, Sula's interpretation is full of problems as well. Anger seems to hover near its irreverence. Where is Sula in her story? Is she outside the world of which Jude is the envy? How would one analyse her voice? In its way, her interpretation, like Jude's, speaks of dependence. Her 'envy' denies Jude's story by replacing it with one that seems to give its teller no place – unlike Jude's, which places the teller in the centre of his tale. Sula's story is still dominated by polarities and raises the disturbing question of the adequacy of women's reading of their own texts.

Nel and Sula represent two kinds of female critics. Nel responds to the male text in the way in which it asks to be responded to. She excretes sympathy, an act of homage, for it. But reviling the text equally participates in the dialectic. Still, Sula's interpretation is preferable to Nel's, for it opens a route out of marginality. Morrison implies that to accept oppression as *the* meaning of Jude's text is to overlook the black man's threat to overt power; worse, his reading makes him complicitous with the victimizers. With his interpretation, Jude has categorized his role to accord neatly with dominant ideology. By portraying himself as a passive victim of outside influence, he gives his world to others.

By refusing the rhetoric of the victim, by turning it inside out, Sula plays with the subversive message of the text and finds its force. She reads the racial struggle as a fear of black power, of the ascendancy in the culture's imagination of black manhood. Furthermore, in regard to Jude's interpretation, Sula suggests some reasons that Jude might find to reproduce his miserable role, to maintain his black man's world. Like the silence of Eve, Jude's complicity suggests his stake in his own oppression. Nurturant criticism, like Nel's, is particularly dangerous for feminist critics of canonical texts; 'milkwarm commiseration' turns sour because it infantalizes. One way out of the dilemma is benign disrespect.

The advantages of covert power rather than the risks of overt authority perhaps explain the attractiveness of Nel's point of view. The collective patriarchal mythology about women encourages readings that keep women apparently absent but imaginatively omnipresent. Rereading the canon involves great costs – its privileged status is undermined – and requires great courage, since one risks being cast out, like Sula, by man and woman alike. Nancy K. Miller, an astute partisan of separatist criticism, presents a counter-argument to the one I have suggested, foreseeing the end of the feminist project in ignoring the sex of the author and in calling the criticism 'gender' rather than 'feminist' criticism. 'If feminists decide that the signature is a matter of indifference, if women's studies become gender studies,' she warns, 'the real end of women in the institution will not be far off. The text's heroine will become again no more than a fiction' (Miller 1982, p. 53). Her apocalyptic vision arises from her political awareness that women's particular perspective, history and culture could once again be hidden if we ignore the sex of the author. I am not advocating indifference, but I am counselling scepticism about gender categories and about signature. Sexual identification, gender-consciousness and signature cannot be confused. Without giving in to assimilative pressures, feminists need to re-evaluate the notorious canon – to discover not only what it excludes but how it constructs what it includes.

One difficulty of this last strategy is that it leads to questions of responsibility. What is women's stake in acquiescence? Why doesn't Eve object to Adam's usurpation? Why does she accept the image of absence? Why does Nel accept subservience? Although undoubtedly strategies for survival in a misogynist culture, theirs are none the less the aspirations of the courtier or of the one who rocks the cradle in order to rule the world. Agreement, echoing and silence are forms of flattery, a rhetoric of subordination. Those who take female writers as their exclusive province and who argue for the absence of significant female subjects in male-authored texts convincingly describe how women feel in patriarchy – silenced, erased, confined, colonized. This view reinforces the way things are, with women inhabiting the margins of power. In Morrison's words, this is 'a whiney tale' – a truth that peaks somewhere between anger and a desire for comfort. By describing how women feel, the tale has gained a place, although secondary, in the canon.

Charlotte Perkins Gilman provides a striking metaphor for the feminist critic who is locked in a patriarchal world. In *The Yellow Wallpaper* (1973) the woman writer, after a post-partum depression, has been confined by her physician husband to a room with barred windows. Both her husband and his co-opted sister infantilize her; they address her in baby talk – inadequate words. She has nothing to do but read the wallpaper of the room, a paper she finds hideous. The paper acts upon her as if it were an example of woman as represented in a patriarchal text; its configurations are mysterious, contradictory, irritating; yet it provokes study. Its pattern cannot be reconciled, so it cancels itself: 'The lame uncertain curves . . . suddenly commit suicide . . . destroy themselves in unheard contradictions.' Some of these contradictions are uncovered in the Marcela story. No wonder, then, that women who try to explicate these contradictions seem as demented as the protagonist of Gilman's tale. But, with increasing scrutiny, the female reader begins to discern another pattern imprisoned behind what she comes to see as the 'outside' pattern. She knows that the shadowy shape is a woman or women trying to escape. The women collaborate to free themselves, not, however, without immense costs. The freed women – many of them – creep away, and the protagonist creeps around her room, seen by her appalled husband as utterly mad, totally out of his reach. And yet the last words of the protagonist are triumphant: '"I've got out at last", said I, "in spite of you and Jane. And I've pulled off most of the paper, so you can't put me back!"'

In the background of patriarchal texts are women trying to escape into readability. Risking being labelled mad, trivial, irrelevant or faddish, feminist critics revise a polarized idea of gendered authorship, seeing the female behind the crumbling paper of the patriarchal text. The text may seem ripped apart – bisexual, unconventional, even insane; it enters a more complex and disunified field of critical scrutiny where its authority seems less secure. Traditional literary works carry stories of a two-sexed world where difference has been mythologized and hierarchized but where other knowledge in the same texts subverts those categories. The canon has been owned by a monopoly, but acts of repossession have begun.

References

Alter, Robert (1981) *The Art of Biblical Narrative*. New York: Basic Books.

Auerbach, Nina (1982) *Woman and the Demon: The Life of a Victorian Myth*. Cambridge, Mass.: Harvard University Press.

Beauvoir, Simone de (1952) *The Second Sex*, trans. H. M. Parshley. New York: Knopf.

Bloom, Harold (1975) *A Map of Misreading*. New York: Oxford University Press.

Cervantes, Miguel de (1964) *Don Quixote de la Mancha*, trans. Walter Starkie. New York: Signet.

Chodorow, Nancy (1978) *The Reproduction of Mothering: Psychoanalysis and the Sociology of Gender.* Berkeley, Cal.: University of California Press.

Daly, Mary (1973) *Beyond God the Father: Toward a Philosophy of Women's Liberation.* Boston, Mass.: Beacon Press.

Dinnerstein, Dorothy (1976) *The Mermaid and the Minotaur: Sexual Arrangements and Human Malaise.* New York: Harper & Row.

Ellmann, Mary (1968) *Thinking about Women.* New York: Harcourt, Brace & World.

Felman, Shoshana (1975) 'Women and Madness: The Critical Phallacy', *Diacritics*, 5, 4 (Winter), pp. 2–10.

Froula, Christine (1983) 'When Eve Reads Milton: Undoing the Canonical Economy', *Critical Inquiry*, 10 (December), pp. 321–47.

Gilman, Charlotte Perkins (1973) *The Yellow Wallpaper.* Old Westbury, NY: Feminist Press.

Hartman, Geoffrey (1980) *Criticism in the Wilderness.* New Haven, Conn.: Yale University Press.

Jehlen, Myra (1981–2) 'Archimedes and the Paradox of Feminist Criticism'. In Nannerl O. Keohane, Michelle Z. Rosaldo and Barbara C. Gelpi (eds), *Feminist Theory: A Critique of Ideology*, pp. 189–215. Chicago, Ill.: University of Chicago Press.

Johnson, Barbara (1980) *The Critical Difference.* Baltimore, Md: Johns Hopkins University Press.

Kolodny, Annette (1980) 'A Map for Rereading, or, Gender and the Interpretation of Literary Texts', *New Literary History*, 11, 3 (Spring), pp. 451–67.

Kramerae, Cheris (1981) *Women and Men Speaking.* Rowley, Mass.: Newbury House.

McConnell-Ginet, Sally, Borker, Ruth, and Furman, Nelly (1980) *Women and Language in Literature and Society.* New York: Praeger.

Marks, Elaine, and Courtivron, Isabelle de (eds) (1980) *New French Feminisms.* New York: Schocken.

Miller, Casey, and Swift, Kate (1976) *Words and Women: New Language in New Times.* Garden City, NY: Doubleday Anchor.

Miller, Nancy K. (1982) 'The Text's Heroines: A Feminist Critic and her Fictions', *Diacritics*, 12 (Summer), pp. 48–53.

Millett, Kate (1969) *Sexual Politics.* New York: Doubleday.

Moers, Kate (1976) *Literary Women: The Great Writers.* Garden City, New York: Doubleday.

Morrison, Toni (1975) *Sula.* New York: Bantam.

Showalter, Elaine (1977) *A Literature of their Own: British Women Novelists from Brontë to Lessing.* Princeton, NJ: Princeton University Press.

Showalter, Elaine (1981) 'Feminist Criticism in the Wilderness', *Critical Inquiry*, 8, 2 (Winter), pp. 179–205.

Spacks, Patricia Meyer (1975) *The Female Imagination*. New York: Knopf.

Trible, Phyllis (1973) 'Depatriarchizing in Biblical Interpretation', *Journal of the American Academy of Religion*, 41 (March), pp. 35–42.

Wittig, Monique (1973) *Les Guerillères*. New York: Avon.

Zeitlin, Froma I. (1978) 'The Dynamics of Misogyny: Myth and Mythmaking in the *Orestia*', *Arethusa*, 2, pp. 150–84.

Index